T0344606

Tourism in Africa

Tourism in Africa

Harnessing Tourism for Growth and Improved Livelihoods

**Iain Christie, Eneida Fernandes,
Hannah Messerli, and Louise Twining-Ward**

A copublication of the Agence Française de Développement and the World Bank

© 2014 International Bank for Reconstruction and Development / The World Bank
1818 H Street NW, Washington DC 20433
Telephone: 202-473-1000; Internet: www.worldbank.org

Some rights reserved
1 2 3 4   17 16 15 14

This work is a product of the staff of The World Bank with external contributions. The findings, interpretations, and conclusions expressed in this work do not necessarily reflect the views of The World Bank, its Board of Executive Directors, or the governments they represent, or the Agence Française de Développement. The World Bank does not guarantee the accuracy of the data included in this work. The boundaries, colors, denominations, and other information shown on any map in this work do not imply any judgment on the part of The World Bank concerning the legal status of any territory or the endorsement or acceptance of such boundaries.

Nothing herein shall constitute or be considered to be a limitation upon or waiver of the privileges and immunities of The World Bank, all of which are specifically reserved.

Rights and Permissions

This work is available under the Creative Commons Attribution 3.0 IGO license (CC BY 3.0 IGO) http://creativecommons.org/licenses/by/3.0/igo. Under the Creative Commons Attribution license, you are free to copy, distribute, transmit, and adapt this work, including for commercial purposes, under the following conditions:

Attribution—Please cite the work as follows: Christie, Iain, Eneida Fernandes, Hannah Messerli, and Louise Twining-Ward. 2014. *Tourism in Africa: Harnessing Tourism for Growth and Improved Livelihoods*. Africa Development Forum series. Washington, DC: World Bank. doi:10.1596/978-1-4648-0190-7. License: Creative Commons Attribution CC BY 3.0 IGO

Translations—If you create a translation of this work, please add the following disclaimer along with the attribution: *This translation was not created by The World Bank and should not be considered an official World Bank translation. The World Bank shall not be liable for any content or error in this translation.*

Adaptations—If you create an adaptation of this work, please add the following disclaimer along with the attribution: *This is an adaptation of an original work by The World Bank. Responsibility for the views and opinions expressed in the adaptation rests solely with the author or authors of the adaptation and are not endorsed by The World Bank.*

Third-party content—The World Bank does not necessarily own each component of the content contained within the work. The World Bank therefore does not warrant that the use of any third-party-owned individual component or part contained in the work will not infringe on the rights of those third parties. The risk of claims resulting from such infringement rests solely with you. If you wish to re-use a component of the work, it is your responsibility to determine whether permission is needed for that re-use and to obtain permission from the copyright owner. Examples of components can include, but are not limited to, tables, figures, or images.

All queries on rights and licenses should be addressed to the Publishing and Knowledge Division, The World Bank, 1818 H Street NW, Washington, DC 20433, USA; fax: 202-522-2625; e-mail: pubrights@worldbank.org.

ISBN (paper): 978-1-4648-0190-7
ISBN (electronic): 978-1-4648-0197-6
DOI: 10.1596/978-1-4648-0190-7

Cover image: © Arne Hoel/The World Bank. Used with permission; further permission required for reuse.
Cover design: Debra Naylor, Naylor Design, Inc.

Library of Congress Cataloging-in-Publication Data
Christie, Iain T., author.
    Tourism in Africa : harnessing tourism for growth and improved livelihoods / Iain Christie, Eneida Fernandes, Hannah Messerli, and Louise Twining-Ward.
        pages cm. — (Africa development forum series)
    Includes bibliographical references and index.
    ISBN 978-1-4648-0190-7 — ISBN 978-1-4648-0197-6 (electronic)
    1.   Tourism—Africa, Sub-Saharan. 2.   Economic development—Africa, Sub-Saharan. 3.   Tourism—Africa, Sub-Saharan—Case studies. 4.   Economic development—Africa, Sub-Saharan—Case studies. I. Fernandes, Eneida. II. Messerli, Hannah, 1957–. III. Twining-Ward, Louise. IV. Title. V. Series: Africa development forum.
    G155.A314C57 2017
    338.47916—dc23
                                                      2014009153

Africa Development Forum Series

The **Africa Development Forum Series** was created in 2009 to focus on issues of significant relevance to Sub-Saharan Africa's social and economic development. Its aim is both to record the state of the art on a specific topic and to contribute to ongoing local, regional, and global policy debates. It is designed specifically to provide practitioners, scholars, and students with the most up-to-date research results while highlighting the promise, challenges, and opportunities that exist on the continent.

The series is sponsored by the Agence Française de Développement and the World Bank. The manuscripts chosen for publication represent the highest quality in each institution and have been selected for their relevance to the development agenda. Working together with a shared sense of mission and interdisciplinary purpose, the two institutions are committed to a common search for new insights and new ways of analyzing the development realities of the Sub-Saharan Africa region.

Advisory Committee Members

Agence Française de Développement
Jean-Yves Grosclaude, Director of Strategy
Alain Henry, Director of Research
Philippe Cabin, Head of Research Publishing Division

World Bank
Francisco H. G. Ferreira, Chief Economist, Africa Region
Richard Damania, Lead Economist, Africa Region
Stephen McGroarty, Executive Editor, Publishing and Knowledge Division

Sub-Saharan Africa

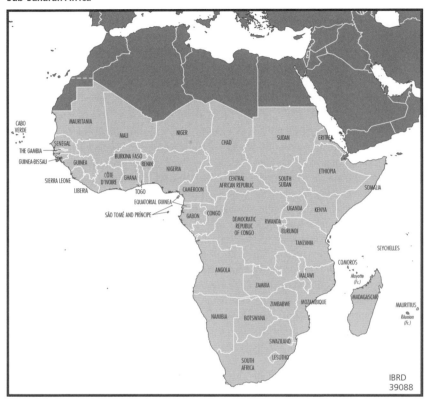

CABO
VERDE

MAURITANIA

MALI

NIGER

CHAD

SUDAN

ERITREA

THE GAMBIA

SENEGAL

GUINEA-BISSAU

GUINEA

BURKINA FASO

BENIN

NIGERIA

SIERRA LEONE

CÔTE
D'IVOIRE

GHANA

TOGO

LIBERIA

CAMEROON

CENTRAL
AFRICAN REPUBLIC

SOUTH
SUDAN

ETHIOPIA

SOMALIA

EQUATORIAL GUINEA

SÃO TOMÉ AND PRÍNCIPE

GABON

CONGO

DEMOCRATIC
REPUBLIC
OF CONGO

RWANDA

BURUNDI

UGANDA

KENYA

TANZANIA

SEYCHELLES

COMOROS

ANGOLA

ZAMBIA

MALAWI

Mayotte
(Fr.)

ZIMBABWE

MOZAMBIQUE

MADAGASCAR

MAURITIUS

Réunion
(Fr.)

NAMIBIA

BOTSWANA

SWAZILAND

SOUTH
AFRICA

LESOTHO

IBRD
39088

Titles in the Africa Development Forum Series

Africa's Infrastructure: A Time for Transformation (2010) edited by Vivien Foster and Cecilia Briceño-Garmendia

Gender Disparities in Africa's Labor Market (2010) edited by Jorge Saba Arbache, Alexandre Kolev, and Ewa Filipiak

Challenges for African Agriculture (2010) edited by Jean-Claude Deveze

Contemporary Migration to South Africa: A Regional Development Issue (2011) edited by Aurelia Segatti and Loren Landau

Light Manufacturing in Africa: Targeted Policies to Enhance Private Investment and Create Jobs (2012) by Hinh T. Dinh, Vincent Palmade, Vandana Chandra, and Frances Cossar

Informal Sector in Francophone Africa: Firm Size, Productivity, and Institutions (2012) by Nancy Benjamin and Ahmadou Aly Mbaye

Financing Africa's Cities: The Imperative of Local Investment (2012) by Thierry Paulais

Structural Transformation and Rural Change Revisited: Challenges for Late Developing Countries in a Globalizing World (2012) by Bruno Losch, Sandrine Fréguin-Gresh, and Eric Thomas White

The Political Economy of Decentralization in Sub-Saharan Africa: A New Implementation Model (2013) edited by Bernard Dafflon and Thierry Madiès

Empowering Women: Legal Rights and Economic Opportunities in Africa (2013) by Mary Hallward-Driemeier and Tazeen Hasan

Enterprising Women: Expanding Economic Opportunities in Africa (2013) by Mary Hallward-Driemeier

Urban Labor Markets in Sub-Saharan Africa (2013) edited by Philippe De Vreyer and François Roubaud

Securing Africa's Land for Shared Prosperity: A Program to Scale Up Reforms and Investments (2013) by Frank F. K. Byamugisha

Youth Employment in Sub-Saharan Africa (2014) by Deon Filmer and Louis Fox

Tourism in Africa: Harnessing Tourism for Growth and Improved Livelihoods (2014) by Iain Christie, Eneida Fernandes, Hannah Messerli, and Louise Twining-Ward

All books in the Africa Development Forum series are available for free at
https://openknowledge.worldbank.org/handle/10986/2150

Contents

Index   279

Boxes

Figures

Maps

Tables

Foreword

For African countries looking to sustain and increase their unprecedented growth rates of recent years, the potential of tourism has not been fully recognized as a vital source of economic and development power that can strengthen and expand the continent's economies. On the wider world stage, tourism contributes more than 9 percent of global GDP, 5.8 percent of exports, and 4.5 percent of investment. African countries are now in their best-ever position to harness the development promise of expanded, sustainable tourism.

Increasing tourist arrivals and spending, even during the recent economic crisis, shows tourism's significant potential for growth. Between 2009 and 2010, despite the global financial slowdown, international tourist arrivals in Africa jumped almost 8 percent, making the region the second fastest-growing in the world after East Asia and the Pacific. As a result, global hotel chains are poised to spend hundreds of millions of dollars in Africa over the coming years to meet rising demand from both international tourists and the continent's own fast-growing middle class.

Tourism can be a powerful development path for Africa. In fact, a welcome key finding of new research suggests that, with effective planning and development, Africa's tourism industry could create 3.8 million jobs over the next 10 years. Already, 1 in every 20 jobs in Africa involves tourism and the travel industry.

With a special analysis of 24 tourism case studies from around the world—spanning Sub-Saharan and North Africa, Asia, Central and Latin America, and the Middle East—this report is a valuable and timely contribution to our efforts to build a sustainable framework for tourism in Africa. It also identifies policies and institutional approaches for African countries to make their tourist industries more competitive and attractive to new investment.

The study shows how tourism barely existed in Thailand in the 1960s and yet now employs 15–20 percent of the country's workforce and how Cancun, Mexico, grew from an uninhabited peninsula into one of the most visited resorts in the world in just 35 years. Mozambique has managed a seemingly impossible transformation of its tourism industry. International tourist arrivals to the country surged 284 percent between 2005 and 2011, and the government forecasts that some 4 million tourists will visit Mozambique each year by 2015. In Cabo Verde, tourism earnings now generate 15 percent of its GDP, and the sector employs roughly one in five workers.

How did these African countries transform their tourism industries? In Mozambique, it took legislative reform, the development of a strategic plan for tourism, and the elimination of unnecessary visas. Cabo Verde attracted significant private investment through political and banking reforms as well as by creating a business-friendly environment for tour operators and other companies.

Many other African countries are on the verge of tourism success. However, as the case studies show, it is by no means easy to develop and sustain successful tourism destinations. African destinations must compete for tourists against Asia and Central and Latin America, which market natural and cultural attractions as well as internationally benchmarked tourist facilities.

For African countries in the early stages of tourism development, the report suggests that governments and the private sector should address security and health concerns associated with political uncertainty and underdeveloped health care infrastructure. According to surveys of hotel developers, African destinations fall short in comparison with Asia and the Americas in perceptions of political, economic, and security risks and the quality of infrastructure, especially in air travel, where the cost, frequency, and routing of African airlines reduces the competitiveness of tourist destinations on the continent.

For those countries looking to scale up tourism, land is often a sticking point. How it is accessed, what tenure is available, what land uses are permitted, and whether investors are treated fairly and consistently are all key questions that surface in the case studies. As tourism grows, planning, standards, and regulations become vital; yet too many can put the brakes on growth and ultimately make tourism less sustainable. Price competitiveness is also significant. Benchmarking studies carried out for this report show that the cost of tours to Africa were 25–35 percent higher than the cost of tours to other regions and that flights to Africa were as much as 50 percent more expensive even where shorter distances were involved.

Lastly, for countries such as Kenya, Mauritius, and South Africa that are deepening and sustaining their tourism success, increasing the share of local value added is imperative. For example, in Tanzania, World Bank trade research notes that most hotel furniture is imported from China, and no trade link existed between local tourism enterprises in the country and the local furniture industry. Another challenge is to manage and cushion the social and environmental impact of large tourism sectors.

While the benefits of tourism development are many, the possible approaches and strategies for development number even more. How can tourism be best developed to address persistent constraints in Africa? This work analyzes persistent constraints and how to resolve them through policy and business reforms that have unleashed tourism potential across other regions of the world. To become competitive worldwide, African governments and the private sector must work together in planning tourism infrastructure, promotion, and financing. Competitiveness also requires the ability to successfully manage growth.

Africa's private companies are increasingly attracting regional and international investment, and the returns on investing in Africa are among the highest in the world. In close alliance with the private sector, governments must also do their part to create better transport, electricity, infrastructure, and other key services to develop tourism for more broad-based growth and improved livelihoods.

This report is the first to examine tourism in Africa comprehensively and regionally and the first to recommend practical, evidence-based measures enabling the sector's economic and development power. This gives new impetus to the continent's development progress by leveraging tourism in pursuit of lasting poverty alleviation and the creation of significantly more jobs and opportunities for all Africans.

Makhtar Diop
Vice President, Africa Region
The World Bank Group

Acknowledgments

This report was developed through the World Bank under the guidance of Makhtar Diop (Vice President, Africa Region), Gaiv Tata (Director, Finance and Private Sector Development, Africa Region), Marilou Uy (Senior Adviser, President's Special Envoy, and former Director, Finance and Private Sector Development, Africa Region), Shanta Devarajan (Chief Economist, Middle East and North Africa Region and former Chief Economist, Africa Region), Irina Astrakan (Sector Manager, Finance and Private Sector Development, Eastern and Southern Africa Region), and Paul Noumba Um (Finance and Private Sector Development, West Africa Region) and was prepared as part of the Competitive Africa: Strategies to Leverage the New Global Economy multisector program led by Vincent Palmade (Lead Economist, South Asia Finance and Private Sector Development) and Tugba Gurcanlar (Trade Specialist, Finance and Private Sector Development, West Africa Region). The core team authoring the report consisted of Hannah Messerli (team leader) with Iain Christie, Louise Twining-Ward, and Eneida Fernandes.

From concept to finalization, the core team benefited from extensive engagement and collaboration with distinguished colleagues across the World Bank Group, including Celestin Monga, Haleh Bridi, MacDonald Benjamin, Dominique Njinkeu, Kirk Hamilton, Punam Chuhan-Pole, Louise Fox, Vincent Palmade, Paul Brenton, Pierre Pozzo di Borgo, Maiko Miyake, David Bridgman, Josephat Kweka, Katrinka Ebbe, and Antia Portillo.

Strategic insights were gained through the generous sharing of expertise by external experts, including Anna Spenceley through the preparation of "Tourism Product Development Interventions and Best Practices in Sub-Saharan Africa," Michael Fishbin and Brian Tress of Ernst & Young through the preparation of "The Sub-Saharan Africa Hospitality Sector Review," and Webster O'Brien and Arik De of SH&E through the preparation of "Competitive Africa: Tourism Industry Research Air Transport Sector Study." These sector studies were complemented by insights from numerous representatives of governments and the private sector across Africa, and of particular note, Anita Mendiratta of Cachet Consulting.

Peer reviewers from the World Bank were Barbara Rippel, Nora Dihel, Phil English, Kirk Hamilton, Guang Chen, Mimi Ladipo, Constantine Chikosi, Parth Shri Tewari, and Shaun Mann. The external reviewers were Uri Dadush (Carnegie Endowment, International Economics Program), Yaw Nyarko (New York University), Yaw Ansu (African Center for Economic Transformation), Chris Rogerson (University of Johannesburg, South Africa), Larry Dwyer (University of New South Wales, Australia), Marina Novelli (University of Brighton, United Kingdom), and Márcio Favilla L. de Paula (United Nations World Tourism Organization, Spain).

The report was edited by Fabienne Stassen and Elizabeth Crompton with support from Martine Bakker, and its production was handled by Jessie McComb.

All involved with the creation and dissemination of this report are appreciative of generous donors who made this comprehensive work and its wide distribution possible. The Multi-Donor Trust Fund for Trade and Development contributed to by the Swedish International Development Cooperation Agency (SIDA), the Department for Foreign and International Development of the United Kingdom (DFID-UK), the Ministry of Foreign Affairs of the Netherlands, and the Swiss State Secretariat for Economic Affairs, managed by Paul Brenton, supported pioneering research and analysis focused on the sector and Africa. The Trade Facilitation Facility, funded by SIDA, DFID-UK, the Ministry of Foreign Affairs of the Netherlands, and the Canadian Agency for International Development, under the direction of Dominique Njinkeu, supported the policy advocacy and implementation activities of this work. The report also benefited from stakeholder engagement across Africa facilitated by Edward Bergman and the Africa Travel Association, and industry engagement globally.

About the Authors

Iain Thornton Christie covered tourism and urban development; land use planning and infrastructure; and private sector development during his career at the World Bank as a manager and adviser. He now consults in these areas with a focus on economic growth and transformation through tourism. In parallel to his core work, Mr. Christie taught at Michigan State, New York, and The George Washington Universities and was a frequent guest lecturer at others. He attended the University of Strathclyde (Glasgow) and has graduate degrees in economics and business from New York and Michigan State Universities, respectively.

Eneida Fernandes has more than 15 years of experience in private sector development for hospitality and tourism. Her work in the Africa Region of the World Bank has included supporting and preparing new private sector development and tourism operations and knowledge products in activities such as support to regional and country-specific studies, design of trust-funded activities for development of cultural heritage sites, institutional capacity building, and trade facilitation activities linked to visas and air transport. Previously Fernandes worked in the Latin America and the Caribbean Region's Sustainable Development Network of the World Bank supporting operation of tourism development activities. Her private sector background includes working in the hospitality sector as a manager and consultant, competency building for youth at risk, implementing best practices in sustainability, and operational capacity building and certification programs.

Hannah R. Messerli is dedicated to using tourism as an economic development tool for emerging economies. As a senior private sector development specialist in tourism at the World Bank, she supports government initiatives to develop private sector capacity in tourism across Sub-Saharan Africa and globally. With more than 20 years of experience in the public and private sectors in tourism planning and development, she has worked in Africa, Asia, Europe, and North and South America. She was a faculty member at New York University and an operations management consultant in Asia and Australia. Messerli has a master's and a doctorate degree in hotel administration and tourism planning from Cornell University and a master's degree in tourism planning and development from The George Washington University.

Louise Twining-Ward is a sustainable tourism specialist with 22 years of international experience in planning, developing, and monitoring sustainable tourism destinations. Currently president of Sustainable Travel International, Louise has lived and worked in more than 30 countries, helping businesses, destinations, and governments to transition to more sustainable management practices. Her special area of interest is the development and use of indicators for monitoring sustainable tourism destination management. Twining-Ward is the author of the UN Women and UNWTO's "Global Report on Women in Tourism 2010" and coauthor of the book *Monitoring for a Sustainable Tourism Transition: The Challenge of Developing and Using Indicators*. She has doctorate and master's degrees in sustainable tourism and in tourism planning and management, respectively, from the University of Surrey in the United Kingdom.

Abbreviations

ADC	Aqaba Development Corporation
AFT	*Agence Foncière Touristique* (Tunisia)
AFTFP	Africa Finance and Private Sector Development (World Bank)
ASEZA	Aqaba Special Economic Zone (Jordan)
DAI	Department of Planning and Investment, *Direction des Aménagements et des Investissements* (Morocco)
FDI	foreign direct investment
FONATUR	National Trust Fund for Tourism Development (Mexico)
GDP	gross domestic product
GSTC	Global Sustainable Tourism Council
IATA	International Air Transport Association
ICT	information and communication technology
ICT	Costa Rica Tourism Board, *Instituto Costarricense de Turismo*
IDB	Inter-American Development Bank
IFC	International Finance Corporation
INFRATUR	Tourism Infrastructure Department (Dominican Republic)
ISO	International Organization for Standardization
ITTOG	Institute of Travel and Tourism of The Gambia
MICE	meetings, incentives, conferences, and exhibitions
NGO	nongovernmental organization
RFP	requests for proposal
SAR	special administrative region
SARS	severe acute respiratory syndrome
SME	small and medium enterprise

SONABA	*Société Nationale d'Aménagement de la Baie d'Agadir* (Morocco)
ST-EP	Sustainable Tourism–Eliminating Poverty
TANAPA	Tanzania National Parks Authority
TDA	Tourism Development Authority (Egypt)
TGST	tourist goods and services tax
TTCI	Travel and Tourism Competitiveness Index
UNCTAD	United Nations Conference on Trade and Development
UNDP	United Nations Development Programme
UNESCO	United Nations Educational, Scientific, and Cultural Organization
UNWTO	United Nations World Tourism Organization
WTTC	World Travel and Tourism Council

All dollar amounts are in U.S. dollars ($) unless otherwise indicated.

Overview

Tourism is a powerful vehicle for economic growth and job creation all over the world. The tourism sector is directly and indirectly responsible for 8.8 percent of the world's jobs (258 million), 9.1 percent of the world's gross domestic product (GDP) ($6 trillion), 5.8 percent of the world's exports ($1.1 trillion), and 4.5 percent of the world's investment ($652 billion) (WTTC 2011). The World Travel & Tourism Council (WTTC) estimates that 3.8 million jobs (including 2.4 million indirect jobs) could be created by the tourism industry in Sub-Saharan Africa over the next 10 years (WTTC 2011).

In Sub-Saharan Africa, the potential for growth in tourism is significant and compelling. Global hotel chains are poised to spend hundreds of millions of dollars in Africa over the next few years to meet rising demand from both international tourists and the continent's own fast-growing middle class.[1] Global international tourist arrivals have been growing steadily at 4–5 percent a year since the 1950s. Between 2009 and 2010, despite the global financial crisis, international tourist arrivals to Sub-Saharan Africa increased 8 percent, making this region the second fastest-growing tourist destination in the world after the Asia Pacific (UNWTO 2010).

Tourism is growing faster in the world's emerging and developing regions than in the rest of the world (UNWTO 2010). The examples of Cabo Verde, the Dominican Republic, the Arab Republic of Egypt, Indonesia, Mauritius, Mexico, Morocco, South Africa, Tanzania, Thailand, Tunisia, and Turkey show how proactive government support can make tourism a powerful and transformative development tool (see part II of the report for individual case studies). In Thailand, tourism barely existed in the 1960s; in 2010 it employed 15–20 percent of the workforce. The Dominican Republic had 1,600 hotel rooms in 1972; in 2011 it had more than 66,000. Tourism accounted for 31.4 percent of exports of goods and services and 7.9 percent of GDP in 2011. Bali, a small island in Indonesia, received 95,000 international tourists in 1973. In 2010 it attracted 1.96 million tourists, who spent $1.9 billion. Cancun, Mexico, grew from an uninhabited peninsula into one of the most visited resorts in the world in just 35 years. In Egypt, from 1990 to 2005, visitor arrivals grew from 2.9 million to 8.6 million, and by 2010, total international arrivals were just short of 15 million.

Mozambique has achieved a seemingly impossible transformation of its tourism industry. International tourist arrivals grew 284 percent between 2005 and 2010. The government expects 4 million tourists a year by 2025. The dramatic growth has been attributed to legislative reform, the development of a strategic plan for tourism, and the elimination of visas for visitors from the Southern African Development Community countries. Tourism in Cabo Verde has also boomed as a result of market-oriented policies, political and banking reforms, and investment incentives. Receipts from tourism in Cabo Verde were $432 million in 2008, constituting 72 percent of all service exports and 15 percent of GDP, while tourism employed an estimated 21 percent of the workforce (27,800 people) directly and indirectly.[2]

Many other countries in Sub-Saharan Africa are on the verge of tourism success. In 2011 tourism directly generated 2.7 percent of the GDP and directly and indirectly accounted for more than 1 in 20 jobs in the region (12.8 million; WTTC 2012). Sub-Saharan Africa has abundant tourism resources. It has expansive beaches, plentiful wildlife, and extensive nature, culture, and adventure opportunities. As disposable incomes rise, domestic travel for leisure purposes is also expected to rise. Between 2001 and 2010, GDP grew an average of 5.2 percent a year, and per capita income grew 2 percent a year, up from −0.4 percent in the previous 10 years. Already more than 10 million people are traveling across international borders every year within Sub-Saharan Africa for shopping, medical needs, sports, religious gatherings, business meetings and conferences, and visits with friends and relatives. For example, 58 percent of all arrivals to Namibia in 2010 were from South Africa and Angola. Regional arrivals to South Africa increased 12.8 percent between 2009 and 2010 (South African Tourism 2010).

Yet it is by no means easy to develop and sustain a successful tourism destination. African destinations compete for tourists against venues in Asia and South America. It is not enough to have interesting natural and cultural attractions and "friendly people." In many African countries a deep-rooted skepticism prevails about the economic and social benefits of tourism, due to a lack of accurate economic data about the sector, genuine concern about the environment, and discomfort with foreign investors and visitors. This report acknowledges the risks that tourism entails, dispels the tourism myths, and lays out an achievable framework for sustainable tourism in Sub-Saharan Africa (figure O.1).

This report, prepared by the World Bank's Africa Finance and Private Sector Development (AFTFP) Tourism Team, synthesizes the results of a World Bank study that drew on five analytical tools for its findings: (a) a 47-country tourism database developed to compare tourism information and competitiveness across Sub-Saharan Africa, (b) a tour operator study that included 47 in-depth interviews with small, medium, and large tour operators in the United States, Europe, The Gambia, and Kenya and an online survey sent to 175 tour operators

Figure 0.1 Framework for Destination Development

in Europe, the United States, and Sub-Saharan Africa,[3] (c) an air transport study that included analysis of international passenger flows and interviews with upper-management airline executives across Sub-Saharan Africa, (d) a survey of tourist hotels that included in-depth interviews with 23 hotel investors, developers, and operators in the United States, Europe, and Africa, and (e) a study of 24 tourism case studies from around the world (including 7 from Sub-Saharan Africa). This study also informed and benefited from the World Bank's Africa Tourism Strategy (World Bank 2010a).

Sub-Saharan African countries with the capacity for tourism can be categorized into three main types according to their level of tourism development: those that are *initiating tourism*, those that are *scaling up tourism*, and those that are *deepening and sustaining tourism*. At the time of writing, most Sub-Saharan African destinations are in the first group. When a country moves up the pyramid, incomes rise, more jobs are created, and the tourism value chain is strengthened.

This report identifies policies and institutional approaches to improve the tourism competitiveness of African countries so that they can move up the pyramid. It clearly explains the opportunities and challenges that tourism offers and suggests strategies based on stories of successful tourism development (including learning from their shortcomings) from across the world.

Performance

Sub-Saharan Africa's share of world arrivals, though still small, is growing. From a small base of just 6.4 million visitors in 1990, Sub-Saharan Africa attracted 30.7 million visitors in 2010. Between 2008 and 2009, tourist arrivals to Sub-Saharan Africa increased 4.4 percent, while arrivals worldwide dropped 3.8 percent. Between 2009 and 2010, tourist arrivals to Sub-Saharan Africa increased 8 percent; the world average was 6.6 percent. Sub-Saharan Africa was the only region where the tourism sector grew during the world economic crisis, and the sector is expected to keep growing.

Tourism is a job-intensive industry. A study by the Natural Resources Consultative Forum found that a $250,000 investment in the tourism sector in Zambia generates 182 full-time formal jobs. This is nearly 40 percent more than the same investment in agriculture and over 50 percent more than in mining. Zanzibar's President Dr. Ali Mohamed Shein has predicted that 50 percent of the island's population will be involved in tourism activities by 2020. He also said that the sector will be a major catalyst in promoting agriculture, employment, and fisheries and in creating more jobs in local industries. Tourism in Zanzibar already provides 11,500 workers with direct employment. An additional 45,000 people are engaged indirectly in the tourism industry (Hamilton and others 2007).[4]

There are already 5.3 million direct tourism jobs across Sub-Saharan Africa (WTTC 2012). By 2021, the WTTC forecasts 6.7 million direct tourism jobs in Sub-Saharan Africa. As travel and tourism touch all sectors of the economy, their indirect employment effects are almost three times as large. The WTTC calculates that the total direct and indirect impact of tourism in Sub-Saharan Africa is 12.8 million jobs. In 2021 more than 16 million people are expected to be employed directly or indirectly as a result of travel and tourism (WTTC 2012).

But tourism is not a panacea. Like other economic activities, it comes with a set of environmental, social, and political risks. If tourism growth goes unmanaged, the natural, cultural, and social assets on which tourism depends can deteriorate. Cabo Verde and Kenya are both feeling the impact of rapid, poorly planned coastal development. It is important to identify the risks and challenges of tourism development and to compare these with alternative options at the outset.

Constraints

The main constraints to tourism development vary by country, but similar patterns of constraints and challenges occur in each of the three stages of tourism development.

In *countries initiating tourism development*, important constraints include basic concerns with security and health that are associated with political instability and underdeveloped health care infrastructure. A 2010 survey of hotel developers found that Sub-Saharan African markets are less attractive than Asian and Middle Eastern markets with regard to the level of risk (political, economic, and security), the image of the region from an investment perspective, the quality and cost of air transport service, and government policy (Ernst and Young 2010). Infrastructure development is a crucial part of initiating tourism development. Air and road connections are the most commonly mentioned constraints on the growth of tourism in Sub-Saharan Africa. Africa's distance from the generating markets creates an acute need for higher-quality and more competitive air access. The cost, frequency, and routing of airlines in Sub-Saharan Africa reduce the competitiveness of its destinations. Visas can also be a basic constraint for many countries. If visas are too expensive or too difficult to obtain, tour operators may opt not to include the country in a regional tour. Where visa requirements have been eased, as in Madagascar and Mozambique, tourism has surged.

Countries scaling up their tourism industry, like Malawi and Zambia, often need to convince policy makers that tourism is of value. Despite the impressive multipliers and track record of tourism in Sub-Saharan Africa, the economic and social importance of the sector is widely underappreciated. Understanding how tourism works, what it is worth, and why it is important is crucial to achieving "destination readiness" for tourism. South Africa has poured resources into its tourism statistics unit and reaped significant results. Basic data include international and domestic arrivals and departures as well as tourist expenditures. Once the basics are in place, data are needed for subsectors of the industry: transportation (load factors and costs per passenger per kilometer, for instance), lodging (including capacity, occupancy, and room rates), small and medium enterprises, national parks (visitation and entry fees), and other areas. More market research, surveys, and systematic monitoring (including benchmark development) are needed to supply these data.

In addition to data, land is often a sticking point during the scaling up of tourism. Fundamental issues include how land is accessed, what tenure is available, what land uses are permitted, and whether investors are treated in a fair and consistent manner. In many Sub-Saharan African countries, such as Angola, it is difficult to access land for development due to unclear ownership. In Maldives, however, long-term leases are available for domestic and foreign investors through a unique leasing program of one resort per island. A similar solution has been used in Cabo Verde. Several countries are identifying specific sites for dedicated tourism development.

As tourism grows, planning, standards, and regulations become vital. But too much regulation and unpredictable behavior by government can inhibit growth and ultimately make tourism less sustainable. In Namibia, for example, more than 50 permits and certificates are required for lodging owners who want to register or renew their registration of their property (HAN 2010). This is expensive and time-consuming and inhibits business growth. A study in South Africa found that compliance costs were three times higher for businesses in tourism than for those in other sectors of the economy (Meny-Gibert 2007).

Price competitiveness is particularly important for destinations wanting to scale up their tourism sectors. Tours to Sub-Saharan Africa cost 25–35 percent more than tours to other parts of the world (Twining-Ward 2010), and flights to Sub-Saharan Africa are almost 50 percent more expensive even where shorter distances are involved. For example, an average round-trip flight to Madagascar from New York costs $2,975, while a flight to China from New York costs $1,173. The reasons for the higher prices include lack of competition in the airline industry, the need for imported goods and services, and high import duties.

The cost of developing hotels and the cost of debt financing also affect tourism competitiveness in Sub-Saharan Africa. In Nigeria, the cost of developing hotels is upward of $400,000 per room for a mid-market hotel; in Ghana the cost is $250,000 per room. Median hotel development costs elsewhere in the world are $200,000 per room for a full-service hotel (Ernst and Young 2010). Higher room rates are the end result.

For *countries that are deepening and sustaining their tourism success*, such as Mauritius and Kenya, human resources and product innovation are particularly important. Sub-Saharan Africa has a large pool of young workers and more than 10 million new job seekers every year (World Bank 2010b). But the level of education is low. Tourism employment requires at least mid-level service sector skills. The hotel and restaurant industry often suffers from a discrepancy between training supply and demand. Whereas tourism training institutes generally focus on hotel management, the current skills gap is often at the operational level. Keeping up with the level of demand for tourism education is a challenge for some African countries. In Ethiopia, for example, only 32 students can be accommodated in the Catering and Tourism Training Institute, despite more than 300 applications. In Namibia, a history of underinvestment in education and poor educational achievement has left young people unprepared to take up new tourism opportunities. In The Gambia, more than 800 students are enrolled in tourism or hospitality courses through the private and public sectors; only one institution, the Institute of Travel and Tourism of The Gambia, provides accredited training (Novelli and Burns 2009). Another challenge is to increase the share of local value added. For example, in Tanzania, a World Bank trade paper notes that most hotel furniture is imported from China and that no trade link exists between local tourism enterprises and the local furniture industry.[5] The last main challenge is to manage and mitigate the social and environmental impact of a large tourism sector. The Mediterranean coastlines of Spain and Italy are good examples of growth that exploded to the point of threatening the viability of the resorts located there. Tanzania's northern circuit is overloaded, and the country is trying to create new areas for tourism growth in the south, in the Selous Reserve, Zanzibar, Pemba, and Mafia Islands.

Strategies

This report gathers 24 case studies from around the world to illustrate how tourism development can succeed. Based on these case studies, 13 strategic areas are highlighted and discussed. Some strategies are more applicable to destinations *initiating tourism*, while others are more applicable to those looking to *scale up tourism* or to *deepen tourism success*. These case studies reveal that, although the needs, challenges, and approaches of tourism destinations change over time, certain basic elements that are needed to initiate, scale up, and deepen tourism success are applicable to most Sub-Saharan African situations.

Initializing tourism development requires certain institutional, infrastructural, and policy foundations. Infrastructure is almost as important as land for tourism. It is needed for the development of tourism and for the welfare of communities. Trunk infrastructure and public utilities are usually provided by the state, as in Turkey. There are exceptions, however. In Punta Cana, the Dominican Republic, investors financed and constructed the airport and the water supply. Focusing their scarce resources on the tourism segment and geographic location of highest potential has proven an effective strategy for many countries at the start of their tourism journey. Such an approach allows for the removal of a critical mass of constraints (including those pertaining to infrastructure, security, and skills) to enable the early arrival of world-class investors who can play a vital role in launching the destination. Such a focused approach can also help to pilot policy reforms (for instance, in land and air transportation). For example, when Indonesia finally let foreign carriers terminate flights in Bali, tourism grew dramatically.

Scaling up tourism development involves planning infrastructure development, promotion, and financing. It also requires the ability to manage growth. This entails scaling up and replicating the successes of the initial tourism zones through countrywide policy reforms and decentralization. Agencies are often created to establish an enabling environment for those interested in investing in land. An example is Uganda's land information service. Alternatively, governments such as Madagascar and Mozambique have prepared special tourism investment zones. Some land banks, such as Tunisia's Real Estate Development Agency (Agence Foncière Touristique), hold land for development. Urban development corporations have also been used to develop land for tourism, drawing on experience from other sectors, where the increased value of land is used as a means of financing utilities (China and India). South Africa and Namibia have adopted conservancy models in which communities play a more active role in the management and leasing of land. Joint-venture projects have been particularly successful in Namibia.

Deepening tourism success involves diversifying products, building human resources, and closely monitoring environmental and social impacts. For countries that have already achieved substantial success in tourism, such as Kenya, the Seychelles, and South Africa, deepening and sustaining success in the face of global competition are constant challenges. Developing new, innovative products and markets, undertaking heritage preservation, upgrading tourism competencies, and planning for social and environmental sustainability are integral to the long-term success of destinations. The Seychelles launched its sustainable tourism label. South Africa launched a new minimum standard for responsible tourism. The Dominican Republic produces locally more than 90 percent of the supplies needed for its tourism sector, giving it a competitive advantage over other islands in the Caribbean. This practice also explains the Dominican Republic's high ratio of jobs to tourist arrivals. Dominican businesses rely on local design and materials for their hotels and lodges, together with international standards in fittings and fixtures. Not only does this practice increase employment, but it also adds value to the tourism experience in the Dominican Republic by providing a distinctive local atmosphere in hotels and lodges.

Recommendations

Throughout this report, recommendations focus on the following:

- Encouraging tourism managers to focus on the value of their product and to be competitive in the international market
- Gaining the essential and strong political support for tourism at the highest levels of government and encouraging government to take the lead in creating effective institutions and in coordinating mechanisms to maintain a dialogue with all stakeholders
- Ensuring the private sector's vital role and the need for government to create an enabling environment for investments and to provide supporting infrastructure for those investments
- Recognizing donors and their capacity to assist the tourism sector in many vital areas, such as infrastructure, training, and pro-poor tourism
- Providing investors with needed information and establishing "one-stop" shops
- Acknowledging the critical role of air transport and the need to liberalize air policies

- Improving connectivity within countries and regions, as well as road and air access to the region, whether through private sector entrepreneurship, government investments, or a combination
- Resolving the current constraints on tourism and considering other countries' solutions to the issues of land availability, investor access to finance, taxes on tourism investments, low levels of tourism skills, lack of security and safety, high crime rates, public health issues, visa requirements, and red tape and bureaucracy
- Assessing the scale of development that is appropriate to the country's assets and management resources and determining where and when development will take place
- Noting that all four pillars of sustainability for tourism—financial, economic, social, and environmental—are essential for sustained tourism growth
- Realizing the potential to finance tourism by appropriating to government the economic rents that tourism generates.

Embracing these strategies consistently is fundamental to tourism development that is economically productive, environmentally sensitive, and protective of cultural heritage.

Case Studies

Tourism has been used as a tool for economic development throughout the world. The case studies included in part II of this report offer an opportunity to learn from previous experience in Africa as well as in other countries. The cases illustrate good practice and lessons learned from experience in tourism as a source of growth and poverty alleviation in developing and emerging countries around the world. Some of them also reveal certain failures. Ultimately, the cases are a tool for Sub-Saharan African countries seeking to explore and learn from the experiences of tourism development in Africa and other significant destinations. Case activities date from the 1970s to the mid-2000s, and the cases were chosen to illustrate a particular challenge or success and the effects of certain planning decisions. The earlier cases provide an extended time frame demonstrating their success or failure and offer perspective on how destinations grow and change over time. The newer cases reflect more recent policies and trends, such as corporate social responsibility, voluntourism, and charitable tourism. Together, the case studies are intended to help countries in Sub-Saharan Africa to envisage a dynamic future for tourism.

The 24 case studies are listed in table O.1, which includes key features of each case. The geographic location of each study is shown in map O.1. While the

Table O.1 Summary of Case Studies

Region and country	Project name	Project category	Salient features of tourism development
Asia			
Indonesia	Bali	Island, large resort	Protection of cultural heritage; institutional framework; airline access and infrastructure development
Indonesia	Nihiwatu	Island ecolodge	Community partnerships; social inclusion and charitable donations
Korea, Rep.	Kyongju	Historic city	Coordination and access; market timing
Maldives	Island resorts	Multi-island, resort development	Transparent evaluation of resort bids; planning framework and environmental controls; business environment; airline access
Singapore	Sentosa Island	Day-trip amusement park and island resort development	Building a resort to appeal to residents and international visitors; importance of training
Latin America and the Caribbean			
Costa Rica	Lapa Rios	Ecotourism	Environmental conservation; tourism certification, including ethics code
Dominica	Jungle Bay	Island ecolodge	Ecotourism integration into world tourism institutions (time-sharing)
Dominican Republic	Puerto Plata	Coastal resort	Political support for tourism; transition from public to private investment; model widely replicated in country; sanitation requirements
Dominican Republic	Future sector growth	Economic and policy analysis	Future dispersion of growth in the country; carrying capacity and diversification of product line
Mexico	Cancun	Coastal resort on uninhabited land	Location and scale; role of public sector developer (FONATUR, Mexico's National Trust Fund for Tourism Development); all-inclusive tourism
Middle East and North Africa			
Egypt, Arab Rep.	Sharm El Sheikh	Coastal development	Product diversification; land acquisition; institutional rationalization
Jordan	Aqaba	Multisector resort and industrial development	New coastal resort development; integration of multisector investment in economic zone
Morocco	Bay of Agadir	Rebuilding of city following earthquake	Mixed-use resort development, residential, commercial and hotel; business environment, open skies, political support; project stopped for political difficulties
Morocco	Coastal cities tourism	Preparing city beach sited for private tender	Strengthening ministry's role as tourism planner; regulation and promotion of private investment; parallel measures in support of resort development
Tunisia	Infrastructure in six zones	Coastal city resort development	Integrated national development; institutional framework, including land bank
Turkey	South Antalya	Large-scale resort	Model widely replicated throughout the country; staff housing problems

(continued next page)

Table O.1 (continued)

Region and country	Project name	Project category	Salient features of tourism development
United Arab Emirates	Dubai	National transformation	New source of growth in face of depleting oil reserves; how to launch a new sector; investment and promotion
Sub-Saharan Africa			
Cabo Verde	National tourism	Transformation in a small country	Market-oriented policies and democratic processes; quality air transport infrastructure, supportive air policies; scale, form, and type compatible with available resources
Kenya	Nairobi	Meetings, incentives, conventions, and exhibitions	Business versus leisure travel, diversification of product line; convention facility investment; targeted marketing
Mauritius	National tourism	Policy framework	Export and investment promotion; training; control of supply; airline policy
Namibia	Wilderness travel	Public-private partnerships	Concessioning community land to private sector; improved wildlife management through conservancies
Rwanda	Sabyinyo Silverback Lodge	Protection of mountain gorillas	Community partnerships with private sector; biodiversity protection
South Africa	Wilderness Safaris and &Beyond	Public-private partnerships	Land management; concessioning community land to private sector
Tanzania	Mt. Kilimanjaro	Mountaineering packages	Poverty reduction analysis; sanitation and management; trade unions for porters, guides, and cooks

Map O.1 Geographic Location of Each Case Study

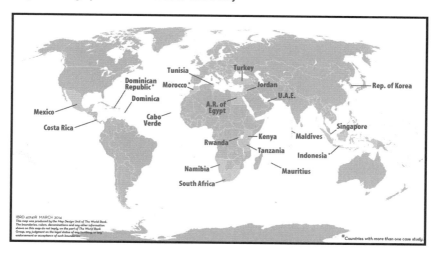

cases come from a wide range of destinations, within and outside of Sub-Saharan Africa, each case was selected to illustrate a specific lesson learned that can be applied to tourism development and planning in Sub-Saharan Africa as well as in other global destinations.

Role of Donors

Much can be done to assist countries wanting to take advantage of their tourism assets. Many actors are involved, including the United Nations World Tourism Organization (UNWTO) and the European Union; multinational donors, such as the World Bank and the African Development Bank; and bilateral donors, such as the U.S. Agency for International Development, the U.K. Department for International Development, and SNV (the Netherlands Development Organization).

The World Bank's Africa Region Tourism Strategy envisions *transformation through tourism: harnessing tourism for growth and improved livelihoods* (World Bank 2010a). The strategy relies on four pillars: policy reforms, capacity building, private sector linkages, and product competitiveness. Working closely with client countries, implementation of the Africa Region Tourism Strategy focuses on interventions in these four areas to address the persistent constraints on the growth of tourism in Sub-Saharan Africa. Combined, these interventions enable high-demand tourism products to compete in the global marketplace. This strategy builds on the lessons learned at the beginning of some countries' tourism journey, when the World Bank helped them by financing the development of tourism zones with high potential (such as Cancun in Mexico, Bali in Indonesia, and Puerto Plata in the Dominican Republic). The lessons gathered in this report highlight how Sub-Saharan African countries can learn from the experience in other countries and achieve growth and improved livelihoods through tourism.

Notes

1. See "Top Hotels Wake Up to Africa Growth Potential," Reuters, August 16, 2011 (http://af.reuters.com/article/topNews/idAFJOE77F08420110816).
2. For further information on Cabo Verde, see Twining-Ward (2010).
3. The survey had a 31 percent response rate.
4. See "Zanzibar Focuses on Tourism to Boost Its Economy and Job Creation," eTN, November 1, 2011 (http://www.eturbonews.com/26124/zanzibar-focuses-tourism-boost-its-economy-and-job-creation).
5. Amit Sharma, consultant, contributed an unpublished paper as input for a diagnostic trade paper examining several sectors, including furniture.

References

Ernst and Young. 2010. "Sub-Saharan Africa Hospitality Sector Overview." Unpublished research for the World Bank Group, Washington, DC.

Hamilton, K., G. Tembo, G. Sinyenga, S. Bandyopadhyay, A. Pope, B. Guilon, B. Muwele, S. Mann, and J. M. Pavy. 2007. *The Real Economic Impact of Nature Tourism in Zambia.* Lusaka: Natural Resources Consultative Forum.

HAN (Hospitality Association of Namibia). 2010. "Documents Needed to Register, Extend Registration, and/or Needed Recurrently for the Operation of an Accommodation Establishment." Unpublished internal document, HAN, Windhoek.

Meny-Gibert, S. 2007. "Counting the Cost of Red Tape to Tourism in South Africa." *SATSA Tourism Tattler Trade Journal* 2.

Novelli, M., and P. Burns. 2009. "Restructuring The Gambia Hotel School into a National Tourism Training Institute." The Gambia Investment Promotion and Free Zone Agency, Banjul.

South African Tourism. 2010. *South African Tourism Annual Report 2010/2011.* Johannesburg: South African Tourism.

Twining-Ward, L. 2010. "Cape Verde's Transformation: Tourism as a Driver of Growth." Unpublished case study for the World Bank, Washington, DC.

UNWTO (United Nations World Tourism Organization). 2010. *UNWTO Tourism Highlights, 2010 Edition.* Madrid: UNWTO.

World Bank. 2010a. *Africa Region Tourism Strategy: Transformation through Tourism; Harnessing Tourism for Growth and Improved Livelihoods.* Washington, DC: World Bank. https://openknowledge.worldbank.org/bitstream/handle/10986/12841/700990 ESW0P1170ing0the0Economic0Pow.pdf?sequence=1.

———. 2010b. "New Jobs for a New Africa: A Strategy for Rapidly Scaling Up Employment in Africa." Strategic Directions for Finance and Private Sector Development, World Bank, Washington, DC.

WTTC (World Travel & Tourism Council). 2011. *Travel and Tourism Economic Impact, 2011.* London: WTTC.

———. 2012. *Travel and Tourism Economic Impact: Sub-Saharan Africa, 2012.* London: WTTC.

Regional Perspective: A Framework for Tourism Development in Sub-Saharan Africa

Chapter 1

Introduction

This report is written for government, state, and local policy makers as well as for donors, potential investors, nongovernmental organizations, and other stakeholders in the tourism sector in Sub-Saharan Africa. It is also written for Sub-Saharan African and other researchers, with the objective of stimulating further analysis of the tourism sector in the region.

Methodology

Like for any industry, the metric that a government should use when deciding on the existence and extent of its tourism industry is the economic value that the sector adds through well-paying jobs, the reasonable levels of public and private investment required, and the limited damage to the country's natural and cultural assets. In economic terms, the objective should be to increase the economic value added of the sector as well as its total factor productivity, making sure that any negative social and environmental effects are priced into the formula. The latter is particularly important for tourism that depends on the careful "exploitation" of cultural and natural assets. In addition to discussing how African countries can become more competitive (by decreasing the cost-quality ratio of the tourism services offered), this report also discusses how countries can generate, sustain, and distribute the economic rents of tourism that is associated with unique cultural and natural assets.

The methodology used in the report follows three analytical steps: benchmarking performance, explaining differences in performance, and identifying ways to improve performance and address constraints on growth.

Benchmarking Performance

Sub-Saharan African countries are categorized into four groups: pre-emerging, potential, emerging, and consolidating. They are then benchmarked with comparable countries by the size and productivity of their tourism industries along the following dimensions:

- The size and growth of their tourism industries based on international tourist arrivals and spending according to data from the United Nations World Tourism Organization (UNWTO)
- The quality-to-cost ratio of packaged vacations established through a survey of tour operators conducted for this report
- The cost of accommodation for a given quality of service based on a study conducted for this report, which includes benchmarking of labor and capital productivity for the hospitality sector in Sub-Saharan Africa (Ernst and Young 2010)
- The cost of air transportation based on a study completed for this report, which also benchmarks the operational performance of airlines as a proxy for productivity (SH&E 2010).

Explaining Differences in Performance

Differences in value added, quality, cost, and productivity among countries are explained to the extent possible by differences in the way tourism actors operate, which, in turn, can be related to factors in their external environment. These external factors include a combination of government failures (for example, policies preventing markets from functioning properly) and market failures (for example, coordination failures and information asymmetries). As these market malfunctions are often the result of a combination of government failures, the report puts greater emphasis on the latter, including the following:

- Political and macro instability, increasing the cost and risk of private investment
- Lack of openness and competition in transport industries (for example, in airline companies), resulting in high costs and poor service
- Problematic and costly tourism visa policies
- Inadequate physical infrastructure, limiting access to key tourism assets
- Unsecured land rights, increasing the cost and risk of private investment
- Overly restrictive zoning laws, preventing the exploitation of natural tourism assets
- Mismanagement by the government of key tourism assets (including hotels, museums, and national parks)
- Policy issues in related industries (for example, a poorly performing construction industry that increases the cost of building hotels)

- Failure to ensure public safety (for example, failure to control malaria or combat crime)
- Restrictive labor market policies (including emigration policies), poor education systems, and the increasing cost of labor
- Policy issues in financial systems, increasing the cost of capital.

Improving Performance and Addressing Constraints on Growth

Because constraints on the growth of tourism vary by country—despite some commonalities—this report includes 24 case studies on the growth of tourism throughout the developing world. The case studies address a range of tourism segments in countries performing at three of the four levels of tourism development identified through the benchmarking exercise. They are designed to reflect the varied characteristics of African tourism. In their totality, they suggest possible solutions to the many issues identified as constraints in African countries, although the solutions would need to be adapted to local circumstances. They show, in particular, how countries can take a pragmatic and proactive approach in a reasonable amount of time and with limited resources to resolve a critical mass of issues from the long and hard list of government and market failures (for example, through the establishment of tourism zones).

These cases also illustrate how countries have dealt with possible negative externalities related to tourism, such as enforcing regulations to limit degradation of the environment, while pursuing possible positive externalities, such as capturing some of the economic rents generated by unique assets through taxes and auctions and supporting first-mover investors who can often put a destination on the global tourism map but frequently face high risks and costs of entry.

Too often in the past, analyses of the tourism sector have not used economic tools that can illuminate constraints on and barriers to growth, identify solutions to increase the value added by the sector, or identify sources of funding to protect the assets on which the sector is based. Several recent World Bank studies of the Africa region have begun to refine and adapt economic tools for the tourism sector.[1] Value chain analysis, a tool useful for identifying market failures and understanding the impact of tourism on the poor, is available for some countries (see box 2.1 in chapter 2 on value chain analysis).

Evidence Base

Five analytical modules provided the platform and inputs for this report:

- *The Sub-Saharan Africa tourism database.* This online research tool covers 47 countries in Sub-Saharan Africa. The database for each country includes geographic, economic, social, and transport indicators; essential economic data on tourism; trends in tourism demand; information on tourism products and activities; a comparative analysis of costs, including flight costs and park entrance fees; a tourism competitiveness ranking; and an analysis of performance, potential, constraints on growth, and available strategies of the tourism sector.

- *The tourism accommodation study.* This study sought to understand the high hotel operating and financing costs and the competitiveness of Sub-Saharan Africa compared with similar international markets. It conducted in-depth interviews with 23 hotel investors, developers, and operators in the United States, Europe, and Africa.

- *The air transport study.* This study sought to explain crucial aspects of the performance of air transport in Sub-Saharan Africa (for example, the high cost of air travel to and within the region), to discuss the constraints on stronger performance, and to identify strategies to achieve global competitiveness in Sub-Saharan African air transport. International passenger flows were analyzed, and high-level airline executives across Sub-Saharan Africa were interviewed.

- *The tour operator study.* This study conducted 47 in-depth interviews with small, medium, and large tour operators in the United States, Europe, The Gambia, and Kenya. It included the results of an online survey, with responses from 51 tour operators in Europe, the United States, and Sub-Saharan Africa.

- *The tourism case studies.* Case studies of 24 tourism destinations worldwide are included in part II of this report. There are seven case studies from Sub-Saharan Africa: luxury wildlife tourism in South Africa; the wildlife conservancy program in Namibia; hiking tourism on Mount Kilimanjaro, Tanzania; beach tourism in Cabo Verde; cultural tourism in Mauritius; conservation tourism in Rwanda; and business tourism in Nairobi, Kenya. Both the successes and shortcomings of each experience provide lessons.

A Note on African Tourism Research

Tourism is of critical importance for economic development, and "it is imperative to take tourism seriously and analyze it no less critically and theoretically than what are considered more legitimate topics and places" (Klak 2007).[2] In his study of research on African tourism, Rogerson (2011) observes that the New Partnership for Africa's Development[3] in its Tourism Action Plan recognizes tourism "as one of the sectors with the most potential to contribute to the economic regeneration of the continent, particularly through the diversification of African economies and generation of foreign exchange earnings." The methodology for Rogerson's study involved a search for relevant material on Google Scholar, a review of chapters in books and proceedings that were not captured by Google Scholar, and an intensive analysis of major tourism journals published in the last decade.

Rogerson notes that notwithstanding the impressive growth in tourism flows to Africa during the last two decades and the policy prominence afforded tourism as a driver of economic development, the volume of academic research on African tourism systems has grown slowly, even with regard to benchmarking African tourism products against global standards of efficiency (Barros and Dieke 2008; Santos, Dieke, and Barros 2009; Barros, Dieke, and Santos 2010). Recent overviews of tourism scholarship in Africa in general and in the 15 countries of the Southern African Development Community[4] underscore the limited scholarship on the tourism-development nexus. Given the potential growth of tourism, Rogerson suggests that careful and strategic policy interventions, grounded in evidence-based research from the African experience, are essential to maximize the role of tourism in national, regional, and local development. Seif and Rivett-Carnac (2010) highlight the need "to anchor research to a canon of literature, so as to achieve greater compatibility between research sites and over time."

Conceptually, investigations of African tourism can employ a diverse set of theoretical frameworks because tourism is both a social and an economic activity. Rogerson also suggests that the United Nations Millennium Development Goals could be used as a framework for research. He lists the following as priorities for research on African tourism:

- Tourism as a tool to protect the environment and cultural heritage
- Implementation of tourism's pro-poor aspects to relieve poverty
- Tourism as a lever for economic growth
- Tourism's intersectoral linkages
- The benefits of different types of tourism (for example, high-end versus package holidays, community-based tourism, heritage tourism, and city tourism)
- Human resource and employment issues for the tourism and hospitality sector
- The nature of the "African tourist," both domestic and regional.

Rogerson concludes that giving voice to new African scholarship in tourism and hospitality suggests the need to establish a world-class tourism and hospitality research center in Africa with an agenda grounded in and informed by contemporary theoretical debates and discourse. The research program should concentrate on the challenges and gaps around the nexus between tourism and development in Africa specifically and in the developing world as a whole.

Notes

1. For links to tourism publications related to Sub-Saharan Africa, see http://www .worldbank.org/afr/tourism.
2. This section of the chapter summarizes the findings of Rogerson (2011), whose bibliography references 116 studies.
3. New Partnership for Africa's Development was adopted by the African heads of state and government of the Organization for African Unity in 2001 and ratified by the African Union in 2002 to address Africa's development problems within a new paradigm. NEPAD's main objectives are to reduce poverty, put Africa on a sustainable development path, halt the marginalization of Africa, and empower women.
4. The 15 countries are Angola, Botswana, the Democratic Republic of Congo, Lesotho, Madagascar, Malawi, Mauritius, Mozambique, Namibia, the Seychelles, South Africa, Swaziland, Tanzania, Zambia, and Zimbabwe.

References

Barros, C. P., and P. U. C. Dieke. 2008. "Technical Efficiency of African Hotels." *International Journal of Hospitality Management* 27 (3): 438–47.

Barros, C. P., P. U. C. Dieke, and C. M. Santos. 2010. "Heterogeneous Technical Efficiency of Hotels in Luanda, Angola." *Tourism Economics* 16 (1): 137–51.

Ernst and Young. 2010. "Sub-Saharan Africa Hospitality Sector Overview." Unpublished research for the World Bank, Washington, DC.

Klak, T. 2007. "Sustainable Ecotourism Development in Central America and the Caribbean: Review of Debates and Conceptual Reformulation." *Geography Compass* 1 (5): 1037–57.

Rogerson, C. M. 2011. "The African Tourism Research Landscape: Current Directions and Gaps." Paper presented to an expert panel workshop for Aga Khan University, Nairobi, January 2012.

Santos, C. M., P. U. C. Dieke, and C. P. Barros. 2009. "Efficiency Measurement Systems in Hotels: Perspectives from Luanda, Angola." *Tourism Review International* 12 (3-4): 303–15.

Seif, J., and K. Rivett-Carnac. 2010. "[Editorial] Tourism Impacts: Lessons for Policy, Programmes, and Projects." *Development Southern Africa* 27 (5): 627–28.

SH&E. 2010. "Competitive Africa: Tourism Industry Research Phase II Air Transport Sector Study." Unpublished report for the World Bank, Washington, DC.

Chapter 2

Why Tourism?

There are new grounds for optimism regarding the economic future of Sub-Saharan Africa. Until the onset of the global economic crisis, gross domestic product (GDP) had grown 5 percent a year, on average, for a decade (World Bank 2011). Growth was widespread even among non-oil-exporting countries and countries experiencing conflict. Although Africa was badly hit by the global crisis, the continent avoided a worse slowdown in growth in 2009 thanks to prudent macroeconomic policies and financial support from multilateral agencies; economic growth rebounded in 2010. The poverty rate in Sub-Saharan African countries declined from 59 percent in 1995 to 50 percent in 2005 (World Bank 2010a). Child mortality rates are declining, the incidence of the human immunodeficiency virus/acquired immune deficiency syndrome (HIV/ AIDS) is stabilizing, and primary education completion rates are rising faster in Sub-Saharan Africa than elsewhere.

Africa's private sector is increasingly attracting investment, with much of the funding coming from Europe and the United States. China, India, and other countries are also investing large sums in the region. Private capital flows are higher than official development assistance, and foreign direct investment is higher than in India. Returns to investment in Africa are among the highest in the world. The public sector has set the conditions for the exponential growth of information and communication technology (ICT), which could transform the continent. The private sector is creating an emerging middle class of hundreds of millions of consumers. The climate for market-oriented, pro-poor reforms is proving robust, and the voice of civil society is increasingly being heard. Interregional cooperation is strengthening, and democracy has taken hold in several countries. Given this scenario, experts view Sub-Saharan Africa as on the brink of an economic takeoff, much like China 30 years ago and India 20 years ago.

Tourism is one of the key industries driving the change. From a small base of just 6.7 million visitors in 1990, Sub-Saharan Africa attracted 33.1 million visitors in 2011 (UNWTO 2012). Tourism contributed $33.5 billion to the economies of Sub-Saharan Africa, accounting for 2.7 percent of the region's GDP (WTTC 2012). Already 1 in 20 jobs is in travel and tourism, and women hold almost

50 percent of tourism sector jobs in Africa (UNWTO 2011). Tourism provides multiple opportunities for economic growth and improved livelihoods.

Ten Reasons to Develop Tourism

Tourism often does not receive the credit it deserves as an economic transformer. Yet the evidence from Thailand, where tourism accounts for 6 percent of GDP, to Mauritius and Cabo Verde, where it accounts for 13 and 15 percent of GDP, respectively, tells a different story and underlines the sector's potential. There are 10 principal reasons for developing tourism assets and placing a country on a path to sustained economic growth of its tourism sector.

Spur Economic Development

The global tourism sector is vast and growing. In 2010, 935 million tourists traveled internationally. They spent $339 billion directly in emerging economies. The total global export income from tourism was over $1 trillion. The average annual growth of international tourist arrivals was 4.1 percent from 1995 to 2010 (UNWTO 2010). The total direct, indirect, and induced impact of travel and tourism on global GDP in 2011 was an estimated $6.3 trillion, with 255 million jobs in the sector, $743 billion in investments, and $1.2 trillion in exports. Tourism's contribution in 2011 represented 9 percent of global GDP, 1 in 12 jobs, 5 percent of investment, and 5 percent of exports. In 2012, although growth was lower than originally anticipated, tourism contributed 2.8 percent of global GDP.[1]

Tourism has demonstrated its economic strength and potential all over the world. In Thailand, tourism barely existed in the 1960s; in 2010 it was worth 6 percent of GDP and employed 15–20 percent of the workforce (figure 2.1).

Thailand is not the only tourism success story. The Dominican Republic, in the Caribbean, had only 1,600 hotel rooms in 1972 but more than 66,000 in 2011; tourism accounts for 31 percent of exports of goods and services and for 7.9 percent of GDP.[2] Bali, a small island in Indonesia, received 95,000 international tourists in 1973; in 2010 Bali attracted 1.96 million tourists, who spent $1.9 billion.[3] Cancun, Mexico, grew from an uninhabited peninsula to one of the most visited resorts in the world in just 35 years: Cancun now has more than 600,000 residents and hosts more than 10 million tourists a year. Its success is attributable to (a) the government's foresight in imagining a grand resort on a deserted peninsula as part of its long-term strategy for economic development, (b) proximity to a very large and wealthy market in North America, especially in Miami, (c) its Caribbean climate and beach assets, and (d) help from Spanish hotel groups skilled in offering all-inclusive vacations, which had previously held little appeal for U.S. tourists.

Figure 2.1 Transformational Effects of Tourism in Thailand

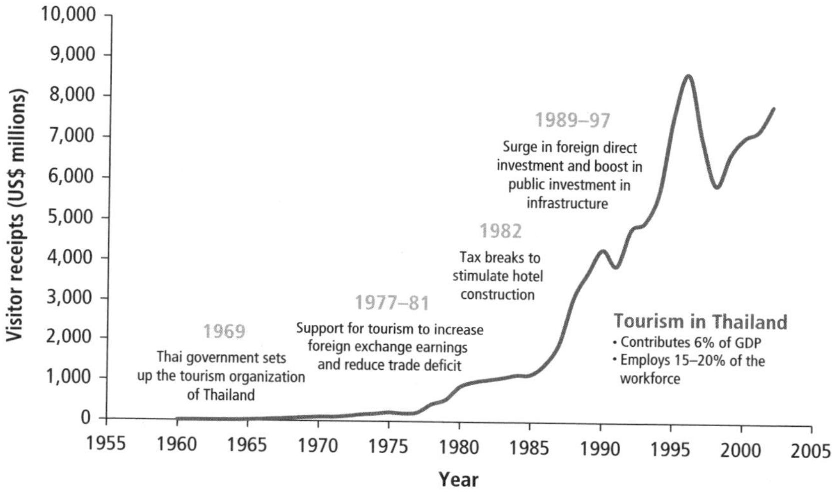

Source: Garcia 2010.

Similar patterns of growth occurred in the Arab Republic of Egypt. In 1970 Egypt attracted fewer than 400,000 tourists; by 1980 the number had reached 1 million. From 1990 to 2005, visitor arrivals grew from 2.9 million to 8.6 million; by 2010 total international arrivals amounted to just under 15 million, and tourist expenditures reached $12.5 billion. Tourism contributes 9.1 percent of Egypt's GDP and has traditionally been the country's largest foreign exchange earner, ahead of worker remittances and petroleum products. According to the World Travel & Tourism Council (WTTC), total direct and indirect employment in the sector amounts to 3.35 million jobs.

Create Good Jobs

More than 200 million people are underemployed in Sub-Saharan Africa, and 10 million more seek jobs every year (World Bank 2010c). As tourism grows, the sector's job creation and income-generating potential rises exponentially (Natural Resources Consultative Forum 2007). Tourism compares well with other sectors regarding the opportunities for small and medium enterprise (SME) development, career advancement, and lifelong learning potential. In Sub-Saharan Africa 1 in 20 jobs is already in travel and tourism (Twining-Ward 2010b). Tourism is also a more efficient job creator than many other sectors due to the multiple downstream effects. A study in Zambia by the Natural Resources Consultative Forum found that a $250,000 investment in the tourism sector generates 182 full-time formal jobs. This is nearly 40 percent more than the same investment in agriculture and over 50 percent more than in mining (Hamilton and others 2007).

Build Remote and Developing Regions

Tourism is growing faster in the world's emerging and developing regions than in the rest of the world. International arrivals in developing countries grew an average of 11 percent a year between 1990 and 2009 (UNDP 2011). The share of international tourist arrivals received by emerging and developing regions increased from 32 percent in 1990 to 47 percent in 2010 (UNWTO 2010).

Accelerate Reform

Tourism accelerates policy and economic reforms that can support SME development and stimulate foreign investment (Wong, Christie, and Al Rowais 2009). In Cabo Verde, tourism took off when the banking sector was reformed, when the escudo was pegged to the euro, and when an attractive package of investment incentives was created (Twining-Ward 2010a). In Rwanda, significant improvements in Doing Business indicators were linked to the desire to increase gorilla tourism. Across Sub-Saharan Africa, destinations are finding that political stability, good governance, and an enabling business environment provide the foundation for tourism growth (UNCTAD 2007).

Improve Infrastructure

In an effort to attract visitors, governments and private sector businesspeople often invest in infrastructure improvements that have positive impacts on the economy and on rural communities. South Africa invested $2.6 billion in upgrading the Johannesburg, Cape Town, and Durban airports in preparation for an influx of sports tourists for the 2010 Fédération Internationale de Football Association (FIFA) World Cup (Agence Française de Développement 2010). For some years hotel managers worldwide have reached out to their surrounding communities to improve the health and welfare of their workers but also to ensure that local people prize the benefits that tourists can bring them, thus protecting tourists from potential resentment of the much poorer local people. In addition, tourists are generally willing to donate money to help local communities. Sun 'n' Sand Beach Resort in Kenya provided water and a health clinic for a neighboring village. The Nihiwatu ecolodge in Sumba, Indonesia, raises $400,000 annually to help 147 villages with health, clean water, and nutrition projects.

Increase Domestic Consumption and Diversify Exports

Tourists create demand for goods and services such as transport, gasoline, retailing, finance, real estate, agriculture, and communications. The WTTC expected tourism to generate twice as much from indirect spending on non-tourism goods and services and from induced supply chain benefits as from direct tourist spending in 2011 (WTTC 2011).

Empower Women, Young People, and Marginalized Populations

Women make up an estimated 70 percent of the world's poor (ILO 2009). Empowering women to participate in economic development at all levels and in all sectors is essential to building strong economies and stable, just societies (UNIFEM and UN Global Compact 2010). Globally, tourism is one of the few economic sectors in which women outnumber men in certain positions and are paid the same. In Africa, a 2010 study by the United Nations World Tourism Organization (UNWTO) and UN Women found that 31 percent of employers in the hotel and restaurant sector were women (UNWTO 2011), compared with 21 percent in other sectors. Young people also derive productive employment from tourism. In Namibia, after just one year of training, an unskilled laborer can learn to be a tour guide, significantly increasing his or her income.[4] By engaging young people in productive employment, tourism can provide an alternative to out-migration, urban poverty, and armed conflict.

Preserve Cultural Heritage and Conserve the Environment

Tourism creates additional value for historic buildings, heritage sites, and the fine and performing arts (Robinson and Picard 2006; World Bank 2001). Cultural heritage is under threat across Sub-Saharan Africa, but tourism provides a source of revenue for its protection. In Ethiopia, for example, the World Bank helped to finance a $35 million cultural heritage project in 2010 that supports and complements private sector investment at major heritage sites and their surrounding communities through tourism planning. Tourism also provides a stimulus for conserving the environment and promoting alternative livelihoods. In 2008 a partnership between the Global Environment Facility of the United Nations Development Programme (UNDP) and the government of the Seychelles established a $3.6 million, six-year biodiversity management project. In Costa Rica, the decision to promote sustainable tourism led to the establishment of a broad spectrum of environmental and social initiatives, including the Costa Rica Certificate in Sustainable Tourism and Blue Flag beaches.

Promote Public-Private Partnerships

Effective tourism planning requires collaboration and partnerships between public and private sectors. Consultation enables participants to take joint responsibility for policy choices, facilitates the collection of economic data, and has positive outcomes for national planning. Public-private partnerships in conservation, infrastructure development, and investment promotion have been used in Sub-Saharan Africa for many years. Examples include the approach taken by Kenya Wildlife Service, SANParks in South Africa, the Madagascar

National Parks Initiative, and Gorongosa National Park in Mozambique (Garcia 2010). The World Wildlife Fund reports that the private sector has invested more than $19 million in tourism joint ventures in communal conservancies in Namibia since 1998 (NASCO 2009).

Improve the National Image

Successful tourism can change external perceptions of a country, improve inter-cultural understanding, and create a positive internal frame of reference for a country. Once war-torn, Rwanda has changed its image because it features mountain gorilla conservation and tourism. With civil strife in the past, Mozambique is now known for its attractive beach resorts. Costa Rica is associated with biodiversity, ecotourism, and environmental consciousness, rather than with the drug trafficking that plagues other countries in the vicinity. The advent of satisfied tourists increases national pride, enhances investor confidence, and serves as an engine of growth for the economy as a whole.

Complexities of Tourism

Tourism's complexity arises from its multisectoral nature as well as its dependence on numerous actors with very different interests in the sector, including those of the international visitors that determine its success. Most, if not all, African destinations depend on the arrival of tourists from countries that are largely outside their sphere of influence.[5] In developing countries, regional and domestic tourism can seldom replace the demand for goods and services that international tourists generate. Such tourism is to be encouraged, however, as it can increase demand, help to diversify accommodation (and thus benefit small, local entrepreneurs), and mitigate seasonality.

In today's globalized market, all tourism products compete on price. Although the prime decision maker is the individual traveler, the volume of tourists to a particular destination is determined to a considerable extent by the world tourism industry, represented by tour operators, travel agents, and transport services in the countries of tourist origin. Destinations can influence these external industry managers through effective and continuing promotion and marketing campaigns but will succeed only if the sale of a high-quality product is competitive in value, not just in price.

Managing Tourism's Risks

Each sector comes with its own set of risks and challenges, and tourism is no exception. The tourism sector, however, is burdened by criticisms that do not reflect reality.

Leakage

A frequent criticism is that the destination receives only a portion of the total cost of a tourist's expenditure. The belief in "leakage" ignores the inputs, entrepreneurship, and risks taken by businesses in the countries of tourist origin. The so-called leakage actually represents the financial returns to businesses that, without the profit incentive, would not undertake the tourism venture. The destination would then be deprived of tourism revenues from all but domestic and, possibly, regional tourists, where leakage would also occur.

A preliminary study in Tanzania estimates that the country captures about half the global value chain in package holidays sold in Europe, but this estimate excludes discretionary spending by tourists. To put tourism in perspective, a global value chain analysis for coffee exports from Tanzania estimates that growers of the best coffee can expect to receive only about 4 percent of the final retail price of the coffee sold in supermarkets in Europe (Mitchell, Keane, and Laidlaw 2009). If basic processing, packaging, and transportation are added, the country still only captures about 8 percent of the final retail price of coffee. As box 2.1 on value chain analysis states, such analysis can identify areas in the chain where the country may be able to derive more benefits from tourism. But, even in the worst cases when a country can provide few local inputs to the value chain, tourism employs local people, among them women and poorly educated workers who would have difficulty finding alternative employment.

Sociocultural Impacts

Tourism has been associated with a variety of social and cultural ills, particularly prostitution. Prostitution is illegal in some countries, whereas child prostitution is illegal nearly everywhere. Tourism is often blamed for fostering both. Prostitution exists openly or clandestinely in most developed and developing countries. In the latter, prostitution is most likely a by-product of unemployment; desperate people, most often women unable to find other work, turn to the oldest profession to feed and house themselves and their dependents. Markets for prostitution exist in all countries—demand for these services exists with or without tourism. Mining is renowned for its camp followers, and most urban areas have concentrations of prostitutes. Ports are also known to be centers of prostitution. Some foreign visitors undoubtedly pay for prostitutes, but the majority travel either as families or as couples and do not use these services. Tourism cannot be blamed for the existence of prostitution, although a small minority of tourists do pay for it.

Child prostitution and child pornography are entirely different from prostitution tourism. They are illegal activities such that those promoting and buying them can be prosecuted in the destination and their home country. Most governments abhor these activities, and many nongovernmental organizations (NGOs) worldwide are working to abate them or take preventive measures to

BOX 2.1

Value Chain Analysis

Value chain analysis is a method for accounting and presenting the value that is created in a product or service at each stage as it is transformed from raw input to a final product consumed by end users. Three issues for the policy and reform agenda typically emerge from the analysis:

- *Product market issues*, for example, trade policy, competition, price distortions, subsidies, licensing, product standards, customs, and property rights regulations
- *Factor market issues*, for example, wages, finance charges, utility markets, and land prices
- *Sector-related issues*, for example, market diversification, research and development, product diversification, and supplier linkages.

Value chain analysis is typically performed in three stages: (a) mapping industry processing chains graphically and quantitatively by disaggregating components such as cost, time, and value added along the various segments of each chain; (b) establishing benchmark indicators for comparing domestic performance against international performance and best practices; and (c) conducting further analysis, such as assessing the relative importance of the issues that affect the performance of the value chain and prioritizing the most binding constraints on the competitiveness of the industry.

The value chain analysis framework identifies a set of priorities—some that are sector-specific and some that apply to the entire economy. Certain issues must be addressed by the private sector, while others fall in the domain of the public sector. In tourism, the analysis involves mapping the transactions and relationships that occur along the tourism supply chain and working with tourism stakeholders to identify bottlenecks in the system and create appropriate market-based solutions.

The World Bank has made value chain analysis a priority in recent years. A value chain analysis for Kenya's tourism sector (World Bank 2010b) highlighted the impact of infrastructure limitations on overall costs; for example, the highest cost within the safari package is inland transport for a weekend excursion. The study found that public sector charges and fees erode private sector profits substantially across all segments of the tourism product. In-country expenditures vary significantly across the different tourism segments. The authors noted that the private sector is responding effectively to demand for customized, small-scale ecotourism packages that offer exclusive wild-life viewing well above the price of such packages in competing African markets. They warned, however, that given the inadequacy of the policy and regulatory environment for conservation and wildlife tourism, the tourism load may strain the sustainability of these ecosystems. Insights such as these, gained through value chain analysis, support the development of the sector from a variety of perspectives.

Source: FIAS 2007.

protect street children. The tourism industry itself has established a Code of Conduct for the Protection of Children from Sexual Exploitation in Travel and Tourism, which is an industry-driven tourism initiative co-funded by the Swiss government's State Secretariat for Economic Affairs and by the private sector within the tourism industry, supported by the End Child Prostitution, Child Pornography, Trafficking of Children for Sexual Purposes (ECPAT) international network; its advisory partners are the United Nations Children's Fund (UNICEF) and the UNWTO. As noted in the Costa Rica case study, since 2008 applicants for certification by the Instituto Costarricense de Turismo's National Accreditation Commission must be signatories to the code of conduct against the sexual exploitation of children and adolescents. Any foreigner traveling for the purpose of child prostitution or pornography is a criminal, not a tourist.

Crime levels are said to rise with tourism. Too often the discrepancy between the tourists' incomes and those of the local people breeds resentment toward the visitors. Again, where unemployment is high and poverty is endemic, crime is more likely to occur. One solution is to strengthen the police force in areas frequented by tourists; a related solution is to identify high-crime areas in the destination and warn tourists to stay away from them. A more effective and long-term solution is to extend the benefits of tourism to local communities living near tourist accommodation. For some time, hotel managers throughout the world have deliberately reached out to their surrounding communities. Whether by offering employment, stimulating the provision of services such as guiding and dry cleaning, supporting local schools, buying hotel inputs from local farmers, donating bed linen and towels when they are replaced in the hotels, booking performers of indigenous song and dance, or creating a market-place for handicrafts and local products within the hotel, the benefits of tourism reach surrounding communities and make the tourist a valued guest rather than a person to be robbed. These same actions are precisely the way to make tourism more pro-poor because direct contact is generally required to engage the poor in tourism.

The fear that foreign visitors might corrupt local cultures arose in the early days of mass tourism and package holidays. In today's globalized world, tourists are far less responsible for introducing local people to different cultures and preferences than are the Internet, movies, music, and so forth.

Negative Economic Impacts

Tourism can fuel higher prices for land in tourist areas. This is the equivalent of the gentrification or rebuilding of depressed urban areas in large cities through-out the world. When land is needed for economic activities that are more expensive than residential or small business can generate, land prices rise, but governments can help to mitigate these negative impacts through zoning and the construction of low-cost housing. Tourism can also lead to increased reliance by locals on imported goods and services, including food, but this can be countered by offering local cuisines to tourists, providing a more authentic experience while encouraging the continued production of local foodstuffs. Most hotels welcome a constant flow of high-quality local foodstuffs for their kitchens because they are almost always less expensive than the imported products.

If tourism growth goes unmanaged, the natural, cultural, and social assets on which tourism depends can deteriorate. Worrisome stories about the overuse of mountain slopes, coastal areas, small islands, and fragile cultural assets have been heard for years. Without question, some countries have not protected their assets as they should. With the growing realization of the fragility of these assets, the increased information about how to protect them, and the international technical and financial assistance that has followed, awareness about establishing limits on the number of visitors has helped to mitigate and stem some of the more grievous misuses of tourism assets. Bhutan controls access to the country as a whole; the Galapagos Islands limit the number of boats and occupants that can visit the site; India forbids the close proximity of vehicles to the Taj Mahal. As the discussion on economic rents in this report shows, countries have tools to acquire funds to protect and improve the assets that attract tourists. A well-balanced package of user fees and policies to protect the assets is essential for successful management of the tourism sector.

Managed sustainably, tourism is an effective development tool. When tourism's environmental, social, and economic constraints are addressed, tourism energizes economies. Costa Rica's eco-country branding has had a positive effect on a multitude of goods and services, from the sale of coffee and furniture to manufacturing. Thailand has bounced back from military coups and a tsunami on the strength of its tourism industry. With the full knowledge that tourism is a complex sector with tentacles that reach into myriad other economic activities, all of which require careful management, countries with tourism assets should prioritize tourism as a development tool.

Competitiveness

Productivity, efficiency, quality, and innovation, together with factor and transaction costs, are central to understanding competitiveness.[6] Productivity is difficult to calculate in the service sector, however, and competitiveness in tourism is especially difficult to measure quantitatively. The World Economic Forum's Travel and Tourism Competitiveness Index (TTCI) uses a combination of 14 qualitative and quantitative indicators to compare the competitiveness of 139 destinations. They include regulatory, infrastructure, and tourism resources indicators. The TTCI ranks countries according to scores for policies;

regulations pertaining to the environment, safety and security, and health and hygiene; indicators for government workers employed in tourism, air transport, ground transport, other tourism, and ICT infrastructure; indicators for price competitiveness, quality of human resources, and national perceptions of tourism; and the strength of natural and cultural resources.

Complexity in measuring competitiveness in tourism arises because the whole is larger than the package of goods and services used by the tourist. The tourist experience is affected by the cultural setting, the attitudes of the local people, the climate, and, simply, the sum of all the experiences the tourist has between leaving his or her home to arriving in the tourism destination and then returning home. The value of the package becomes more important to the tourist than its price. A receptive local population can, therefore, create great value for the tourism product, although it is difficult to measure.

Competitiveness in tourism is depicted in this report as a pyramid (figure 2.2). At the bottom lies the destination with only the most essential tourism facilities. As tourism becomes accepted, the destination must provide additional and improved facilities to expand its base. Finally, at the peak of the triangle, the destination's quality determines its competitiveness. The challenge, then, is to remain on top. To climb the quality pyramid, destinations must put the fundamentals in place, replicate their successes, and manage them for sustainable outcomes.

Many primary tourism assets in Sub-Saharan Africa are expensive to access, poorly managed, and deteriorating. Furthermore, numerous tour operators consider service standards to be particularly low in Sub-Saharan Africa, resulting in visitors having a disappointing perception of value for money. Long-haul

Figure 2.2 Framework for Destination Development

visitors are generally happy to pay park entrance fees if they are confident that they are being used for park maintenance, but they expect the quality of the experience to match the cost. Even in well-known destinations in Sub-Saharan Africa, public reinvestment in tourism attractions is often insufficient to maintain and improve their quality. Other assets in Sub-Saharan Africa are deteriorating or lie dormant because of lack of access, operational and management know-how, signage, marketing, or funding. Ethiopia has seven United Nations Educational, Scientific, and Cultural Organization (UNESCO) world heritage sites, four national parks, and distinctive historic products based on ancient Axumite civilizations, but it is still underperforming relative to other areas of East Africa (Mitchell and Coles 2009). Cameroon and Gabon have significant natural tourism resources but have failed to exploit them because of lack of access, lack of involvement of local communities, and insufficient funding.

The World Bank's Africa Region Tourism Strategy states that many destinations in Sub-Saharan Africa fail to deliver high-quality service because tourism ministries lack the know-how and leadership to develop and implement policies and effective plans; tourism associations fail to address the training needs of their members; and a disconnect exists between tourism schools and the skills needed by tourism businesses. If mature destinations want to command and maintain tourism's appeal, greater attention needs to be paid to the quality-value equation. While high-end tourists are prepared to pay top dollar for the "trophy value" of a vacation in Sub-Saharan Africa, persons in the important middle section of the market need to feel that they are getting value for their money. Professional tourism services result in higher guest satisfaction and a broader mix of tourism products.

Role of the Government

A high-quality product can only flourish in a country where the tourism sector is well managed. This point was made in the World Bank's tourism sector study for Senegal (Crompton and Christie 2003, 30):

> Whether Senegal becomes a major tourism destination will depend on the quality of sector administration. Tourism is essentially a private sector activity but is highly dependent on public sector support. Tourism cuts across many sectors and there is often little communications between them. Among the ministries with functions or activities related to tourism, in addition to the Ministry of Tourism, are those ministries responsible for finance, land, public works, transport, agriculture, labor, culture, national parks, immigration and customs, and commerce. To be successful, tourism requires coordination and complementarity of actions within the government and between the government and the private sector, civil society in general, and, in

particular, with local communities that are specifically impacted by tourism, where NGOs can facilitate the process. Only a continuing dialogue between the public and private sectors can lead to successful tourism management.

The government's primary role in tourism should be to develop the strategy for the sustainable growth of the sector, to formulate policy, to create the conditions for public investment, and to provide an enabling business environment to complement private sector activity. A policy that encourages private investment will be conducive to long-term private investment; a policy of command and control will likely stifle long-term investment. Governments play a key role in creating an attractive environment for investors and tourists; they build highways, repair bridges, upgrade airports, improve cultural heritage sites and pedestrian areas, and support events and festivals. They ensure that hospitals provide good health care and that potable water is available. Governments also play a role in improving the investment climate over time if they create healthy financial markets, maintain transparent land transactions with a reliable land registry, recognize the importance of training and promote public and private training solutions, and provide appropriate incentives for investment.

Strong political support for tourism is often the starting point for destination development. Political support from the top is needed to remove policy bottlenecks, mobilize resources for infrastructure investments, and coordinate actions across ministries and with the respective local governments. For example, in Egypt, many regulations stood in the way of tourism development, but the creation of the Tourism Development Authority in 1991, as an agency of the Ministry of Tourism, was crucial to alleviating the problem. In the case of Cancun, Mexico, the government's foresight in imagining the resort was fundamental to the destination's success. In Mauritius, with falling sugar prices and severe competition in textiles, the government set out to diversify its economy and generate export-led growth, focusing particularly on tourism. To address the distance from major markets, the government set up its own airline, Air Mauritius, and developed pooling arrangements with other major airlines.

The World Economic Forum's TTCI contains a regulatory subindex that measures how governments prioritize tourism, how much they spend on tourism as a percentage of the total budget, how effective their marketing and branding are, and how comprehensive monthly and annual tourism data collection is. The results of the data collected from six Sub-Saharan African and six other destinations are shown in table 2.1.

The total TTCI rankings for 139 countries place Mauritius, one of Sub-Saharan Africa's brightest tourism stars, first in the world. The government not only prioritizes tourism but also ranks third in the world for travel and tourism expenditures, and the public and private sectors combined rank eighth for the effectiveness of their marketing and branding. Sub-Saharan African

Table 2.1 Travel and Tourism Competitiveness Index (TTCI) Ranking for Selected Countries, 2011
regulatory subindex, prioritizing tourism

Country	Government prioritization of tourism	Government expenditure on travel and tourism	Effectiveness of marketing and branding	Compre-hensiveness of annual tourism data	Timeliness of monthly and quarterly tourism data	Total score
Cameroon	118	112	130	126	123	135
Costa Rica	13	24	14	58	72	19
Dominican Republic	23	1	34	28	12	7
Egypt, Arab. Rep.	46	21	42	40	46	22
Indonesia	71	13	58	28	12	15
Kenya	41	20	19	72	46	18
Mauritius	5	3	8	44	12	1
Morocco	11	64	12	28	1	23
Mozambique	48	94	54	28	98	63
Tanzania	95	30	74	88	109	90
Thailand	16	85	20	111	12	38
Zambia	53	105	59	98	123	111

Source: WEF 2011.
Note: Scores are ranked for 139 countries. Lower numbers are higher performers.

destinations score particularly low in the areas of "comprehensiveness" and "timeliness" of tourism data, which handicaps efforts to manage the sector effectively. Even Mauritius ranks forty-fourth in "comprehensiveness of annual tourism data." Among the remaining Sub-Saharan African countries for this regulatory subindex, Kenya and Tanzania rank among the region's best tourism performers; Mozambique and Zambia are in a second category; and Cameroon is ranked as a country "initiating tourism." With greater government support, all of these countries should have a better-performing tourism sector. Overseas marketing representation is another indicator of the level of political support for tourism; it creates a distinct advantage in reaching international markets. Only 15 out of 47 Sub-Saharan African countries have dedicated overseas marketing offices.

Regularly scheduled consultations among tourism representatives enable participants to take joint responsibility for policy choices and to develop a common vision. Open communication and an environment of mutual respect and understanding are critical to effective public-private nonprofit sector partnerships in tourism. In East Asian countries, consultation has enhanced decision making, strengthened government, and generated greater consensus, transparency, and follow-through for market reforms. Various examples of institutional coordination and mechanisms for consultation among the plethora of actors in the tourism sector are evident throughout the world.

Examples of Governments' Success in Tourism Development

Forming a multisector technical group can improve the coordination of tourism, as can the creation of a working group to perform the analyses needed to inform decision making. Aware that a strategy for tourism was essential for the implementation of sound policies for the sector, the Senegalese Ministry of Tourism itself organized the *journées nationales de concertation* in 2002. Participants represented a cross-section of society, including decision makers, tour operators, members of parliament, researchers, and journalists. Most states in the Caribbean Community have created statutory bodies that regularly bring together public and private sector representatives for specific tourism responsibilities, most often for promotion and marketing, but also for broader tourism management issues. The Antalya development project in Turkey established two coordinating committees—one in Ankara, the other in Antalya—to ensure coordination between the central government, developers, local government, and community stakeholders.

Many of the policy and practice areas that apply to tourism are derived from other sectors; examples include labor laws, building codes, and commercial and other regulatory legislation. A multisectoral stakeholder coordination committee, such as the Private Sector Advisory Group set up in Ghana, can help to mitigate this issue. The Private Sector Advisory Group has been able to make proposals that no single group could have comfortably made. It has since expanded into a business roundtable and private sector foundation with an ambitious agenda to improve the business environment. In Mauritius, for example, the government strongly encouraged open dialogue with the private sector through the establishment of a Joint Economic Council. Similar initiatives exist in Cameroon, Côte d'Ivoire, Madagascar, Senegal, Uganda, and Zambia.

The case study of Morocco's public support for private action describes a successful capacity-building program for a critical government agency: the Department of Planning and Investment (Direction des Aménagements et des Investissements, DAI) of the Ministry of Tourism. As a result, the DAI initiated sustainable, integrated coastal resort developments through public-private partnerships. By the project's closing, the DAI had prepared four large land development concessions on about 1,500 hectares that would create 30,000 new beds and 100,000 direct and indirect jobs. The final agreements for the concessions included clauses to protect environmentally sensitive areas, natural habitats, and cultural properties within and near the future resorts and set environmental guidelines for resort management.

Role of the Private Sector

The critical investments financed by the private sector are, traditionally, in accommodation and related tourism services. Although the capital that gives value to natural and cultural assets stems from the private sector, tourism cannot operate successfully without considerable government support. The government must provide supporting infrastructure as well as appropriate policies to create an enabling environment for private investment.

Management may well be the most critical factor in the quality of a hotel[7] and, therefore, in the price it can charge in the international tourism market. The responsibilities of a hotel manager are onerous and have become more complex, as ICT plays an increasingly prominent role and social and environmental issues determine the acceptability of the accommodation to local communities and to environmentally minded tourists. In Sub-Saharan Africa, many hotels have to provide their own infrastructure services, such as power, water filtration and treatment, solid waste removal, and sewage treatment and disposal, to compensate for the unreliability of public services. Such investments necessarily raise a hotel's capital and operating costs, raise prices for the tourists, and adversely affect competitiveness.

The lack of availability of sufficiently long-term local financing for tourist accommodation and related services constrains the growth of tourism in Sub-Saharan Africa. Local people, other than the elites, often cannot raise investment funds from personal sources. Two consequences can arise from the lack of domestic capital markets: in some countries with strong tourism assets, foreign private investment may dominate the hotel sector and, in others, tourist accommodation and services may be of low quality, making the destination uncompetitive in the international market. A notable exception is Mauritius, where most hotels, even the most luxurious, are locally owned because profits from sugar and textiles were reinvested in the hotel sector; currently, Mauritius has four hotels classified as "leading hotels of the world."

Management contracts can provide technical assistance and transfer knowledge to local investors who are able to raise the capital for a hotel but do not have the expertise to manage it. Such assistance can be particularly helpful to countries initiating tourism.

The private sector often establishes its own professional associations—for example, hotel owners or managers, restaurant owners, and transport owners associations. These organizations enable the exchange of useful knowledge and some centralization of functions, particularly in ICT. The Caribbean has a long history of support for its "small hotels," enabling them to share databases, promotion, advertising, and even purchasing.

Although the private sector has a difficult enough job simply managing its own properties, it must establish partnerships with government to ensure the success of the sector. In some cases, the private sector will finance large infrastructure projects, such as an airport, in partnership with the government. Most frequently, the partnerships occur when the private sector participates actively in the coordination committees and mechanisms. In many countries, the public and private sectors join forces to promote and market the sector; the government allocates budgetary funds to create an overall image of the country and its tourism assets, while the private sector promotes specific tourist accommodation and services.

Role of Donors

Tourism ministries are often underfunded, and getting tourism started involves a significant commitment of resources. Tourism master plans, technical assistance for strengthening institutions and formulating strategy, training for hotels, restaurants, and tourism services, the provision of water and sewage treatment plants, improved health care and sanitation training, particularly in local communities serving tourism, upgraded transport access to tourism destinations, and a new or upgraded airport or port facilities are some of the investments needed to launch tourism or expand it to the next development stage. These investments will benefit many other sectors, but tourism provides the economic justification for the expenditures. In some cases, donor assistance may be the only source of funding.

In Bali, for example, the government was instrumental in developing the first tourism master plan that made Bali a top site for tourism. The master plan for Bali was commissioned in 1970 and compiled by a French consulting group, funded by the UNDP, and supervised by the World Bank. In the Dominican Republic, a department of the central bank, using funds from the World Bank, implemented the first project. In Tunisia, the government identified several sites for tourism development and then invited the World Bank to support the development of infrastructure and site planning. An Italian consulting firm conducted the preparatory studies, funded by the UNDP and executed by the World Bank. In each case, an "anchor development" site was identified and given initial stimulus and support. When the project was successfully launched, this success improved investor confidence and stimulated the growth of the entire destination.

In the area of infrastructure, external assistance is requisite. Tourism is far more dependent on a range of infrastructure services (power, potable water, waste management, telecommunications, and all forms of transport and related services) than most economic activities. Furthermore, the absence of any one infrastructure service can seriously impede the marketability of the tourism product and can damage the resource base of the asset. As previously noted, many resort hotels and accommodation in isolated areas already provide basic infrastructure services for their guests within the hotel gates, adding to the capital and operating costs of tourist accommodations and thus raising the costs of visiting.

Addressing Africa's $93 billion infrastructure deficit will require two concerted efforts:

- Promoting policy measures and institutional reforms by governments and public utilities to address numerous inefficiencies that together hemorrhage some $17 billion of infrastructure resources annually
- Harnessing greater domestic and external public resources and, through the above policy and institutional reforms, providing an attractive business environment for private investment, including for public-private partnerships (World Bank 2010a).

In addition to its role as a direct investor, the World Bank will work to address the policy and institutional inefficiencies and will assist in improving the overall public finance framework, including infrastructure planning, project screening, and project execution. The Bank's program in Africa will emphasize sustainable infrastructure by helping countries to develop clean energy strategies that improve both infrastructure and the environment. The World Bank is increasingly focusing on regional infrastructure projects, including transport corridors, larger power generation projects, cross-border transmission lines, fiber-optic backbone, and aviation and maritime transportation. The World Bank, with its clients worldwide, cannot provide Sub-Saharan Africa's infrastructure needs alone. Other donors are urgently required to help to modernize the continent's infrastructure and connect its poorest regions with existing networks. Tourism can provide the stimulus and economic justification for part of that infrastructure investment.

Notes

1. WTTC, Economic Data Search Tool (http://www.wttc.org/research/economic-data-search-tool/).
2. Based on UNWTO statistics. See the case study on Puerto Plata for more information.
3. Based on UNWTO statistics. See the case study on Bali for more information.

4. Results of personal interviews at the Namibia Academy for Tourism and Hospitality suggested that young people can earn five times more as a tour guide than as a farm laborer.

5. This section draws from IFC, World Bank, and MIGA (2000).

6. In *The Competitive Advantage of Nations,* Porter (1990) introduces the concept of "National Diamond." The competitiveness of a nation is modeled using four inter-related influences: factor conditions, demand conditions, related and supporting industries, and firm strategy and rivalry. Porter defines competitiveness as "the ability of entrepreneurs (of a country) to design, produce, and market goods and services, the price and nonprice characteristics of which form a more attractive package than that of competitors."

7. As Mark Twain noted, "All saints can work miracles, but few could manage a hotel."

References

Agence Française de Développement. 2010. "Modernizing O. R. Tambo International Airport." http://www.afd.fr.

Crompton, D. E., and I. T. Christie. 2003. "Senegal: Tourism Sector Study." Africa Region Working Paper 46, World Bank, Washington, DC.

FIAS (Foreign Investment Advisory Service). 2007. *Moving towards Competitiveness: A Value Chain Approach.* Washington, DC: World Bank.

Garcia, A. 2010. "Public-Private Sector Partnership: An Emerging Mechanism in Tourism Development." In *Africa Tourism Strategy: Transformation through Tourism,* Part 2. Washington, DC: World Bank.

Hamilton, K., G. Tembo, G. Sinyenga, S. Bandyopadhyay, A. Pope, B. Guilon, B. Muwele, S. Mann, and J. M. Pavy. 2007. *The Real Economic Impact of Nature Tourism in Zambia.* Lusaka: Natural Resources Consultative Forum.

IFC (International Finance Corporation), World Bank, and MIGA (Multilateral Investment Guarantee Agency). 2000. "Tourism and Global Development." World Bank, Washington, DC.

ILO (International Labour Organization). 2009. "Global Employment Trends for Women." ILO, Geneva.

Mitchell, J., and C. Coles. 2009. *Ethiopia: Enhancing Private Sector and Community Engagement in Tourism Services.* London: Overseas Development Institute.

Mitchell, J., J. Keane, and J. Laidlaw. 2009. *Making Success Work for the Poor: Package Tourism in Northern Tanzania.* Final Report. London: Overseas Development Institute.

NASCO (Namibian Association of Community-Based Natural Resource Management Support Organisations). 2009. *Namibia's Communal Conservancies: A Review of Progress and Challenges in 2009.* Windhoek: NASCO and World Wildlife Fund.

Natural Resources Consultative Forum. 2007. "Zambia Economic and Poverty Impact of Nature-Based Tourism, Economic Sector Work." Report 43373-ZM, World Bank, Washington, DC.

Porter, M. E. 1990. *The Competitive Advantage of Nations.* New York: Free Press.

Robinson, M., and D. Picard. 2006. *Tourism, Culture, and Sustainable Development.* Paris: UNESCO.

Twining-Ward, L. 2010a. "Cape Verde's Transformation: Tourism as a Driver of Growth." Unpublished case study for the World Bank, Washington, DC.

———. 2010b. "Sub-Saharan Africa Tourism Industry Research, Phase II Tour Operator Study." Unpublished report for the World Bank, AFTFP, Washington, DC.

UNCTAD (United Nations Conference on Trade and Development). 2007. *FDI in Tourism: The Development Dimension.* Geneva: United Nations.

UNDP (United Nations Development Programme). 2011. "Tourism Poverty Strategies in the Integrated Framework for Least Developed Countries." Discussion Paper, UNDP, New York, April.

UNIFEM (United Nations Development Fund for Women) and the UN Global Compact. 2010. *Women's Empowerment Principles: Equality Means Business.* New York: United Nations.

UNWTO (United Nations World Tourism Organization). 2010. *UNWTO Tourism Highlights, 2010 Edition.* Madrid: UNWTO.

———. 2011. *Global Report on Women in Tourism 2010.* Madrid: UNWTO.

———. 2012. *UNWTO Tourism Highlights, 2012 Edition.* Madrid: UNWTO.

WEF (World Economic Forum). 2011. *The Travel and Tourism Competitiveness Report, 2011: Beyond the Downturn.* Geneva: World Economic Forum.

Wong, M., I. T. Christie, and S. Al Rowais. 2009. "Tourism in South Asia: Benefits and Opportunities." World Bank, PREM, Finance and Private Sector Development Unit, South Asia, Washington, DC.

World Bank. 2001. *Cultural Heritage and Development: A Framework for Action in the Middle East and North Africa.* Washington, DC: World Bank.

———. 2010a. *Africa's Future and the World Bank's Role in It.* Washington, DC: World Bank.

———. 2010b. *Kenya's Tourism: Polishing the Jewel.* Washington, DC: World Bank, Finance and Private Sector Development, Africa Region.

———. 2010c. *New Jobs for Africa: A Strategy for Rapidly Scaling Up Employment in Africa.* Strategic Directions for Finance and Private Sector Development. Washington, DC: World Bank, June.

———. 2011. "Africa's Future and the World Bank's Support to It." World Bank, Washington, DC. http://siteresources.worldbank.org/INTAFRICA/Resources/AFR_Regional_Strategy_3-2-11.pdf.

WTTC (World Travel & Tourism Council). 2011. *Travel and Tourism Economic Impact, 2011.* London: WTTC.

———. 2012. *Travel and Tourism Economic Impact: Sub-Saharan Africa.* London: WTTC.

Chapter 3

Tourism Performance and Potential in Sub-Saharan Africa

Tourism is a $3 billion a day business that creates 3.4 percent of the world's jobs directly and 8.8 percent of all jobs when its combined direct, indirect, and induced impacts are calculated. Although the sector shrank 4 percent in 2009 as a result of the global economic crisis, it bounced back quickly, demonstrating its resilience to external shocks. By 2020 there are expected to be 1.6 billion international tourists worldwide, up from 1 billion in 2010 (figure 3.1). The average annual growth rate of international tourism is 4.1 percent. Although mature, developed destinations in Europe and the United States are expected to grow only 3 percent a year to 2020, emerging destinations in East Asia and the Pacific and in the Middle East are expected to grow 6–7 percent.

Africa's share of world arrivals, though still small, is growing. In 1995 Africa received just 3.6 percent of world tourist arrivals; by 2010, Africa's market share had increased to 5.2 percent. Sub-Saharan Africa received 3.3 percent of world tourist arrivals. Longer-term forecasts provided by the United Nations World Tourism Organization (UNWTO) predict that the region will receive 77 million arrivals by 2020 (compared with just over 30 million in 2010); of these, 50 million will be intraregional visitors (table 3.1).

Sub-Saharan African Countries' Share of the World Tourism Market

Within Sub-Saharan Africa, the performance of tourism destinations varies considerably by region (figure 3.2). East and Southern Africa attract more tourists and contribute more to gross domestic product (GDP) than West and Central Africa (table 3.2). Moreover, within each region, certain countries dominate in attracting tourists: in East Africa, Zimbabwe receives 16 percent of international arrivals, Mozambique 15 percent, and Kenya 15 percent; in Southern Africa, South Africa is the leading destination, receiving 66 percent of all tourist arrivals to the region, compared with Namibia's 9 percent; in West Africa,

Figure 3.1 International Tourist Arrivals Worldwide, by Region, 1950–2020

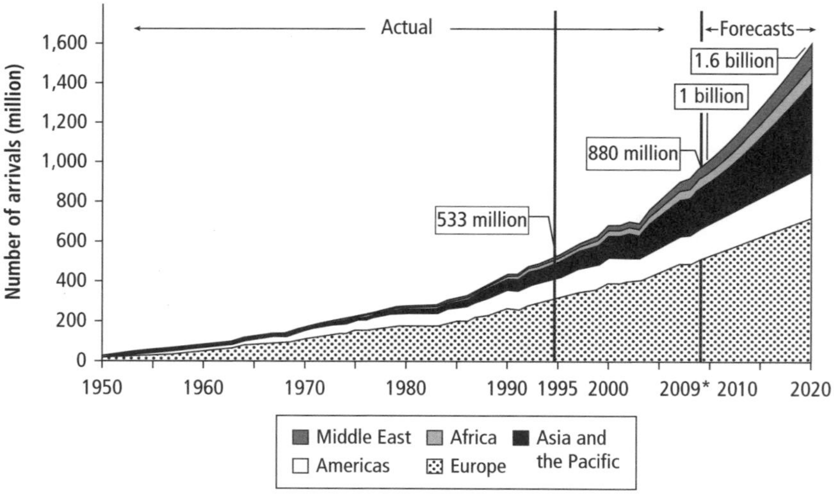

Source: UNWTO 2010.

Table 3.1 International Tourist Arrivals Worldwide, by Region, 1990–2010
millions

World region	1990	1995	2000	2005	2009	2010	Change (%) 2008–09	Change (%) 2009–10	% of total arrivals, 2010
Europe	261.5	304.1	385.6	439.4	461.5	476.6	−4.9	3.3	50.7
Americas	92.8	109.0	128.2	133.3	140.6	149.8	−4.9	6.4	15.9
North America	71.7	80.7	91.5	89.9	92.2	98.2	−5.7	6.6	10.5
Rest of Americas	21.1	28.3	36.7	43.4	48.4	51.6	−3.4	6.6	5.5
Asia and the Pacific	55.8	82.0	110.1	153.6	180.9	203.8	−1.7	12.7	21.7
Africa	14.8	18.9	26.5	35.4	46.0	49.4	3.7	7.3	5.2
Sub-Saharan Africa	6.4	11.6	16.2	21.5	28.4	30.7	4.4	8.0	3.3
North Africa	8.4	7.3	10.2	13.9	17.6	18.7	2.5	6.2	2.0
Middle East	9.6	13.7	24.1	36.3	52.9	60.3	−4.3	14.1	6.4
Total	435.0	528.0	675.0	798.0	882.0	940.0	−3.8	6.6	100.0

Source: UNWTO 2011.

Table 3.2 International Tourist Arrivals and Receipts in Sub-Saharan Africa, by Region, 2010
number of arrivals unless otherwise noted

Region	Total tourist arrivals	Total long hauls	Receipts (US$, million)	Average contribution to GDP (%)
Southern Africa	10,626,127	2,509,893	8,599	3.4
East Africa	11,905,651	3,944,858	6,332	5.5
West Africa	4,419,061	1,748,555	2,676	2.0
Central Africa	1,075,408	654,168	631	1.7
Total	28,026,247	8,857,474	18,238	2.6

Sources: World Bank 2012; UNWTO 2011; WTTC data.

Figure 3.2 Tourist Arrivals in Africa, by Region, 2010

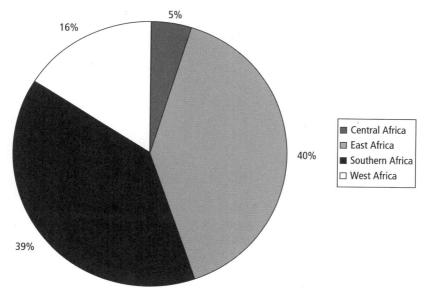

Source: UNWTO 2013.

Senegal and Nigeria are the dominant destinations, together accounting for 78 percent of visitors to the region.

The primary international source markets for Sub-Saharan African countries are France, the United Kingdom, the United States, Germany, and Portugal (map 3.1). France was the top long-haul source market for Africa in 2009 and

Map 3.1 Top Sources of Tourists in Africa, by Country, Most Recent Data Available

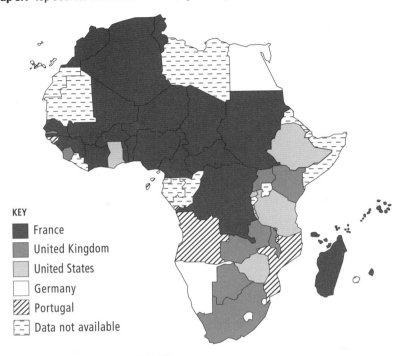

KEY

- ■ France
- ■ United Kingdom
- ▨ United States
- □ Germany
- ▨ Portugal
- ⊡ Data not available

Source: World Bank, Africa House, and ATA 2010.

was particularly dominant in West Africa. The most popular destinations in Sub-Saharan Africa for French tourists are Mauritius and Senegal. France is also the top market for Madagascar, Mali, and the Seychelles. The United Kingdom has long-standing links to Kenya, South Africa, and The Gambia; the United Kingdom is also the top source market in Tanzania and Zambia. Emerging destinations for U.K. visitors are Cabo Verde, Mozambique, Namibia, Uganda, and Zambia. The United States is the top source market for Ethiopia, Ghana, Rwanda, Uganda, and Zimbabwe, with South Africa receiving the most U.S. tourists. Emerging source markets for Sub-Saharan Africa include Australia, Brazil, China, Italy, the Russian Federation, and Spain.

Value of Tourism to Sub-Saharan African Economies

The value of tourism to Sub-Saharan African economies varies widely. In 2011 tourism contributed 2.7 percent directly to GDP in Sub-Saharan African countries, compared with 4.3 percent of GDP in Southeast Asia, 4.4 percent in the Caribbean, and 3.0 percent in the Middle East.[1] However, average regional figures fail to show the high level of dependence that some countries have on tourism (map 3.2). For example, tourism activities account for 44 percent of GDP in the Seychelles and for 16 percent of GDP in Mauritius.

On a subregional basis, tourism contributes most to East Africa's GDP (5.5 percent), followed by Southern Africa (3.4 percent) and West Africa (2 percent), with Central Africa trailing at just 1.7 percent. Tourism provides other benefits as well:

- An average of 6.4 percent of total exports across Sub-Saharan Africa

- Almost half of all service exports (49.7 percent), compared with 16.7 percent in the Caribbean, 5.6 percent in Southeast Asia, and 6.2 percent in the Middle East

- Approximately $33.5 billion in direct tourism receipts.

Map 3.2 Contribution of Tourism to GDP in Sub-Saharan Africa, Most Recent Data Available

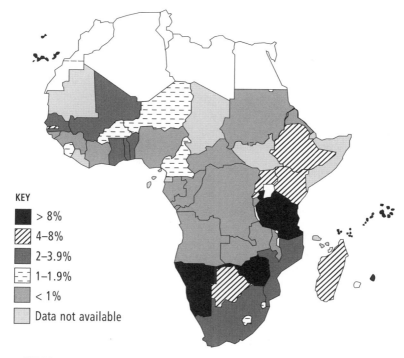

KEY

- > 8%
- 4–8%
- 2–3.9%
- 1–1.9%
- < 1%
- Data not available

Source: UNWTO 2013.

Southern Africa receives almost 40 percent of all the tourism receipts ($13 billion a year), of which 91 percent go to South Africa, compared with 5 percent to Botswana, 2 percent to Namibia, and just 1 percent each to Lesotho and Swaziland. In East Africa, Kenya, Mauritius, and Tanzania receive more than $1 billion in tourist receipts. In West Africa, Ghana and Nigeria are the biggest tourism earners, accounting for 60 percent of all West African receipts.

Tourism Employment

More than 200 million people are underemployed in Sub-Saharan Africa, and 10 million more seek jobs every year. There are an estimated 5.3 million direct tourism jobs across the region.[2] Because travel and tourism touch all sectors of the economy, tourism's total direct and indirect impact on employment in Sub-Saharan Africa is 12.8 million jobs. By 2022, the World Travel & Tourism Council (WTTC) forecasts that Sub-Saharan will have 6.8 million direct jobs in tourism and more than 16 million people employed directly and indirectly through tourism.[3] However, to generate the potential new jobs that are forecast in tourism, investment in Sub-Saharan Africa needs to grow.

Tourism Investment

Investment flows in tourism, and especially foreign direct investment (FDI), are difficult to identify. First, "tourism" is an aggregation of many activities, making it difficult to assess comprehensively. Second, in national accounts, "tourism" does not appear as a formal industry classification; its subcategories, such as hotels and transport, are found within "real estate" or are aggregated under "transport, communications, and storage," making it difficult to quantify the size of assets and flow of investments. Third, transnational corporations can operate in tourism in nonequity modes such as with management contracts or franchises. These modes do not appear in FDI data, even though they may resemble FDI in areas such as managerial control, technology and knowledge transfer, and access to markets. Finally, the collection of tourism data has been poor in developing countries. Improved data collection and classification systems are needed so that policy makers can design meaningful policies to position tourism as an engine of growth.

Tourism is the one service sector in which African countries have a trade surplus. In South Africa, for example, tourism-related sales abroad earn more foreign exchange than do exports of gold. In Tanzania, export earnings from tourism exceed those from gold or agriculture (UNCTAD 2007). Yet FDI in tourism is not only poorly studied and understood, it is also controversial. Foreign ownership in tourism, it is argued, is widespread, preventing pro-poor growth because of the leakages that occur and the lack of backward linkages from the investment. The United Nations Conference on Trade and Development (UNCTAD) found that FDI in tourism is still rather low in developed and developing countries compared with FDI in other economic activities, including other service industries. For example, outward FDI in tourism from the United Kingdom, the third largest tourism-spending country, was $34 billion in 2004, or 2.5 percent of that country's total outward FDI. For the United States, home to most of the world's largest tourism-related transnational corporations and the second largest source of outward FDI flows in tourism, tourism's share was just 1.5 percent of total outward FDI stocks.

In 2007 UNCTAD conducted a survey of 300 hotel groups and 1,350 hotels. Based on the results of that survey, FDI in hotels is concentrated in Latin America, although at a low level, and only 7 percent is in Sub-Saharan Africa. Sub-Saharan Africa undoubtedly has the potential to attract higher levels of FDI for tourism. However, experience across the continent is mixed. UNCTAD's recent case studies on FDI and tourism in Sub-Saharan Africa show that the percentage of FDI for tourism can range between 0.2 and 36 percent. The WTTC 2011 data reveal that South Africa received by far the most foreign direct investment ($6.1 billion) in the Sub-Saharan African region. Ghana attracted the highest tourism FDI in West Africa: $270 million, amounting to 4 percent of total investment. In East Africa, Kenya attracted $404 million in tourism FDI and Uganda received $165 million in 2011. As indicated in UNCTAD's East and Southern African country case studies, FDI has become a significant source of investment capital in the tourism sector.

Ministries of tourism have an important role to play in creating a hospitable environment for tourism projects. Investors typically need a wide base of information about the economy, tourism trends, tourism plans, and regulations. Sub-Saharan Africa falls behind in the area of communication and coordination between policy makers working on tourism, investment, competition, and trade issues. Better dialogue between these entities would help to address the situation. Several countries around the world have set up "one-stop tourism promotion agencies" that consolidate the information typically required by an investor. The contribution made by tourism in creating beneficial links to small and medium enterprises as well as domestic enterprises depends on the size and breadth of the domestic economy and on the maturity of the tourism service sector (UNCTAD 2009).

Notes

1. WTTC, Economic Data Search Tool (http://www.wttc.org/research/economic -data-search-tool/).

2. WTTC, Economic Data Search Tool (http://www.wttc.org/research/economic
-data-search-tool/).
3. WTTC, Economic Data Search Tool (http://www.wttc.org/research/economic
-data-search-tool/).

References

UNCTAD (United Nations Conference on Trade and Development). 2007. *FDI in Tourism: The Development Dimension*. Geneva: United Nations.

———. 2009. *Foreign Direct Investment in Tourism: The Development Dimension*. Geneva: United Nations. http://web.idrc.ca/en/ev-115746-201-1-DO_TOPIC.html.

UNWTO (United Nations World Tourism Organization). 2010. *UNWTO Tourism Highlights, 2010 Edition*. Madrid: UNWTO.

———. 2011. *UNWTO Tourism Highlights, 2011 Edition*. Madrid: UNWTO.

———. 2013. "Statistical Annex." In *UNWTO World Tourism Barometer*, Vol. 11, April. Madrid: UNWTO.

World Bank. 2012. Sub-Saharan Africa Tourism Database. World Bank, Finance and Private Sector Development Unit Africa Region, Washington, DC.

World Bank, Africa House, and ATA (Africa Travel Association). 2010. "Relative Market Share of Top Five Source Markets." *State of Tourism in Africa* 1 (1): 2.

WTTC (World Travel & Tourism Council). 2011. *Travel and Tourism Economic Impact, 2011*. London: WTTC.

Chapter 4

Essential Tourism Services

Accommodation

Calculations based on United Nations World Tourism Organization (UNWTO) data for 40 of the 47 countries in Sub-Saharan Africa suggest that there are about 390,000 hotel rooms in the region.[1] Unbranded guesthouses and lodges dominate, and just 10 percent (35,200) of rooms meet international standards. South Africa has about half the region's stock of international standard accommodation. Other destinations with established hotel investment markets are Kenya, Mauritius, and the Seychelles. Mauritius has 104 hotels with more than 80 rooms. According to research conducted by Ernst and Young (2010), Nigeria, Senegal, Tanzania, and Zambia have maturing hotel markets.

World Bank research found vacations in Sub-Saharan Africa to be on average 20–30 percent more expensive than vacations in other regions, even when airfares are not included (Twining-Ward 2010). The differences are particularly noticeable in mid-range products. High hotel costs are due primarily to the high costs of hotel development and the cost of debt financing. In Nigeria, the cost of hotel construction is upward of $400,000 per room for a mid-market hotel; in Ghana, the cost is $250,000 per room. Median hotel development costs elsewhere in the world are $200,000 per room for a full-service hotel (Ernst and Young 2010).

To develop a hotel in Sub-Saharan Africa, 40–50 percent equity contributions may be needed in addition to collateral of 1.5 to 2 times the loan amount. International brands have considerable pull in obtaining financing, but many parts of Sub-Saharan Africa are high risk, which means that interest rates are also high.

The survey of hotel developers found four main areas where Sub-Saharan African countries fall short in their investment climate compared with Asian and Middle Eastern markets: (a) risk management (political, economic, security); (b) image of the region from an investment perspective; (c) airline service; and (d) government policy (Ernst and Young 2010). To attract high-quality investors, such as luxury safari operators, destinations need to provide stable land tenure, political stability, suitable infrastructure, an attractive business environment, and a commitment to tourism (World Bank 2009).

Table 4.1 Top Six Countries in Sub-Saharan Africa, by Number of Hotel Rooms

Country	Total number of hotel rooms	Number of international hotel rooms	Average occupancy (%)	Year of most recent recorded data
South Africa	61,417	9,850	57	2007
Tanzania	31,365	1,588	43	2005
Kenya	24,354	2,284	92	2007
Cameroon	24,803	673	17	2006, 2007
Ghana	24,410	902	75	2005, 2008
Malawi	20,871	120	61	2004, 2006

Sources: World Bank 2012; UNWTO 2013.

The occupancy rates and profitability of hotels in Sub-Saharan Africa show great disparities. For example, Kenya and Cameroon have almost the same number of rooms, and yet average occupancy is 80–90 percent in Kenya and only 17 percent in Cameroon (see table 4.1).[2] Twenty-three international hotel corporations operate in Sub-Saharan Africa. Of these, Accor, Hilton, InterContinental, and Starwood are the largest. There are also numerous subsidiary brands.[3] There are nine regional brands, of which Laico, Protea, Serena, and Sun International are the largest.[4]

The survey of accommodations in Sub-Saharan Africa revealed that RevPar, a primary benchmark for the hotel industry based on average daily rates divided by occupancy, saw a downturn in 2008 and 2009 because of the economic crisis. Data from January to July 2010, however, showed a 6.1 percent increase in RevPar in Kenya, 5.5 percent in Mauritius, and 39.3 percent in South Africa. The dramatic change in South Africa's RevPar was due to the World Cup football tournament in June and July 2010 (Ernst and Young 2010).

Despite the impediments, the accommodation sector in Sub-Saharan Africa is expanding rapidly. Accor, InterContinental Hotel Group, Rezidor Hotel Group, which operates the Radisson Blu chain, and Starwood are among those looking to capitalize on the continent's need to expand its underdeveloped hotel industry. In the last four years, Rezidor alone has added 33 hotels to its operations on the African continent. Among projects in the planning stage are a $40 million upscale Radisson Blu hotel in the Mozambican capital of Maputo and a 120-room, $42 million lodge in South Africa's Kruger National Park, both expected to open in 2013.[5]

Air Transport

Africa's distance from source markets creates an acute need for higher quality and more competitive air access. Air and road connections are the most commonly mentioned constraints on the growth of tourism in Sub-Saharan Africa.

Map 4.1 Top 75 Airline Routes to Sub-Saharan Africa, by Daily Seat Capacity, August 2010

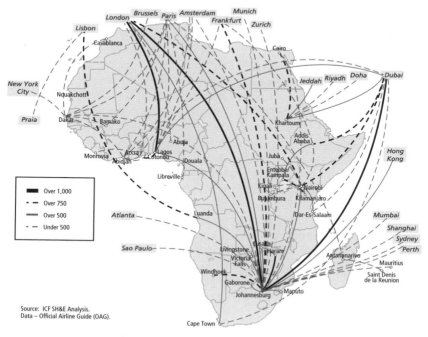

Source: ICF SH&E Analysis.
Data – Official Airline Guide (OAG).

Source: SH&E 2010.

The high cost, irregularity, and routing of airlines around Sub-Saharan Africa reduce the competitiveness of its destinations. Despite comprising 15 percent of the world's population, the continent is served by only 4 percent of the world's scheduled air service seats (map 4.1). Nevertheless, signs of positive developments in air transport are emerging. Between 1998 and 2009, the supply of airline seats grew 6.5 percent a year, and Cabo Verde, Ethiopia, Mozambique, and Tanzania all experienced double-digit growth in the number of air service seats.

Key hubs in Sub-Saharan Africa are Addis Ababa, Johannesburg, and Nairobi; Accra, Abuja, Dakar, Dar es Salaam, and Lagos are developing into regional hubs. Additionally, the Emirates' hub in Dubai has become an increasingly important staging point for intra-Africa travel.

Long-haul connections are dominated by a small number of foreign carriers, such as Air France, British Airways, Brussels Airlines, Emirates, KLM, SWISS, and Virgin. Airline routings are strongly connected to former colonial interests and to countries with a common language. British Airways and Virgin dominate routes to Ghana, Kenya, Nigeria, and South Africa. Air France dominates routes to Madagascar, Mali, Mauritania, and Senegal.

Foreign airlines play a disproportionate role in air traffic to and from the region because of their frequency of service and operational stability. Many former national carriers, such as those of Ghana and Zambia, are gone, although a few still operate in cooperation with international carriers (including Kenya Airways with KLM).

South African Airways dominates the Southern African market. East Africa's most successful airlines are Ethiopian Airlines and Kenya Airways. They serve both intra-African and intercontinental flights with successful hub and spoke operations. Combined, they carried almost 6 million passengers and generated revenues of $2 billion in 2009 (SH&E 2010). High population density and higher gross domestic product have led to particularly strong growth in West Africa's seat capacity over the last few years, as seen by the arrival of African Sky and Arik Air. The purpose of transnational partnerships is to fly underserved routes while achieving efficiencies of scale. Mauritius, for example, credits some of its tourism success to pooling agreements with major carriers such as British Airways and Air France.

The tour operator benchmarking study compared the price of tours to Sub-Saharan Africa with the price of similar tours to other parts of the world and found that charter tours were 20–30 percent more expensive to Sub-Saharan Africa than to comparable destinations in other parts of the world.

Flights were found to be almost 50 percent more expensive to Sub-Saharan Africa even where shorter distances were involved (figure 4.1). The study found

Figure 4.1 Average One-Way Fares, by World Region

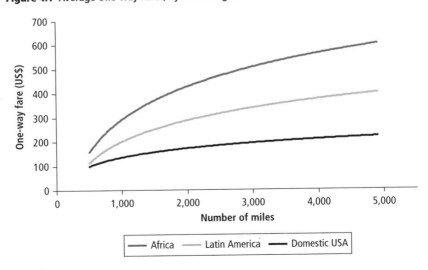

Source: SH&E 2010.
Note: Data for Africa include intra-Africa and Africa–Middle East fares.

Table 4.2 Prices of Tours and Flights to Sub-Saharan Africa and Comparable Destinations

Country	Length of tour (number of nights)	Name of tour	Type of tour	Tour operator	Price per adult (US$)	Tour price per night (US$)	Roundtrip (US$)
Madagascar	17	Madagascar Encompassed	Standard	Gap Adventures	3,549	208	2,975
Malawi	9	Best of Malawi	Private	Cox and Kings USA	5,495	611	2,290
Ethiopia	7	Ethiopian Odyssey	Private	Cox and Kings USA	3,245	464	1,374
China	18	Silk Road Adventure	Standard	Gap Adventures	2,999	166	1,173
Indonesia	8	Bali to Borobudur	Private	Cox and Kings USA	4,265	533	1,644
India	7	Indian Experience	Private	Cox and Kings USA	2,280	326	984

Source: Twining-Ward 2010.
Note: Data for Africa include intra-Africa and Africa–Middle East fare.

that an average round-trip flight to Madagascar from New York cost $2,975, while a flight to China from New York cost $1,173. A flight to Malawi cost $2,290, whereas a flight to Indonesia cost $1,644 and a flight to India cost $984. Safari tours to Sub-Saharan Africa were found to be 38 percent more expensive than safaris to other destinations, such as Borneo, Galapagos, or India. Cultural tours were 34 percent more expensive in Sub-Saharan Africa than in destinations such as the Arab Republic of Egypt and Indonesia. For example, a 10-day tiger-watching trip to India with Cox and Kings UK cost $3,703 in 2010, while a similar trip to Namibia cost $5,039. The primary reasons for the higher price of tours to Africa were the cost of air fares and the cost of accommodations (Twining-Ward 2010). Table 4.2 compares the costs to tourists of visiting Sub-Saharan Africa versus other countries.

Charter Service

Charters provide some relief from the high fares on scheduled airlines. Permission for charters in certain countries, however, is given only after arduous negotiation. In Zambia, for example, each flight must be approved, making planning difficult. Beach clubs and resorts have long used charter services with back-to-back planeloads servicing a single property. Charters serve Italian tourists visiting Zanzibar and British tourists visiting The Gambia. Some countries are currently using them as substitutes for scheduled carriers. São Tomé and Príncipe has successfully chartered Euro Atlantic Airways to fly a Boeing 757 once weekly between Lisbon and São Tomé and Príncipe and between São Tomé and Príncipe and Luanda. This arrangement allows São Tomé and Príncipe to maintain its crucial business, tourism, and visiting friends and relatives (VFR) market link to Portugal, as well as its increasingly important link to Angola, without the associated start-up and fixed costs of owning a national airline. Some charter airlines, such as Corsair, have evolved to provide scheduled service. Where an "open-skies" environment exists, such as in Kenya or Maldives, charters can be a useful solution, especially if there is high seasonality or an infrequent need for service.

Internal Air Transport

Capacity between regions in Africa is still limited. Less than 15 percent of intra-Africa seat capacity is devoted to flights between regions, and most African carriers do not fly daily due to a combination of regulations and lack of proper-size aircraft. The high growth of passenger demand, albeit from a small base, has put upward pressure on prices. Average one-way fares were found to be twice as expensive in Africa as in Latin America and four times as expensive as domestic flights in the United States (SH&E 2010). The least expensive non-stop flight offered from Bamako to Nairobi on Kenya Airways was found to be more than twice as expensive as the least expensive flight between Tokyo and Bangkok on Delta. The route structure in Africa is focused on existing, proven traffic and does not facilitate new connectivity or stimulate Sub-Saharan African aviation. Air service, particularly in West and Central Africa, is expensive and provides infrequent and irregular schedules, often with multistop itineraries.

Factors that contribute to the higher fares include higher airport taxes and charges, inefficiencies due to small market size, ineffective management of airlines and airports, and the power of a monopoly or duopoly to set artificially high rates (SH&E 2010). The seasonal nature of tourism in some areas further exacerbates the cost and routing issues.

As an example of private sector initiative, air access for luxury resorts in Kenya and Tanzania has become a value added component. Wilderness Safaris, the luxury tour operator, set up Wilderness Air (previously Sefofane Air Charters) to overcome the challenge of poor roads and long distances, allowing them to expand their product range. At the other price extreme, low-cost "no frills" carriers provide efficient local and intraregional services in Sub-Saharan Africa. South African Airways launched its own brand of low-cost carrier, Mango, which competes with Kulula in the South African market. Low-cost airline Fly Dubai, which flies to Sudan, Egypt, and Djibouti, has announced that it will fly to Addis Ababa, providing service for the many expatriate Ethiopians working in Dubai and enabling persons living in Dubai to visit Ethiopia. Other airlines, including Kenya Airways' Jambo Jet and EasyJet's FastJet, also offer service to Ethiopia.

Security

Security is another concern. The International Air Transport Association (IATA) reports that the airline accident rate in Africa (1:471,000) is twice that in the rest of the world (Brogden 2009). The analysis of the African airline industry found that 16 national African airlines are subject to a partial or total ban on flying in Europe (and often North America) because of poor safety and security records (SH&E 2010). Yet there are also notable success stories regarding security. In Cabo Verde, Sal Airport has achieved Category 1 classification by the U.S. government, which permits direct flights from the United States. Because one delayed plane can eliminate a tour operator's profits, the excellent reputation of Cabo Verde's aviation authority has made the country an attractive destination for tour operators.

Recommendations for Improved Air Transport

As noted, the private sector has taken several initiatives to compensate for the overall deficiencies in the costs and routing constraints of internal and intraregional air travel. Aviation has been slower to liberalize than other sectors in Sub-Saharan Africa, and further liberalization of internal, intraregional, and international flights will improve the accessibility of the region for tour operations. The impact of airline liberalization can be significant. For example, when Garuda Indonesia finally allowed foreign carriers to terminate flights in Bali, tourism grew sharply. Air access is a critical enabler of tourism and is crucial for island destinations.

The case studies in part II on Cabo Verde, Bali, Maldives, and Morocco clearly demonstrate the importance of liberalized airline policies. Cabo Verde is a remarkable success story that clearly illustrates the need for and benefits of significant investment in aviation infrastructure. Policy reforms are important to increase the number of flights and tourists, but, without efficient airports, tourism cannot even get under way. In the last two decades, Cabo Verde has invested in its airports with considerable success. Several have been modernized, runways have been improved, and passenger and freight terminals have been built. It now has four international airports, on Santiago, Sal, Boa Vista, and São Vicente. Direct flights are available to six major European cities and two cities in the United States. Cabo Verde is served by TAP, the Portuguese airline, from Lisbon, Rome, Milan, and Bologna. Connections to the United Kingdom are via charters; TUIfly and Thomson fly to Manchester and Birmingham. JetAirFly provides cheap flights to Cabo Verde from Brussels. ArkeFly (the charter carrier of Dutch TUI) connects Cabo Verde to the Netherlands. TAAG Angola Airlines connects Cabo Verde with Angola and Brazil.

Connections to Paris and Madrid are offered by TACV (Cabo Verde Airlines), which was the first carrier to offer a direct flight to and from the United States (Boston Logan Airport) and to Brazil (Fortaleza). In 2010 the U.S. carrier Delta Airlines began twice-weekly flights to Cabo Verde from Atlanta, as a refueling stopover on the way to East and Southern Africa. Thus key to Cabo Verde's tourism success has been its policy reforms, investments in air transport infrastructure, high-level airline safety, and open-skies policy.

The gaps revealed in African air coverage relate mainly to intra-African connectivity, which is particularly strong in West and Central Africa. Key lessons can be learned from certain Indian, Latin American, Southeast Asian, and East Asian experiences. Policy options range from smaller focused efforts to a national commitment to support aviation and its related infrastructure. In the short term, addressing visa regimes through policy changes, enhancing cooperation between governments in specific African regions, and increasing the transfer of knowledge and best practices would strengthen the local airline industry (SH&E 2010). Although the SH&E consultants recommended that airlines establish a transnational strategic partnership, which would be tasked with achieving overall gains for regional aviation rather than for a single country or carrier, they recognized the political difficulties of such a venture. As an alternative, they suggested strategies such as bilateral partnership agreements, pan-African code shares, and charters for essential service routes such as Lisbon to São Tomé and Príncipe. They also advocated establishing technical and financial cooperation agreements through various assistance programs and noted that joint purchasing of equipment and services, for example, would benefit participating airlines.

Road Transport

Internal air service is also important to compensate for the difficulties of road transport. In many destinations only seasonal access to some parts of the country is possible. Poor roads add to the cost of operating tours and increase operating costs because of vehicle and mechanical damage and pollution (Spenceley 2010). Road quality and accessibility are a challenge for tour operators in The Gambia, Kenya, Senegal, and Zambia, among others.

A survey conducted in 2007 in Kenya found that traffic jams in Nairobi cost all drivers combined as much as $746,000 a day through increased fuel consumption, mechanical damage, and pollution. Although improvements have been made, Nairobi's traffic is still congested. By contrast, Namibia and South Africa have overcome this problem through consistent investment and infrastructure development. As a result, both destinations now attract large numbers of self-drive tourists (Twining-Ward 2010).

Tour Operators

The tour operation sector in Sub-Saharan Africa is thought to include some 2,500 to 3,000 ground operators, providing direct employment for 35,000 to 40,000 people (Twining-Ward 2010).[6] In 2010, 31 million tourists arrived in Sub-Saharan Africa; of these, about 16 percent (4.9 million) arranged their trip using a tour operator, suggesting that tour operators are responsible for between $2 billion and $3 billion in spending annually in Sub-Saharan Africa. Interviews with tour operators in the United Kingdom and the United States indicate that a higher proportion of travelers to Sub-Saharan Africa use tour operators than travelers to other parts of the world because of the greater complexities of obtaining visas, booking accommodation, and making tour arrangements.

Charter tours constitute 10–15 percent of the tour operation market and are used predominantly by Northern European visitors, middle-aged couples, and families. Visitors to Sub-Saharan Africa mostly favor custom tours, which constitute an estimated 50–70 percent of the market. Custom tours are particularly popular with the U.S. market and with older, more experienced travelers. Group and overland tours appear to be popular with U.K. and French visitors and younger travelers. Group tours make up approximately 12–17 percent of the market.

Tour operators were asked to identify the countries they thought had the greatest potential for tours over the next five years (map 4.2). The countries considered to have the most potential were Botswana, Cabo Verde, Namibia,

Map 4.2 Tourism Potential in Sub-Saharan Africa, 2009

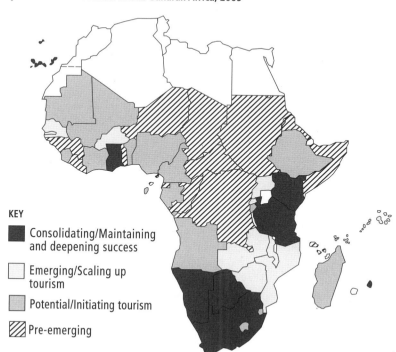

KEY

- Consolidating/Maintaining and deepening success
- Emerging/Scaling up tourism
- Potential/Initiating tourism
- Pre-emerging

Source: World Bank 2011.

South Africa, and Tanzania. Destinations described as emerging were Benin, Ethiopia, Ghana, Madagascar, Malawi, Mali, Mozambique, Rwanda, Uganda, and Zambia.

Notes

1. Data from World Bank (2012), sourced from the most recent available UNWTO e-statistics (http://www.e-unwto.org/home/main.mpx).
2. UNWTO 2008 statistics (http://www.e-unwto.org/home/main.mpx).
3. Accor includes Sofitel, Novotel, Mercure, Ibis, Club Med, and Hotel Formule 1. Starwood includes Sheraton, Four Points, St. Regis, The Luxury Collection, and Le Méridien. InterContinental Hotels Group includes InterContinental, Crowne Plaza, Holiday Inn, and Holiday Inn Express.
4. The nine brands are African Pride Hotels, Beachcomber Hotels, The City Lodge Group of Hotels, Laico Hotels and Resorts, Protea Hotels, Serena Hotels, Southern Sun Hotels, Sun International, and Three Cities.
5. "Top Hotels Wake Up to Africa Growth Potential," *Reuters Africa*, August 16, 2011. http://af.reuters.com/article/topNews/idAFJOE77F08420110816.
6. Employment opportunities include jobs as drivers, guides, porters, mechanics, naturalists, reservation agents, accountants, and managers.

References

Brogden, L. 2009. "Development Trends in the Airline Industry." Presentation of the IATA regional vice president, Africa, Windhoek, March 3.

Ernst and Young. 2010. "Sub-Saharan Africa Hospitality Sector Overview." Unpublished research for the World Bank, Washington, DC.

SH&E. 2010. "Competitive Africa: Tourism Industry Research Phase II Air Transport Sector Study." Unpublished report for the World Bank, Washington, DC.

Spenceley, A. 2010. *Tourism Product Development Interventions and Best Practices in Sub-Saharan Africa. Part 1: Synthesis. World Bank Tourism Industry: Research and Analysis Phase II.* Washington, DC: World Bank.

Twining-Ward, L. 2010. "Sub-Saharan Africa Tourism Industry Research, Phase II Tour Operator Study." Unpublished report for the World Bank, AFTFP, Washington, DC.

UNWTO (United Nations World Tourism Organization). 2013. *Tourism Factbook.* UNWTO, Madrid. http://www.e-unwto.org/content/v486k6/?v=search.

World Bank. 2009. "Competitive Africa: Strategies to Leverage the New Global Economy." Concept Note, World Bank, Washington, DC.

———. 2011. *Africa Region Tourism Strategy: Transformation through Tourism, Harnessing Tourism for Growth and Improved Livelihoods.* Washington, DC: World Bank.

———. 2012. Sub-Saharan Africa Tourism Database. World Bank, Finance and Private Sector Development Unit, Africa Region, Washington, DC.

Chapter 5

Tourists and Tourism Products in Sub-Saharan Africa

Tourists to Sub-Saharan Africa can be divided into four main groups according to the purpose of their visit: leisure, business, visiting friends and relatives (VFR), or others. Leisure tourists make up approximately 36 percent of the market. Business travelers constitute about 25 percent of international arrivals (Twining-Ward 2009; see figure 5.1). Data on tourists visiting friends and relatives is not collected by all countries but is likely to make up about 20 percent of arrivals. The "other" category includes several important niches, such as sports tourism, visits for medical treatment, and attendance at meetings or conventions.

There are three main categories of leisure tourists:

- High-end tourists who book expensive once-in-a-lifetime trips to places such as Kenya, the Seychelles, South Africa, and Tanzania
- Niche tourists who arrange overland or cross-continental trips and adventure, cultural heritage, diving, and bird-watching tours
- Lower-end charter tourists who take holidays to beaches in The Gambia, Kenya, and Senegal.

According to the operators interviewed, Sub-Saharan Africa is bypassing a large portion of the middle-income market, despite the significant opportunities that exist to attract this income segment. This is the result of the perception that the cost of a tour to Sub-Saharan Africa is high in relation to its value.

Business tourism is another important and growing segment, one that is less seasonal than leisure tourism and more resilient to political change. Business tourists tend to stay longer and to use high-end hotels and restaurants. Kenya, for example, has successfully diversified its leisure tourism market by developing business tourism and now ranks second behind South Africa for business meetings in a market worth $24 million. The transport study consultants found that up to 55 percent of passengers on African airlines are traveling for business, compared with just 15 percent for tourism and 30 percent for visiting friends and relatives (SH&E 2010).

Figure 5.1 Typical Mix of Passengers on African Carriers, Intercontinental Flights

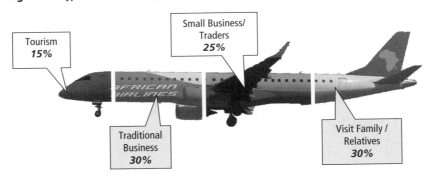

Source: SH&E 2010.

Intraregional travel is also growing strongly. The UNWTO forecasts that 75 percent of all tourists to Africa will be intraregional African travelers by 2021 (UNWTO 2010). South Africa is the largest source market for intraregional travel. The pattern of short-haul travel in Sub-Saharan Africa is closely related to trading partners, nearest neighbors, relative incomes, and ethnic similarities.

Tourism Products

Long-haul tourism thrives on new destinations, innovative products, and novel experiences. Recent market studies have found that "Generation Xers" (persons born between 1961 and 1980) are looking for unique experiences that lead to personal fulfillment. They are living longer than earlier generations, control 70–80 percent of the wealth, and value more active lifestyles that include long-haul travel (SNV 2009). Sub-Saharan Africa has a world-class inventory of tourism resources, including white- and black-sand beaches, coral reefs, mountains, deserts, wildlife, cultural heritage sites, and vibrant creative industry activities (World Bank 2012). Traditional opportunities are offered in safari, beach, business, and diaspora tourism (map 5.1).

Safari Tourism

The safari is the primary tourism product for East Africa and Southern Africa. The large diversity of destinations and the high value associated with "big five" game viewing give East and Southern Africa a competitive advantage over other areas of Sub-Saharan Africa and the rest of the world in the delivery of safari products.

Map 5.1 Tourism Product Opportunities in Sub-Saharan Africa

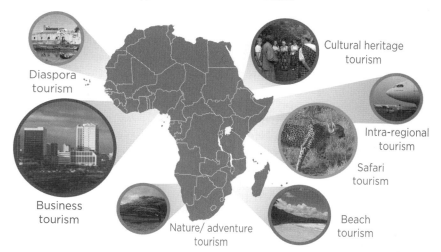

Diaspora tourism

Cultural heritage tourism

Business tourism

Intra-regional tourism

Safari tourism

Nature/ adventure tourism

Beach tourism

Source: World Bank 2011.

Beach Tourism

Beaches are an important secondary product in East and West Africa and, to a lesser extent, in Southern Africa. However, visitor preferences are changing. With increased concern about exposure to the sun, fewer long-haul visitors wish to spend their holiday lying on the beach. Beach-focused destinations, such as the Seychelles, have had to work hard to diversify their tourism offerings.

Business Tourism

Business travel is a growth area for Sub-Saharan Africa. Unlike leisure travel, the flow of business travel depends on the dynamism of the economic activity in the destination. Business tourists, on average, tend to spend more daily than the other categories of tourists and are less seasonal than leisure tourists.

Diaspora Tourism

This market is predominantly composed of middle-income, African American adults between the ages of 30 and 70, who wish to learn about their own cultural heritage by visiting the countries and regions of their ancestors. City tours, visits to historic sites, arts and crafts shopping, and trips to slave trade memorials are components of diaspora tourism. Once in the destination, travel is mostly by tour bus. In addition, intra-Africa diaspora travel is a growing market.

Nature and Adventure Tourism

TUI Travel PLC Adventure Brands quotes a 2009 U.K. government survey predicting that in the next few years adventure travel will increase 70 percent, "activity" or "off-the-beaten-track" holidays will increase 100 percent, and adventure and eco-friendly discovery travel will increase 300 percent (TUI Travel 2010). Africa's varied terrain and remote locations make it an ideal location for many nature-based adventure sports. Dune boarding in Namibia, nature tourism in Zambia (Hamilton and others 2007), camel expeditions in Mali, cultural heritage tours in Ethiopia, kayaking on the Zambezi River, and lemur tracking in Madagascar offer new adventure opportunities. Given the adventurous tendencies of persons from Generation X (persons born between 1961 and 1980) and from Generation Y (persons born between 1981 and 2000), adventure travel is likely to increase, with Sub-Saharan African countries catering to their demands.

Cultural Heritage Tourism

Cultural heritage tourism is one of the fastest-growing segments of the tourism industry worldwide. Of all international leisure tourism, 40 percent has a cultural component (Ebbe 2008). Given Sub-Saharan Africa's rich traditions in music, art, and dance, cultural tourism presents a substantial opportunity for growth. Already, Ghana has marketed itself as a heritage destination by making its slave trade monuments into tourism destinations; Mali and Senegal have promoted their music festivals; Burkina Faso, through its film festival, which is attended by people from all over the world, has created a cultural product from a national passion.

Tourists are particularly attracted to United Nations Educational, Scientific, and Cultural Organization (UNESCO) World Heritage sites. UNESCO reports that Sub-Saharan Africa is severely underrepresented on the World Heritage list. Underrepresentation is due not to a lack of sites but to unexplored opportunities. A study conducted by the African World Heritage Fund in 2009 identified 160 undeveloped cultural heritage sites across the region. Many of the official World Heritage sites in Sub-Saharan Africa are listed as "in danger." A press release in 2006 noted that, although Sub-Saharan Africa only had 8 percent of World Heritage sites (65 sites), the region had 43 percent of the World Heritage sites listed as "in danger" (UNESCO 2006). Five years later, 40 percent of "in danger" World Heritage sites are still in Sub-Saharan Africa; of these, five are in the Democratic Republic of Congo. Developing cultural heritage opportunities in Sub-Saharan Africa will involve identifying potential sites, establishing preservation plans, and ensuring that existing sites are managed better (Robinson and Picard 2006; World Bank 2001).

Domestic Travel

Growth in gross domestic product per capita has led to the emergence of a new middle class of African consumers who have discretionary income to travel (McKinsey and Company 2010). Under the right conditions, the tourism sector can tap this wealth. Currently, domestic travel in South Africa is contributing to tourism growth; Kenya has already given priority to domestic travel, and Ghana and Zimbabwe are starting to do the same.

Intraregional Tourism

More than 10 million people are traveling across national borders every year within Sub-Saharan Africa for business meetings and conferences, medical reasons, religious journeys, shopping, sports events, and visiting friends and relatives (Twining-Ward 2009). South Africa is the largest source of intraregional leisure travelers in Sub-Saharan Africa. Nigeria is a potential regional tourism powerhouse, and Kenya also shows potential as a large source market for intraregional travel.

Wellness, Health, and Retirement

Opportunities for wellness, health, and retirement tourism in Sub-Saharan Africa are growing. South African hospitals are a draw for intraregional visitors, and Mauritius and the Seychelles leverage wellness opportunities in their marketing campaigns. Cabo Verde has attracted second-home buyers.

References

Ebbe, K. 2008. "Cultural Heritage and Tourism: Synergies for Local Economic Development." Internal document, Washington, DC, World Bank.

Hamilton, K., G. Tembo, G. Sinyenga, S. Bandyopadhyay, A. Pope, B. Guilon, B. Muwele, S. Mann, and J. M. Pavy. 2007. "The Real Economic Impact of Nature Tourism in Zambia." Natural Resources Consultative Forum, Lusaka.

McKinsey and Company. 2010. *Lions on the Move: The Progress and Potential of African Economies*. Washington, DC: McKinsey Global Initiative.

Robinson, M., and D. Picard. 2006. *Tourism, Culture, and Sustainable Development*. Paris: UNESCO.

SH&E. 2010. "Competitive Africa: Tourism Industry Research Phase II Air Transport Sector Study." Unpublished report for the World Bank, Washington, DC.

SNV (Netherlands Development Organization). 2009. *The Market for Responsible Tourism Products with a Special Focus on Nepal and Latin America*. Amsterdam: SNV.

TUI Travel. 2010. *A Passport to Adventure*. London: TUI Travel.

Twining-Ward, L. 2009. "Sub-Saharan Africa Tourism Industry Research: Analysis of SSA Tourism Database." Unpublished report for the World Bank, Washington, DC.

UNESCO (United Nations Educational, Scientific, and Cultural Organization). 2006. "Launch of Africa World Heritage Fund." Press release, UNESCO, Paris. http://whc.unesco.org/en/news/253.

UNWTO (United Nations World Tourism Organization). 2010. *UNWTO Tourism Highlights, 2010 Edition.* Madrid: UNWTO.

World Bank. 2001. "Cultural Heritage and Development: A Framework for Action in the Middle East and North Africa." World Bank, Washington, DC.

———. 2011. *Africa Tourism Strategy: Transformation through Tourism, Harnessing Tourism for Growth and Improved Livelihoods.* Washington, DC: World Bank.

———. 2012. Sub-Saharan Africa Tourism Database. World Bank, Finance and Private Sector Development Unit, Africa Region, Washington, DC.

Chapter 6

Constraints on and Solutions for Tourism Growth

Given its strong and varied tourism assets and encouraging economic progress, Sub-Saharan Africa could be on the verge of a breakthrough in tourism development. The tourism sector in the majority of Sub-Saharan African countries is not performing up to its potential. Nevertheless, 8 countries have highly successful tourism sectors and 10 others could be successful in the foreseeable future; another 15 are waiting in the wings. This suggests that opportunities exist to grow the tourism sector, especially if constraints on growth are simultaneously addressed. Because the market failures that constrain tourism also constrain other segments of the economy and because tourism has backward linkages to sectors like agriculture, construction, and light manufacturing as well as significant pro-poor benefits, such a strategy could have a truly transformative effect on the macroeconomies of Sub-Saharan African countries. To be truly transformative, the determining factor will be the scale of investment in tourism.

A Typology of Sub-Saharan African Countries by Level of Tourism Development

To understand which Sub-Saharan African destinations are the highest performers and why, the Africa Finance and Private Sector Development (AFTFP) unit of the World Bank developed a typology ranking 47 Sub-Saharan African countries by their level of tourism development. Based on five key indicators, the methodology—described in chapter 1—entailed an analysis of the tourism sector's current situation, future prospects, and macroeconomic setting.[1] This typology can be seen as a diagnostic categorization, identifying the current status of all Sub-Saharan African countries, in contrast to the categories of strategic action that group recommendations for improving tourism.

Table 6.1 Sub-Saharan African Countries, by Level of Tourism Development and World Bank Income Ranking

Level of tourism development	Low income	Lower-middle income	Upper-middle income
Pre-emerging	Central African Republic, Chad, Comoros, Democratic Republic of Congo, Eritrea, Guinea, Guinea-Bissau, Liberia, Niger, Somalia, Togo	Republic of Congo, Equatorial Guinea, Sudan	None
Potential	Benin, Burundi, Ethiopia, Madagascar, Mali, Mauritania, São Tomé and Príncipe, Sierra Leone	Angola, Cameroon, Côte d'Ivoire, Lesotho, Nigeria, Swaziland	Gabon
Emerging	Burkina Faso, The Gambia, Malawi, Mozambique, Rwanda, Senegal, Uganda, Zambia, Zimbabwe	None	The Seychelles
Consolidating	Kenya, Tanzania	Cabo Verde, Ghana	Botswana, Mauritius, Namibia, South Africa

Sources: World Bank 2009, 2010a.

The typology produced four distinct groups of countries:

- Pre-emerging
- Potential
- Emerging
- Consolidating.

The results are shown in table 6.1.

Tourism can potentially create millions of jobs, among other economic benefits, if it is developed successfully. Yet, so far, just 8 of Sub-Saharan Africa's 47 nations have achieved significant tourism success and employ 4 percent or more of their workforce in tourism. Another 10 countries could achieve that same success in the foreseeable future, with 15 others lined up behind. Standing in the way of successful and sustainable tourism development in Sub-Saharan Africa are some persistent constraints, discussed below. Presented with them are examples of how countries facing the same challenges have resolved these issues; where there are no good examples, the issue is followed by a recommendation.

The characteristics of the four groups are as follows:

- *Pre-emerging.* These 14 countries have *not yet developed* their tourism sectors, and their market failure is almost complete. They have little governance or security, have shown little interest in tourism, and have poor short- to medium-term prospects for tourism growth. This group also includes three countries with little or no data on tourism: Equatorial Guinea, Liberia, and Somalia.

- *Potential.* These 15 countries *initiating* tourism have shown some interest in tourism but lack adequate governance of the sector. They have some basic infrastructure for tourism but still face market failures pertaining to regulation, resources, and institutions, which also affect the macroeconomy.

- *Emerging.* These 10 countries are *scaling up* tourism. They have solid institutions, are prioritizing tourism, and are performing reasonably well with regard to quality and competitiveness. The market failures that are evident—for example, the high costs of access to the destination, financing, and hotel construction, together with continuing difficulties in access to land—are mostly related to government failures, although the small scale of tourism contributes to the high costs of access.

- *Consolidating.* Eight countries are working on *deepening and sustaining* success. They have relatively mature tourism sectors, are committed to tourism, and have the highest economic and tourism performance in Sub-Saharan Africa. The management quality and capability of the private sector are reflected in the accolades that selected hotels and operators receive.[2]

Countries at the lower levels of tourism performance should note that success in tourism is not dependent on income level. As table 6.1 shows, two low-income countries are among the highest performers in Sub-Saharan Africa, and nine are in the "emerging or scaling up" category.

Common Constraints

With varying degrees of seriousness, several constraints are common to most Sub-Saharan African countries, regardless of their level of tourism development. These issues are among the macroeconomic market failures that also constrain tourism in many countries outside Sub-Saharan Africa. Those that have been discussed in previous chapters of this report are treated summarily in this section.

As noted in chapter 2, the tourism sector has multiple complexities because it is not self-contained and depends on a range of international and national actors. Negative criticisms are frequently launched against tourism; not all are justified, and some are exaggerated. Nevertheless, the sector requires careful and expert management to address the risks it can pose. As an export industry, a tourism destination competes against every other destination worldwide on price. Therefore, Sub-Saharan Africa's tourism sectors must maintain competitiveness through the following:

- Quality of tourism assets
- Standards of visitor accommodation

- Efficiency and safety of transport to, from, and within the country
- Adequacy of a variety of infrastructure components
- Receptiveness of local populations to tourists
- Skills of the range of officials and employees with whom tourists interact
- Safety and security of the destinations.

As noted in chapter 4, the limited and costly access to Sub-Saharan African destinations from major supplier markets and the infrequent, irregular, and inadequate transportation within countries have major implications for the competitiveness of Sub-Saharan African countries with other destinations worldwide. As noted in chapter 1, tourism is highly dependent on a range of infrastructure facilities. These are often lacking or inadequate in many Sub-Saharan African countries, yet the absence of any one component of infrastructure—for example, potable water—can seriously hamper tourism development or impose heavy capital and operating costs on private sector managers of the tourism product.

Several entities are primarily responsible for the success of the sector, as discussed in chapter 2. The government is an essential supporter that must throw its political support behind the sector, initiate the formulation of a strategy for it, and play the crucial coordinating role between the different public sector agencies involved and the relevant private for-profit and nonprofit entities and local communities. The government must also address market failures that affect the tourism sector and create an enabling environment for private investment. Above all, it must provide political stability. However, no tourism sector could exist without the private sector's investment in accommodation, attractions, and tourism services and facilities and without its knowledge transfer. In addition, local communities must be receptive to and benefit from the tourists who step into their communities. External donors can provide the critical capital and technical assistance needed to support the sector and help to raise it from one development level to the next. Without any one of these active participants, the sector cannot grow to its full potential or, if in the early stages of tourism development, even begin to create tourism packages for visitors. The previous chapters have provided examples of how these major players have successfully participated in the development of tourism in a range of countries.

IHS Global Insights[3] assigns a risk rating to every country based on a set of criteria for each of the following six categories: political, economic, legal, tax, operational, and security. Sub-Saharan African countries have a higher average risk than other countries (Ernst and Young 2010). Low levels of demand, weak domestic multipliers, and problematic business environments make it more expensive to operate tourism businesses in Sub-Saharan Africa than in other regions of the world. In addition to the constraints listed above, other barriers exist to the tourism trade in Sub-Saharan Africa. These barriers are discussed next, followed by examples of how some countries have overcome them.

Availability of Land

Ensuring that public and private land is available for tourism development is essential but often involves conflicting political, socioeconomic, technical, legal, and institutional vested interests. The existence of common land rights and "common pool resources" complicates the issue (Hardin 1968). Serious opposition can come from local people with traditional rights to the land but no legal title. The questions of who owns land, who owns the resources on it, and how rights are transferred are central to business and tourism development. The land has to be available on a long-term basis, either through ownership or lease, and be clear of legal and other claims.

A tourism master plan, generally undertaken by a foreign consulting firm and often funded by a donor,[4] may be the most efficient method of identifying prime tourism land for development. The results are more likely to be perceived as stemming from an objective and technical analysis than if they are the product of a government agency. Successful master plans identify high-value areas for tourism development as well as areas that could be developed at successive stages in the future; they also zone areas for alternative uses. Such plans identify areas that require environmental impact assessments and evaluate the country's environmental management capacity.

The master plan assesses the quality of tourism assets and recommends how they might be improved. It should also analyze local construction costs, the availability of materials and technical know-how, and the likely price levels at which accommodations could be constructed. It should evaluate the destination's competitiveness versus similar destinations and include a market survey of potential supplier markets. The consultants typically suggest an appropriate institutional framework for the plan's implementation and the country's technical assistance requirements and should suggest sources of financing, including potential donors. During the production of the master plan, with the assistance of the government, the consultants should convene stakeholders two or three times during the process to deliver their findings and encourage inputs. The objective of this participatory process is to give as many stakeholders as possible a sense of ownership of the eventual plan.

Frequently land will have to be purchased by the government or a statutory body for tourism development. In many countries, the developers are not allowed to purchase the land outright, in which case long-term leases of up to 99 years are the norm. More favorable conditions for developers will apply when countries are at the lower stages of tourism development. The government's incentives for tourism development may range from investing in the basic infrastructure for a large development to merely providing external access roads and utilities to the outskirts of the project. In cases where the government has created the right conditions for development, it may simply invite bids from the private sector for the whole or specific aspects of the project.

Since nationwide, comprehensive land reform is, at best, a long-term endeavor for most developing countries, governments have often relied on shorter-term practical solutions to facilitate access to secured land for investors. These include, as discussed below, land agencies created to establish an enabling environment for investment. In many countries, the state also has the right to expropriation or eminent domain. These rights can be used to relocate residents from tourist areas, but are generally only exercised in extreme situations, as they can create severe social and community impacts and are not compatible with sustainable tourism. Similarly, customary or religious land rights may not be codified but must be treated with respect, and adequate compensation must be paid for any change in ownership, so that no stakeholders feel alienated as a result of the tourism development.

Examples of How Other Countries Resolved Land Issues

No one land policy is right for every destination. Every situation is different and depends on landownership laws and regulations. Three of the case studies in part II provide examples of how the Arab Republic of Egypt, Namibia, and South Africa resolved issues related to the availability of land for tourism. A summary of the Egyptian case and information about approaches taken by other countries follow.

Land Access

Access to land was the primary constraint on expansion of the tourism industry near the Red Sea and on the Sinai Peninsula in Egypt. During the 1990s, the evolution of Egypt's institutional and regulatory framework for tourism gradually overcame opposition from the petroleum industry, the military, and the ministries of the interior, agriculture, and environment. When the Ministry of Tourism and the Tourism Development Authority were finally able to establish sites for tourism development, private investment surged; the Red Sea hotels now include the Four Seasons, Hyatt Regency, Marriott, Le Méridien, and Ritz Carlton.

Land Agencies

Uganda has a land information service. Some governments, such as Madagascar and Mozambique, prepare special tourism investment zones. Land banks, such as Tunisia's Real Estate Development Agency (Agence Foncière Touristique), hold land for development. Urban development corporations have also developed land for tourism, as was the case in the early days of Jamaican tourism. These corporations generally are experienced in other sectors and apply the increased value of the developed land to finance the utilities for the project (China and India).

Development Zones
As part of a plan to facilitate further foreign investment, the government of Cabo Verde bought large tracts of uninhabited land on Sal and Boa Vista islands to create two types of dedicated tourism development areas: integrated tourism development areas, which are areas with special tourism value, and zones for the conservation and protection of tourism, which are areas with high biodiversity and tourism value. Establishing these zones allowed the government to earmark prime coastal sites for tourism development and environmental protection. The process was successful in attracting investors but disenfranchised local landowners, causing considerable discontent.

Leasing
One hundred of the Maldives' many islands have been leased for tourism. The leasing model consists of auctioning uninhabited islands in a bidding process, with criteria published in advance and evaluated by independent and disinterested persons. Not only is the bidding process transparent and public, but it also gives significant weight to environmental considerations such as the setback from the high-water mark, height limits for buildings, and protection measures to prevent beach and coastal erosion. As an incentive for local participation, a consortium that includes local investors can secure longer leases than can be made available to foreign investors (World Bank 2005).

Access to Finance

Access to finance can be a critical constraint on tourism growth. In many Sub-Saharan African countries, commercial banks are not equipped to fund large tourism projects or may elect not to do so because tourism projects tie up funds for long periods and are less attractive than short-term business loans. Smaller types of tourism establishments, such as restaurants or gift shops, may face similar challenges in accessing finance. Small businesses such as lodges that expand incrementally require heavy up-front funding and only reach stable cash flows after a few years of operation. Inappropriate funding can imperil the financial stability of these ventures, but, at the same time, local financial institutions tend to avoid such high-risk ventures. Resolving the issue of finance for hotels and tourism facilities as well as microfinance for small and medium enterprises (SMEs) is vital for tourism.

Examples of How Other Countries Resolved Access to Finance Issues

In an effort to address this constraint, some countries have developed specialized hotel financing institutions that operate like mortgage lenders, while others have relied on nonbank financial institutions, such as insurance companies or pension funds. Urban development corporations may use incremental taxes to fund expansion. This involves basing real estate taxes on future increases in real estate value (for examples, see Peterson 2006).

In the Dominican Republic, access to finance was a considerable constraint. The government had to mobilize separate funds from the World Bank and the Inter-American Development Bank. These funds were made available as lines of credit to the central bank and then channeled through commercial banks and blended with the commercial banks' own funds to ensure their financial involvement in the subprojects.

Taxes on Tourism Investments

Many private investors in tourism complain that the government taxes them beyond their capacity to pay. When the tourism sector appears to be profitable and yet continues to require government expenditures on infrastructure, training, and promotion, for example, governments are often tempted to look for more tax revenues from entities in the tourism sector. As an example, SMEs in Zanzibar are unable to achieve economies of scale because of high taxes and complex tax structures that favor larger hotels. Taxes and levies constitute 12.8 percent of the total value chain for meeting, incentives, conferences, and exhibitions (MICE) tourism in Nairobi, Kenya, undermining private sector reinvestment in the tourism sector (World Bank 2010c).[5]

Examples of How Other Countries Handled the Imposition of New Hotel Taxes

Industry concern about taxation of its activities is so great that the World Travel & Tourism Council (WTTC), as part of its New Millennium Vision, included taxation in its program to eliminate barriers to growth. The WTTC stated that travel and tourism "generates more tax revenue than any other industry"; consequently, the "WTTC has developed principles, tools, and a research capability to work with governments to evaluate intelligent taxation approaches" (WTTC n.d.).[6] Similarly, the UNWTO Business Council sponsored a worldwide study on the effects of taxation on the tourism industry, which is published as *Tourism Taxation: Striking a Fair Deal* (UNWTO 1998). The theme of the study is that taxes can either stimulate or stifle tourism growth. Clearly, a balance needs to be struck between the need for private sector investments to be profitable and survive and for central and local governments to be able to provide the sector's required social and physical infrastructure and to preserve tourism assets from tourism revenues.

Tax issues should be discussed in a coordinating mechanism that the government establishes with the private for-profit and nonprofit sector. Governments should also discuss any proposed tax increases on tourism entities in this forum before introducing them. When tourism operations are sufficiently profitable to pay such taxes, they are warranted. When they are not, they can be waived temporarily. There have been cases in the Caribbean where the hotel association has paid for independent auditors to audit the books of affected hotels and present a report to government showing that groups of hotels are not profitable enough to pay new taxes. This example also demonstrates the value to tourism entities of having their own associations that can speak on behalf of a subsector in one voice to government.

Low Level of Tourism Skills

Sub-Saharan Africa has a large pool of young labor and more than 10 million new job seekers every year (World Bank 2010d), but the average educational attainment is low and tourism employment requires mostly mid-level service sector skills. Having an educated, skilled labor force is at the core of tourism innovation and competitiveness (Zeng 2008). The tour operator study conducted for this report identified service standards as a critical constraint on operations, particularly in high-cost destinations, such as Tanzania. The chief weaknesses are in business skills, understanding visitor needs and expectations, customer service, and online communications. Hotel companies noted that low education levels, lack of prior experience, cultural differences, and poor health meant that employees were less productive in many Sub-Saharan African countries. Another factor in Sub-Saharan Africa is that an employee's first language may not be English, French, Portuguese, or Spanish; it is usually a tribal language.

Tourism ministries in Sub-Saharan Africa frequently lack the know-how and leadership to implement effective training plans. In addition, disconnects often

Table 6.2 Types of Skills and Training Needed in Sub-Saharan Africa

Type of skills	Target group	Type of training needed	Type of course
Vocational skills	Entry-level employees in the tourism industry	Front desk management, reception, maintenance, housekeeping, food service, food preparation, and bartending	Train-the-trainer courses that train people to become "vocational skills consultants;" apprenticeship programs and day release
Public sector skills	Employees who work for public entities, parastatal entities, or nongovernmental organizations related to tourism, including wildlife reserves and national parks	Destination planning and destination management	Workshops and seminars that include monitoring and evaluation and are repeated on a regular basis
SME management skills	Owners and managers of small-scale private sector tourism enterprises	Financial management, operations management, human resources management, sales and marketing management	A series of courses that are short in nature, broad in scope, and designed for owners and managers with a high school education
Management of executive skills	Upper- and middle-management employees in large corporations or medium-size enterprises in hospitality and transport	Hotel management, food and beverage management, hotel financial management, and human resources management	In-house management training programs to develop a "culture of tourism"

Source: Adapted from Spenceley and Rozga 2007.

exist between tourism school curricula and the skills needed by tourism businesses. As a result, the level of service, even in developed destinations, is often inadequate in Sub-Saharan Africa. As shown in table 6.2, training is needed in all areas and at all levels, from vocational to managerial. This is true for all tourism subsectors, including airlines, where the study identified a lack of skilled professionals in the area of network planning, revenue management, maintenance, safety, aerospace purchasing, and quality control. The hotel study found that two to three foreign workers are usually employed at each full-service hotel to ensure international standards of operation; more are needed at luxury hotels (Ernst and Young 2010). The informal sector can also benefit from training, such as for handicrafts, which can boost the incomes of local communities—particularly when hotel managers allow them to sell their crafts within the hotel grounds.

Some tourism training institutes tend to focus on hotel management, when the critical skills gap is often at the operational level. The challenge for training schools is to ensure that tourism education is up to date, of a high standard, and in line with sector needs. Keeping up with the level of demand for tourism education is a challenge for some Sub-Saharan African countries. In Ethiopia, for example, only a fraction of students each year can be accommodated in the Catering and Tourism Training Institute, despite more than 300 applicants (Spenceley and Rozga 2007). By contrast, in The Gambia, more than 800 students are enrolled in tourism or hospitality courses throughout the private and public sectors. However, the majority of graduates in The Gambia are not sufficiently well trained or prepared to work in hotels (Novelli and Burns 2009).

Examples of Successful Training Programs in Sub-Saharan African Countries

Well-trained and motivated hotel employees perform well in Sub-Saharan Africa. For example, the hotel study conducted for this report found that housekeepers clean, on average, 14 rooms in an eight-hour shift. Considering the poor availability of hospitality training opportunities in Sub-Saharan Africa, this is not significantly different from European housekeepers, who clean 18 to 22 rooms in eight hours (Ernst and Young 2010).

The Institute of Travel and Tourism of The Gambia (ITTOG) offers professional courses in all sectors of the tourism industry, with special emphasis on travel agencies, accommodations, tour operations, tour guiding, group operations, event management, and general tourism business management. Close links with the University of Amsterdam in the Netherlands and South Nottingham College in the United Kingdom have resulted in course improvements and visiting lecturers. The ITTOG is also supported by the Center for Responsible Tourism in the United Kingdom, and with its help, the ITTOG promotes the teaching of responsible tourism as a core activity. The ITTOG also hosts professional and college groups from developed countries who study issues related to pro-poor and responsible tourism, using The Gambia as a case study. The two-way partnership is mutually beneficial.

Training is a public and private sector responsibility. Many hotel managers accept employees trained in formal hotel or tourism training programs but consider their training complete only when they have gone through the hotel's own training program. Many hotels train their own staff without requiring any formal training at all. Examples of private sector tourism training programs in Sub-Saharan Africa include Accor Academy and Sun International's training center for its staff in South Africa. Accor Academy trains 135,000 students a year using video game modules. The innovative, job-specific content of their training has been found to enhance employee loyalty and pride.[7] The Sun International program, summarized in table 6.3, supports continuous development from tertiary education through to job-specific training,

Table 6.3 Sun International Formal and Informal Learning

Type of learning	Example
Formal learning	
Learning event	Workshops, scheduled courses, conferences, seminars
E-learning and distance learning	Virtual classrooms, CD-ROM, Web courses, structured Web learning, workbooks and guides, Web conferencing
Structured work experience	Job rotations, secondments, job shadowing, project management
Certification and qualifications	Sun International certification, professional certification, academic qualifications
Structured coaching and team effectiveness	Structured mentoring, structured coaching, team effectiveness activities, external coaching
Informal learning	
On-the-job and experience learning	Work within role, exposure to other departments and roles, special assignments and projects, action learning
Knowledge management	Best practices, reference and reading material, information repositories, access to internal experts, internal standards and documented processes
Mentoring and communities of practice	Buddies, mentors, and peers; informal professional networks; common interest groups; lunch talks
External experience	Relationships with outside professionals, speaking engagements, professional memberships, executive directorships

Source: Sun International 2011.

foundation training for managers, elective training, and targeted development for promising potential employees (Sun International 2011).

Labor Policy

Having proper labor policies in place from the start helps to protect workers and guest laborers from exploitation. Having too much labor protection can, however, stifle job creation. In Namibia, following independence, many new labor laws were enacted to protect disadvantaged Namibians from exploitation. According to private sector interviewees, current and new employment regulations in Namibia make it harder, not easier, for businesses to employ more workers. Although the tourism sector has been successful in getting special treatment concerning work hours and vacation days in the past, dispute resolution is time-consuming and costly. The new Namibian Labor Act is likely to slow hiring and increase its cost. It will hinder companies' ability to select suitable employees and make it harder for companies to fire incompetent workers. In a fast-paced tourism industry, these measures will be a severe hindrance to Namibia's ability to be internationally competitive.

Comparison of Tourism Jobs with Those in Other Sectors

Not all jobs in tourism are good, although most tourism jobs compare favorably to work in sugar fields, mines, logging, and some manufacturing, among other labor-intensive employment. Tourism activities normally provide greater employment opportunities for women than other sectors.

Lack of Security and Safety As Well As High Crime Rates

Eighteen Sub-Saharan Africa countries are classified as "fragile states" on the fiscal 2011 rating list of the World Bank's Country Policy and Institutional Assessment.[8] These states are diverse and include countries that face severe development challenges, such as conflict, recovery from conflict, political instability, weak institutional capacity, and poor governance, as well as some island economies. Their common characteristics include the inability to mobilize domestic resources, dependence on external resources, poor levels of human development, low population density, weak infrastructure, concentration of exports in a few products, and high risk of conflict. Tourism development in fragile and postconflict countries involves a unique set of challenges.

In the list of countries in table 6.1, 12 of Sub-Saharan Africa's fragile states are in the "pre-emerging" category, five (Angola, Burundi, Côte d'Ivoire, São Tomé and Príncipe, and Sierra Leone) are in the "potential or initiating" category, and Zimbabwe is in the "emerging or scaling up" category. Two states that are not classified as "fragile"—Equatorial Guinea and Niger—are classified as "pre-emerging." When successful, as in The Gambia, tourism can be a tool for peace building, poverty alleviation, and infrastructure investment, as it improves the country's image as an investment destination, among other benefits.

News of security concerns can result in immediate cessation of tourism activities in a country. Tour operators in the tourism research survey conducted for this report noted a reduction in the number of tours in Kenya, Madagascar, and Zimbabwe when internal troubles arose. High crime rates have the same effect on visitors as internal conflict. Particularly in the early days of tourism in the Caribbean, hotels were gated and placed behind high walls, keeping tourists inside. Many luxury hotels in Sub-Saharan Africa follow the same practice. Today, however, numerous tourists visit a country to experience its culture and other attractions, such that they leave the hotel and mix with the local population.

Examples of Countries That Have Overcome Tourism Losses Caused by Internal Conflict and Crime

Kenya successfully combated negative images associated with its elections by significant spending on promotion and stabilization measures. In Mali insecurity in the north of the country has severely reduced tourist visitation, and now the south of Mali has begun a strong marketing campaign to disassociate itself from the north's troubles. Caribbean countries undertook intensive public education campaigns to instill in the local people a realization of the benefits that tourism brings to the islands and their role in maintaining a flow of tourists. As discussed in chapter 2, hotel managers throughout the world have realized the importance of extending tourism benefits to the surrounding communities, from which they mostly draw their staff, and have encouraged local people to think of tourists as the source of their improved way of life.

Public Health

The public health situation in a destination is critical to a tourist's welfare. Many travelers are put off from undertaking a journey when, prior to leaving home, they must endure injections and then remember to take preventive medicine regularly during travel. Several Sub-Saharan African countries have malaria in at least some regions of the country. Other more serious diseases are prevalent or break out periodically in a few countries. High-class medical care may be available in the capital and other big cities, but not in less traveled regions. Clearly, improvements in public health are of primary value to the local population; without them, the number of foreign visitors will not expand, and visitors will be less willing to explore more remote parts of the destination. As a first, essential step, the tourism sector can train its staff to meet high hygiene standards in accommodation and food establishments and educate them about the benefits of improved hygiene. Tourism facilities can also encourage their staff to instruct their families and persuade members of the local community to introduce better hygiene in their homes. The tourism sector can have a positive ripple effect in improving the basic health of its employees and their associates.

Visa Requirements

Streamlined processing of visas and work permits is a crucial enabler of tourism.[9] The World Bank's Africa Region Tourism Database project researched the visa requirements for 47 countries in Sub-Saharan Africa (map 6.1). A clear

Map 6.1 Visa Requirements in Sub-Saharan Africa

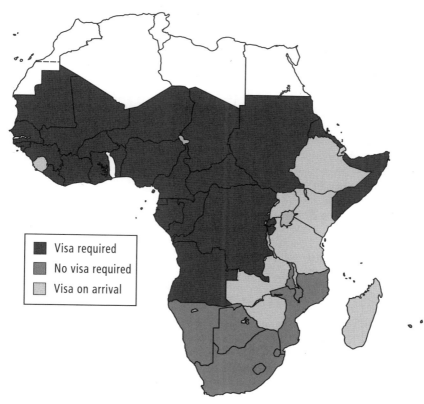

■ Visa required
■ No visa required
□ Visa on arrival

Source: SH&E 2010.

correlation was found between ease of visa processing and tourism performance. Countries with more mature tourism sectors had removed visa requirements for their key source markets. In contrast, countries with complex visa requirements had less developed tourism sectors. Visas can be a particular constraint for small countries. If the visa is too expensive or too difficult to obtain, tour operators may opt not to include the country as part of a regional tour.

When visas are expensive and passports must be sent for processing prior to travel, visitors are deterred. Independent travelers who may not have the time or access to an embassy or consulate to have their passport processed will be most adversely affected. Greater numbers of passengers can have a multiplier effect that compensates for the loss of visa revenues. Moreover, as foreigners spend across the economy, the effect is much broader than a fee that simply makes a small contribution to the overall national budget.

Examples of Countries That Have Expedited the Visa Process

The aviation study examined travel between the United States and the Republic of Korea to show how visa waiver programs can dramatically increase inbound arrivals (SH&E 2010). Following civil unrest in 2008, Kenya dropped its visa fees and increased its marketing budget. The result was a strong recovery in the number of tourist arrivals.[10] Madagascar implemented a similar policy in an effort to increase arrivals following political unrest and announced that tourists staying for less than 30 days could receive a free visa on arrival at the airport. Mozambique's recent tourism boom is also credited to changes in visa policies that allow visitors from the Southern African Development Community countries to enter without a visa. As figure 6.1 shows, most visa-free countries are in Southern Africa, but visas can be purchased on arrival at the airport in most countries in East Africa.

Red Tape and Bureaucracy

Planning for and regulating tourism development is crucial to sustainability, but too much regulation and unpredictable behavior by government and others inhibit growth and, ultimately, make tourism less sustainable. In Namibia, for example, more than 50 permits and certificates are required for lodging owners to register or reregister their accommodation establishment (HAN 2010). This is expensive and time-consuming, and it inhibits business growth.

Research across 2,000 businesses in South Africa by the Strategic Business Partnerships for Growth found that the costs of complying with regulations are up to three times higher in the tourism industry than for other businesses. The survey established that tourism firms of all sizes face higher regulatory costs than firms in general, tax compliance is more burdensome, and municipal regulations are a far greater problem in this sector than in others. The reason for the higher costs was the considerable number of government departments and statutory bodies responsible for different aspects of industry regulation. A strong case for simplification and streamlining exists in this area.

Bribes and corruption also make doing business expensive and problematic in Sub-Saharan Africa. In the Democratic Republic of Congo, spontaneous "fees" can increase aircraft landing rights from $1,000 to more than $12,000 for some flights (SH&E 2010). The Central African Republic has a similar revenue-generating system: it charges airlines a "development fee" that doubles the landing cost (SH&E 2010). In Kenya, 75 percent of businesses report having to make "informal payments" to get things done; an estimated 12 percent of all payments are "informal" (SBP 2006).

Recommendations for Reducing Red Tape and Bureaucracy

The two countries charging spontaneous fees, the Central African Republic and the Democratic Republic of Congo, are classified as "fragile states" and in this report's classification are "pre-emerging" tourism destinations. Obviously, correcting these irregularities might not be the first, and certainly would not be the only, recommendation made to their governments in the context of encouraging tourism. Kenya, Namibia, and South Africa, however, are among Sub-Saharan Africa's 10 best-performing tourism destinations (table 6.4). Issues of excessive and duplicative regulation and "informal payments" should be eliminated to help these tourism sectors to become more profitable and more efficient. If they are not addressed, the long-term consequences for the sector would have a negative effect on prices and deter private investment.

Table 6.4 Performance of Tourism Sectors in Sub-Saharan Africa, 2011

Country	Total tourism receipts (US$, million)[a]	Direct contribution of tourism to GDP (%)		Direct travel and tourism employment (number of workers)		Year of total tourism receipts and report data[c]
		2011[b]	Forecast for 2021[b]	2011[b]	Forecast for 2021[b]	
Group 1: Consolidating						
Botswana	513	2.9	3.1	28,500	40,100	2008
Cabo Verde	352	15.0	17.9	27,800	43,900	2008
Ghana	919	2.6	2.4	114,400	136,000	2008
Kenya	752	5.4	4.8	247,300	272,500	2008
Mauritius	1,454	12.8	13.6	69,000	90,500	2008
Namibia	382	2.9	5.1	20,900	47,100	2008
South Africa	7,638	2.9	3.2	569,800	762,900	2008
Tanzania	1,260	5.0	4.2	432,100	463,800	2009
Subtotal	13,270	n.a.	n.a.	1,509,800	1,856,800	n.a.
Group 2: Emerging						
Burkina Faso	62	1.4	1.1	57,900	60,000	2008
Gambia, The	83	7.8	6.4	44,100	49,900	2008
Malawi	27	4.5	3.8	128,300	146,000	2007
Mozambique	190	3	2.7	240,100	331,400	2008
Rwanda	202	3.1	2.7	54,200	62,500	2008
Senegal	250	5.1	4.7	125,200	147,900	2006
Seychelles	278	25	21.4	11,000	11,000	2007

(continued next page)

Table 6.4 (continued)

Country	Total tourism receipts (US$, million)[a]	Direct contribution of tourism to GDP (%) 2011[b]	Forecast for 2021[b]	Direct travel and tourism employment (number of workers) 2011[b]	Forecast for 2021[b]	Year of total tourism receipts and report data[c]
Uganda	667	3.9	3.3	202,100	251,100	2009
Zambia	146	2.5	2.4	25,300	29,500	2008
Zimbabwe	294	5.1	5.4	38,300	56,500	2008
Subtotal	2,199	n.a.	n.a.	926,500	1,145,800	n.a.
Group 3: Potential						
Angola	285.0	1.7	1.7	68,200	94,700	2008
Benin	209.0	2.5	2.6	41,200	58,700	2008
Burundi	1.3	2.4	1.7	36,000	31,100	2008
Cameroon	177.0	2.4	2.3	95,300	117,900	2007
Côte d'Ivoire	118.2	2.5	2.5	106,200	129,100	2007
Ethiopia	377.0	5.3	4.0	1,080,100	1,109,100	2008
Gabon	9.0	1.1	1.6	4,600	9,200	2004
Lesotho	34.0	4.3	5.2	19,100	26,500	2008
Madagascar	308.0	5.3	5.5	193,700	264,800	2009
Mali	221.0	4.5	4.3	79,400	76,700	2007
Mauritania	42.7	—	—	—	—	2007
Nigeria	221.0	1.4	1.6	765,200	1,163,100	2008
São Tomé and Príncipe	7.7	3.9	2.4	2,700	2,500	2008
Sierra Leone	34.0	3.4	3.5	33,400	43,200	2008
Swaziland	32.2	2.3	2.4	5,800	7,000	2007
Subtotal	2,077.1	n.a.	n.a.	2,530,900	3,133,600	n.a.
Group 4: Pre-emerging						
Central African Republic	9.0	2.1	1.8	15,000	16,800	2008
Chad	63.6	1.5	1.6	24,600	31,100	2007
Comoros	18.8	2.8	2.5	4,900	6,600	2007
Congo, Dem. Rep.	26.2	0.9	0.8	109,600	131,400	2007
Congo, Rep.	54.0	1.5	1.7	11,500	16,100	2007
Equatorial Guinea	—	—	—	—	—	—
Eritrea	26.0	—	—	—	—	2009
Guinea	1.5	1.9	1.7	35,400	40,800	2008
Guinea-Bissau	2.8	—	—	—	—	2006
Liberia	—	—	—	—	.—	—
Niger	45.0	1.8	1.6	14,300	18,800	2008
Somalia	—	—	—	—	—	—

(continued next page)

Table 6.4 (continued)

Country	Total tourism receipts (US$, million)[a]	Direct contribution of tourism to GDP (%)		Direct travel and tourism employment (number of workers)		Year of total tourism receipts and report data[c]
		2011[b]	Forecast for 2021[b]	2011[b]	Forecast for 2021[b]	
Sudan	331.0	1.1	1.3	121,500	179,100	2008
Togo	34.0	3	2.5	23,200	24,500	2007
Subtotal	611.9	n.a.	n.a.	360,000	465,200	n.a.
Grand total	18,158.0	n.a.	n.a.	5,327,200	6,601,400	n.a.

Sources: World Bank 2012; UNWTO 2013; WTTC Economic Data Search Tool, http://www.wttc.org/research/economic-data-search-tool/.
Note: n.a. = not applicable. — = not available. Indicators used to determine destination groups were international arrivals relative to population (World Bank 2012); tourist receipts per long-haul tourist arrival (UNWTO data); forecasted growth in tourist arrivals from 2011 to 2021 (WTTC economic forecast data); Doing Business rank for Sub-Saharan Africa (World Bank 2010b); Travel and Tourism Competitiveness Index for tourism regulation, infrastructure, and tourism resources (WEF 2009).
a. UNWTO data.
b. WTTC data (as of 2013).
c. Most recent data available.

Notes

1. Indicators used to determine destination groups are international arrivals relative to population (World Bank 2012); tourist receipts per long-haul tourist arrival (UNWTO data); forecasted growth in tourist arrivals 2010 to 2020 (WTTC data); Doing Business rank for Sub-Saharan Africa (World Bank 2010b); Travel and Tourism Competitiveness Index for tourism regulation, infrastructure, and tourism resources (WEF 2009).

2. The Leading Hotels of the World (http://www.lhw.com/), for example, lists a number of vanguard hotels in Sub-Saharan Africa: 12 in South Africa, 4 in Mauritius, and 1 each in Botswana, Kenya, the Seychelles, Tanzania, Uganda, and Zimbabwe.

3. See http://www.ihs.com/products/global-insight/country-analysis/global-risk.aspx.

4. Examples include the United Nations World Tourism Organization and the European Union, multinational donors such as the World Bank and the African Development Bank, and bilateral donors such as the U.S. Agency for International Development, the U.K. Department for International Development, and SNV (the Netherlands Development Organization).

5. Incentives tourism refers to trips that an employer offers as a reward to its top-performing employees.

6. The WTTC New Millennium Vision is available at http://fama2.us.es:8080/turismo/turismonet1/economia%20del%20turismo/turismo%20zonal/lejano%20oriente/ASIA%20PACIFIC%20TRAVEL%20AND%20TOURISM%20IN%20THE%20NEW%20MILLENIUM.PDF.

7. See "Accor Celebrates 25 Years of the Hospitality Industry's Largest Corporate University," January 17, 2011 (http://www.hospitalitynet.org/news/154000320/4049814.html).

8. The Bank's definition of fragile states is based on the Country Policy and Institutional Assessment rating.
9. Australia pioneered the instant e-visa system several years ago. The airline inputs travelers' data at check-in, and the visas are ready by the time they arrive in Australia.
10. Kenya's arrivals dropped 32 percent in 2008 and then bounced back up 24 percent following the recovery policies in 2009.

References

Ernst and Young. 2010. "Sub Saharan Africa Hospitality Sector Overview." Unpublished research for the World Bank Group, Washington, DC.

HAN (Hospitality Association of Namibia). 2010. "Documents Needed to Register, Extend Registration, and/or Needed Recurrently for the Operation of an Accommodation Establishment." Unpublished internal document, HAN, Windhoek.

Hardin, G. 1968. "The Tragedy of the Commons," *Science* 162 (3859): 1243–48.

Novelli, M., and P. Burns. 2009. "Restructuring The Gambia Hotel School into a National Tourism Training Institute." The Gambia Investment Promotion and Free Zone Agency, Banjul.

Peterson, George E. 2006. "Leasing Land and Land Sale as an Infrastructure Financing Option." Policy Research Paper 4043, World Bank, Washington, DC.

SBP (Strategic Business Partnerships for Growth). 2006. "Counting the Cost of Red Tape for Tourism in South Africa, Strategic Business Partnerships for Growth in Africa." ComMark Trust, Johannesburg.

SH&E. 2010. "Competitive Africa: Tourism Industry Research Phase II Air Transport Sector Study." Unpublished report for the World Bank, Washington, DC.

Spenceley, A., and Z. Rozga. 2007. "IFC Tourism Training Network, Market Research Report." International Finance Corporation, Washington, DC; Global Business School Network, London.

Sun International. 2011. "Human Capital." http://suninternational.investoreports.com /sun_ar_2010/reports/joint-report-of-the-chief-executive-and-chief-financial-officer /human-capital/.

UNWTO (United Nations World Tourism Organization). 1998. "Tourism Taxation: Striking a Fair Deal." UNWTO Business Council, Madrid.

———. 2013. *Tourism Factbook.* UNWTO, Madrid. http://www.e-unwto.org/content /v486k6/?v=search.

WEF (World Economic Forum). 2009. *Travel and Tourism Competitiveness Report 2009: Managing in a Time of Turbulence.* Geneva: WEF.

World Bank. 2005. "Maldives Investment Climate Assessment: South Asia Region." World Bank, Washington, DC.

———. 2009. "World Bank List of Economies (Country Classification)." World Bank, Washington, DC. http://www.iqla.org/joining/World-Bank_Classification-List _2009.pdf.

————. 2010a. *Africa Region Tourism Strategy: Transformation through Tourism, Harnessing Tourism for Growth and Improved Livelihoods.* Washington, DC: World Bank.

————. 2010b. *Doing Business 2010.* Washington, DC: World Bank.

————. 2010c. *Kenya's Tourism: Polishing the Jewel.* Washington, DC: World Bank, Finance and Private Sector Development Unit, Africa Region.

————. 2010d. "Scaling Up Support for Agriculture: Africa Region Action Plan." Internal draft document, World Bank, Washington, DC.

————. 2012. Sub-Saharan Africa Tourism Database. World Bank, Finance and Private Sector Development Unit, Africa Region, Washington, DC.

WTTC (World Travel & Tourism Council). n.d. "Asia-Pacific Travel and Tourism in the New Millennium: A World Travel and Tourism Council Vision." WTTC, London:

Zeng, D. Z., ed. 2008. *Knowledge, Technology, and Cluster-Based Growth in Africa.* Washington, DC: World Bank.

Chapter 7

Strategic Decisions for Tourism Sustainability

Governments contemplating initiating tourism or moving tourism from one development stage to the next need to make strategic decisions from the outset about three main issues:

- Scale of tourism development
- Sustainability of the sector
- Financing of tourism and economic rents.

These decisions should be made in consultation with all of the stakeholders in tourism at the national and regional levels, even when an expansion of tourism is foreseen only for a particular region of the country. When a major change is contemplated, the interdependence of the sector's several branches requires a countrywide assessment of its likely impacts on the resources and services available to the rest of the sector.

Scale of Tourism Development

Before embarking on a program to initiate or scale up tourism, governments have to decide on the scale of the development. One of the most significant planning decisions is size: whether to build large resorts, boutique hotels, mid-sized projects, ecolodges, or some combination. The scale of the development will determine the extent of the transformation that the investment can achieve. However, as noted below, if the development exceeds the capacity of the country to absorb the assets and the resources available to manage the sector, the consequences will be negative. Related issues are the income market that the destination should target. If several parts of the country are suitable for tourism development, planners will have to decide whether to consolidate their efforts in one location or disperse tourism developments to several regions. Several countries that have very large, successful destinations, such as the Dominican

Republic and Mexico, opted to start with an anchor project in one location. A government—or a public-private tourism authority or statutory body—will also have to decide whether to treat tourism development as an immediate once-and-for-all activity or as a continuing program with investments scheduled over a series of 5- to 10-year periods.

Political and equity considerations will shape decisions, as will the quality and value of the nation's tourism assets. In general, foreign corporations own large-scale projects, depending on the amount of investment capital that is available for tourism in the destination; smaller resorts normally reflect area traditions; and medium-sized projects tend to capture mid-market consumers. Ideally, the planners will be able to diversify the tourism product by enhancing and promoting a combination of tourism assets: resorts, mountains, national parks, wildlife, cultural, adventure, health and wellness, festivals, and other purposes (such as for meetings, incentives, conferences, and exhibitions, known as MICE tourism), and sports (such as fishing, sailing, and golf), among others. Master plans conducted by independent consultants can be very helpful in providing guidance on the scale of tourism development and in suggesting planning techniques for managing the development sustainably. Some considerations about the scale of tourism follow.

Critical Mass

A certain quantity of accommodation is needed to create the critical mass needed to convince airlines to establish routes and tour operators to promote the destination. The first investors will need either incentives, such as infrastructure investment from government, or special concessions if they are to risk their capital without this critical mass. A "first mover" may face the same risks when a country that has one or more established resort areas decides to expand its tourism potential by opening a new tourism area. Jamaica successfully developed a new resort area in Negril on the west coast. It is currently opening another in the southwest to relieve the pressure on Montego Bay and Ocho Rios, to diversify the tourism product, and to create employment.

Large-Scale Projects

The case studies in part II show that large projects have delivered substantial jobs and tax and foreign exchange revenues. They have also contributed to a positive national investment climate in tourism and other sectors. Projects like Aqaba in Jordan, Cancun in Mexico, and Dubai in the United Arab Emirates are sometimes criticized for being too big and too impersonal, but they created the critical mass that forged a brand and created a profitable flow of tourists. Their large scale also made it easier to lower costs, generate economic returns, and address national weaknesses in training, promotion, and social inclusion. Mexico initiated two large-scale resort developments (Cancun and Zihuatanejo) almost simultaneously on the Caribbean and Pacific coasts. In Cancun, developers opted for concentrated growth on a deserted island, originally as a hub for the Caribbean coast (the Mayan Riviera); today the intense development extends 100 kilometers south. Alternatively, in Zihuatanejo they opted for much more decentralized growth on the Pacific coast. Each has been successful in its own way and attracts different market segments.

The World Bank has implemented more than 300 tourism projects in 86 countries since the 1960s (Hawkins and Mann 2007), and the number of projects continues to grow. World Bank interventions financed the takeoff of tourism in the Dominican Republic (World Bank 1974, 1979; National Statistics Office 2010), Indonesia (Bali), Morocco, Tunisia, and Turkey. The intervening 20 years have shown that planned resorts (a) have economies of scale in construction, (b) provide the infrastructure to stimulate investment, (c) become magnets for tourism development, and (d) are models that can be replicated in other countries. On this last point, Puerto Plata, initially a public investment program in the Dominican Republic, spawned several privately sponsored projects, such as Punta Cana. Notably, Playa Dorada in Puerto Plata was itself subsequently privatized.

Small-Scale Projects

Smaller-scale projects can range from ecolodges in sensitive ecological areas to boutique hotels in resort areas, cities, or near a natural asset. As a result of their scale, they can be designed to be more compatible with the environment and the social fabric of a community than a large-scale resort. Individuals with a passion and vision often drive these smaller projects. Such projects typically take longer to break even without the critical mass of rooms but, depending on the market they cater to, may have a deeper and more effective local value chain.

Nihiwatu Resort on Sumba Island in Indonesia, for example, took 10 years to assemble its land package, but the community payback is now significant. Costa Rica created certification programs for ecotourism lodges to guarantee their sustainability but is now building larger hotels on beach sites reserved for larger operations. Smaller projects may be financially successful over time and often have valuable community outreach programs, but they are difficult to scale up enough to generate significant economic returns for the country.

For tourism to benefit a community significantly, individual projects must adopt specific measures to incorporate the interests of local communities into the project's design and implementation. The Sustainable Tourism–Eliminating Poverty (ST-EP) initiative of the United Nations World Tourism Organization (UNWTO) identifies seven key ways that tourism can help to fight poverty and foster social and economic inclusion in developing countries:

- Employment of the poor in tourism enterprises
- Supply of goods and services to tourism enterprises by the poor

- Direct sales of goods and services to visitors by the poor (informal economy)
- Establishment and running of tourism enterprises by the poor
- Taxes on tourism income with proceeds benefiting the poor
- Voluntary giving by tourism enterprises and tourists to the poor (travelers' philanthropy)
- Investment in infrastructure stimulated by tourism, which benefits the poor.

With the help of the U.S. Agency for International Development (USAID), the tourism project in Pays Dogon, Mali, includes a visitor center as well as nature and cultural trails that benefit local communities and offer a philanthropic element. In Tanzania, the Mulala Cultural Tourism Enterprise in Arusha demonstrates how public and nonprofit sector partnerships can assist women in poor communities to develop small tourism projects around their lifestyle, farms, and village resources. In Kenya, mountain climbing has provided pro-poor employment and income-generation opportunities for tour guides.

Mount Kilimanjaro, a world heritage site, is the highest mountain in Africa at 5,895 meters. A network of tour operators, porters, and guides makes it one of the best-organized mountain hikes in Africa. The estimated income from Mount Kilimanjaro is about $50 million a year, of which about $13 million (28 percent) is pro-poor, providing income for about 400 guides, 10,000 porters, and 500 cooks.

Clusters

Tourism is naturally a clustering activity, as tourism products are composed of many different types of facilities and services. Porter (1998) explains that clusters often extend laterally to include government and other institutions. Clustered products also tend to have higher levels of innovation, productivity, and management. The Aqaba Special Economic Zone in Jordan is an example of clustered development. Developing new growth poles, composed of a cluster of businesses, can also assist with decentralizing tourism, while achieving beneficial scale.

Excessive Expansion

Increasing the number of tourists can be counterproductive. Projects in Mauritius, the Seychelles, and Zanzibar had ambitious targets for increased arrivals, often without considering the infrastructure needed to make expansion possible or the impact on traditional tourists. Zanzibar currently has 9,000 beds and is considered relatively developed, but it has set a highly ambitious target of 25,000 beds by 2020. Mauritius has always had a significant share of the luxury tourism market but may not be able to retain its image as a luxury destination with the large increase in hotel rooms that is planned. Large numbers of tourists are characteristic of low-cost destinations because they lead to congestion and management problems that require significant investment (larger airports, more buses, more hotels, waste management capacity, utilities, and so forth). A luxury market depends heavily on the sense that the asset is only available to the wealthy few—at least in the peak season. In Cabo Verde, development has occurred so quickly that regulations and monitoring have been unable to keep up, which has led to ecological and social stress. Large numbers of tourists spending smaller amounts of money have forced staff pay and room rates down in the Arab Republic of Egypt and Turkey. Alternatives to expanding the number of tourists are to attempt to extend the tourist season (Spenceley 2010) by enhancing attractions and creating out-of-season festival, sporting, and cultural events and to increase tourist yield by maximizing opportunities for tourists to purchase locally produced goods and services.

Monitoring

To understand the impact of tourism and prevent serious damage to the product, particularly in a situation of rapid growth, governments must monitor tourism's various impacts on tourists, the businesses of tourism, the local population, and the natural assets on which tourism is based. Monitoring must be carried out in coordination with the private sector, nongovernmental organizations (NGOs), and local communities. Tourists' overall reactions to the visit can be captured in visitor satisfaction surveys with carefully targeted questions. Occupancy rates, prices, and the profitability of accommodation provide clear insights into whether the size of the sector is appropriate to the demand. Water quality, beach sand profiles, and coastline should be monitored regularly in resort destinations. Wildlife surveys and park biodiversity should be monitored to ensure that resources are not under stress. The views of the population at-large and local communities in areas of tourism concentration need to be collected, even if only informally. Such monitoring, performed regularly, should reveal whether a tourism sector can expand or should remain at a size that preserves its asset base and continues to attract satisfied tourists at acceptable income levels for the destination. Effective monitoring can only be undertaken with current, accurate, and appropriate databases, measured against equally accurate benchmarks.

Sustainability of the Sector

The four pillars of successful tourism development are financial, economic, social, and environmental sustainability. Without any one of these four conditions, the sector will falter.

Financial Sustainability

The success of any sector depends on the financial viability of investments and businesses. Investors and business owners need to integrate a clear path toward financial sustainability into their business, investment, or development plans from the beginning. In addition to responsible investors, the sustainability of the investments in accommodation and tourism services depends on the competence of the private sector together with the creation of a supporting policy environment, the provision of infrastructure by government, and the acceptance of tourism by the local population. Investors in the tourism sector must carefully assess the risks to their bottom line from all of the constraints discussed in chapter 6. They must also assess the local investment climate, the degree of seasonality, and the competition from overseas markets and from other established or imminent competing local investments.

Financial sustainability is particularly important in community-based tourism and ecotourism projects in which environmental and cultural sustainability are considered essential to success. Community tourism ventures are frequently started as philanthropic projects to integrate communities into mainstream tourism, but project implementers do not always have the business skills or knowledge needed to integrate financial sustainability planning into their endeavor. Many community tourism businesses fail due to careless financial planning that does not incorporate sufficient funds for the maintenance of business assets or consider cash flow challenges stemming from seasonality. Detailed financial sustainability plans, including demand and cash flow estimates, help investors—whether from the private sector or from development programs—to understand the true costs of developing a community tourism business and help businesses to plan for the future. Financial sustainability planning allows community members to benefit adequately and sustainably from tourism and should be integrated into any tourism investment regardless of the size and impact.

Financial sustainability needs to be institutionalized as a crucial element of tourism sector development, whether for large-scale development or small-scale ecotourism ventures. By creating a culture that has entrenched ideas about financial sustainability, countries will benefit from a lower rate of business failure, increased interest in investment, and higher levels of economic sustainability.

Economic Sustainability

Tourism is a cross-sectoral activity in which visitors spend money directly in hotels and often disburse substantial funds outside the hotel. Estimates of expenditures outside the hotel vary according to the type of hotel and local circumstances but can range from half to nearly double expenditures in the hotel. These direct expenditures, which are induced as a result of the investment in accommodation, give tourism operations their relatively high economic returns.

According to the World Travel & Tourism Council (WTTC), tourism's main comparative advantage over other sectors is that visitor expenditures have a "flow-through" or catalytic effect across the economy in terms of production and employment creation. Even during the building stage, tourism creates local jobs in the construction sector. If the country is sufficiently developed, the investment can generate local demand for furniture and furnishings and even for capital equipment. Tourism also generates demand for transport, telecommunications, and financial services. Through the consumption of local products in tourist accommodation and through visitor expenditures outside that accommodation, tourism can catalyze the development of small businesses in the production and service sectors, increase the demand for handicrafts, and generate linkages to agriculture, fisheries, food processing, and light manufacturing, such as the garment industry. Tourism can also create links to the informal sector. Notably, tourism can provide an economic base for a region whose only development options are its cultural and natural resources, whether coastal, mountain, or wildlife.

Each new production or service activity that is either started or expanded to meet actual or potential tourism demand will require new investment. But where capacity is underutilized or people are underemployed, tourism can generate new sources of income without significant new investments. Furthermore, the range of products and services that can be developed to satisfy tourism demand makes tourism a catalyst for entrepreneurial activity.

The lack of a comprehensive economic overview of the tourism sector has resulted in a limited understanding of its role. The WTTC has long promoted the development of credible economic assessments of the size, significance, and net contribution of tourism activity through the use of tourism satellite accounts. Since 1993, the UNWTO has actively pursued the same objective within the United Nations System of National Accounts. The objective is to measure the true economic impact of tourism in each country and to inform the policy decisions of governments and the investment decisions of private industry.

Sound government policies will help to extract the maximum economic benefits from tourism. As the discussion of economic rents later in this chapter suggests, various types of financing may be available to help governments to maintain a healthy and productive sector.

Social Sustainability

Some societies experience a sense of alienation from tourism, in particular when the visitors from other countries seem so different from themselves and physical and economic barriers prevent the local people from participating in the benefits of tourism. Hotels are often criticized for being foreign-owned and for not employing locals at the higher managerial levels, although this is less and less the case. In Mauritius, for example, the industry has predominantly been locally or regionally owned and managed from the outset; local investors continue to diversify out of other sectors, principally sugar and manufacturing, and into tourism. The perception of foreign-dominated hotel management is increasingly disappearing. Indeed, few hotels are sufficiently profitable to pay expatriate salaries. In Mauritius, at least one five-star hotel, part of a large local chain, is 100 percent locally owned and managed; no foreigner is employed on its staff. In Côte d'Ivoire, nationals and citizens dominate tourism services, the latter being Ivorians of foreign extraction who have elected to live in Côte d'Ivoire. Insufficient research has been conducted on this issue in Africa, but in the Caribbean, where the same concern is occasionally still voiced, ownership and management are predominantly local or regional for all ranges of accommodation and services.

A real issue in tourism throughout developing countries is how to extend the sector's benefits to the poor and local communities. Donors and NGOs have initiated many community-based projects aiming to establish links to traditional tourism. Some of the failures can be attributed to not involving the private sector in these initiatives at an early stage. Private sector involvement at the design stage ensures that local goods and services will be purchased and expectations will be fulfilled. Hotel managers or owners, in such varied destinations as Figi and the Eastern Cape in South Africa, have consciously involved the local community in their activities, occasionally with outside technical assistance. Links to local communities can be established by employing local people and sourcing goods and services from the community, supporting the establishment of small-scale or microenterprises to supply hotel needs, and upgrading training and skills for specific jobs, such as guides. Interdependence between the local community and the tourist accommodation generally improves relations between the two, and the benefits are mutual. Other initiatives are designed to empower local people to host tourists in their communities and thus give value to natural or cultural assets owned by the local community. Hosting may include reception facilities for daytime visits or overnight accommodation for tourists.

Sustainability considerations have graduated from being a minor additional component of resort development to being a central aspect of corporate risk management. Corporate social responsibility is seen as a mechanism for managing sustainability risks, in particular by gaining the support of the local community for the business that is conducted on its doorstep. Corporate social responsibility programs include corporate giving, travelers' philanthropy, and community initiatives, such as those undertaken by Nihiwatu Resort, Indonesia. More than 500 guests at Nihiwatu have contributed to funding local projects, with guest and organization donations amounting to almost $400,000 annually. The resort has helped more than 20,000 people living in 147 villages in a 110-square-kilometer area near West Sumba with agriculture projects, health projects, schools, and wells. In 2010 Nihiwatu was awarded the top prize at the Virgin Responsible Travel Awards as well as the award for reducing poverty most effectively. The combined resources of Nihiwatu and the Sumba Foundation have resulted in a powerful mechanism for delivering local water, electricity, and health care services.

Pro-poor tourism helps to extend the benefits of tourism to local communities. The Overseas Development Institute in the United Kingdom, the International Finance Corporation, the World Bank, and SNV (the Netherlands Development Organization) developed the pro-poor value chain analysis used for tourism. Value chain analysis is a useful technique for tracking pro-poor impacts in the tourism supply chain. World Bank value chain analysis in Kenya, Mali, Mozambique, Tanzania, and Zanzibar has allowed agencies and stakeholders to understand better how the poor can benefit from tourism and how obstacles to their participation can be removed. The pro-poor objective of value chain analysis is to identify interventions that harness markets and create larger-scale impacts than can be achieved through localized community development (Mitchell and Ashley 2009). "Pro-poor income" is defined as the wages and profits earned by poor households across the entire value chain. By "following the dollar," the analysis focuses on key points along the chain where interventions could expand income opportunities for the poor in the commercial service sector. The aim is to support market-based interventions by analyzing how the poor currently engage, how their positions can be improved, and how changes in value chain performance would affect them. Table 7.1 outlines the steps in the pro-poor value chain analysis.

Environmental Sustainability

Although often referred to as a "smokeless" industry, the dependence of tourism on natural resources makes any negative impacts more conspicuous. Water pollution, ecological disruption, land degradation, and congestion typify negative environmental externalities associated with poorly planned tourism. Often, however, pollution and degradation from external sources negatively affect the sustainability of tourism's own investments. Tourism can only be sustainable if the natural assets on which it is based are protected from degradation. This is particularly true in Africa, variously marketed as a nature, wildlife, resort, and cultural heritage destination. Consequently, a well-managed tourism sector will protect its natural resource base in new developments and mitigate negative impacts on the environment from previous developments and from external sources. When carefully managed, tourism can become a tool for protecting the environment and for financing conservation. Projects such as the Great Limpopo Transfrontier Park in Mozambique demonstrate the power of tourism to address a broad range of sustainability issues. The park forms part of a transfrontier conservation area where ecosystems are protected, the welfare of local

Table 7.1 Steps Involved in Pro-Poor Value Chain Analysis

Phase and step in the process	What to do?	Why?
Phase 1: Diagnosis		
Step 1	Prepare	To define the destination, type of potential target group, and assessment team and partners
Step 2	Map the big picture: enterprises and other actors in the tourism sector, links between them, demand and supply data, and the pertinent context	To organize a chaotic reality and understand the overall system
Step 3	Map where the poor do and do not participate	To avoid erroneous assumptions about the poor and take account of the less visible suppliers
Step 4	Conduct fieldwork interviews in each node of the chain, with tourists and service providers, including poor current and potential participants	To provide data and insights for steps 5 to 8
Step 5	Track revenue flows and pro-poor income, estimate how expenditure flows through the chain and how much accrues to the poor, and consider their returns and factors that enable or inhibit earnings	To follow the dollar through the chain down to the poor and assess how returns can be increased
Phase 2: Scope and prioritization of opportunities		
Step 6	Identify where in the tourism value chain to seek change: which node or nodes?	To select areas ripe for change, drawing on steps 1 to 5, and to ensure that steps 6 to 8 are focused on priority areas
Step 7	Analyze blockages, options, and partners in the nodes selected and generate a long list of possible interventions	To think laterally and rationally in generating the range of possible interventions
Step 8	Prioritize interventions on the basis of their impact and feasibility	To generate an intervention shortlist, comprising interventions most likely to deliver impact
Phase 3: Feasibility and planning		
Step 9	Ensure intervention feasibility and planning	To package selected interventions for funding and implementation

Source: Mitchell and Ashley 2009.
Note: These steps are iterative and cannot be entirely sequential—for instance, some initial thinking from step 6 (where to focus) will help to concentrate on resources within step 5.

communities is enhanced, and the natural and cultural assets are conserved and converted into renewable tourism resources.

The task of managing tourism's assets sustainably will generally exceed a ministry of tourism's technical and manpower resources. Therefore, the government needs to establish regulatory measures and control systems to ensure that the government department supervising the environmental aspects of a new project is well equipped to monitor and advise those working in the tourism and other sectors. Because environmental regulations can delay or even derail a poorly designed project, the agency supervising environmental regulations should have a prominent position in government. In Tanzania, for example, responsibility for the environment is assigned to the vice president's office, in the Environmental Division. The National Environmental Management Council is responsible for all aspects of environmental policy and planning.

Many countries have already produced environmental development plans that can serve as models for other nations, although they must be adapted to local circumstances. In Sub-Saharan Africa, South Africa and Tanzania, among others, have published environmental plans. Any country will have to address four environmental areas for tourism:

- *Environmental impact assessments* should be provided for any investment in the tourism sector. Although difficult to quantify, many environmental impacts are measurable. Trained government officials in the country's environmental department should evaluate these plans. If the assessment does not satisfy the reviewer, he or she needs to have the authority to request that certain aspects of it be redone.

- *Coastal zone management* helps to define and zone coastlines to restrict development in sensitive areas. The conflicting interests of tourism, fishing, and boating should be resolved in an integrated management plan. The construction of accommodation and other construction on the coast should be subject to setback regulations that take into account sea level rise and conform to a land use plan for the coastal area. Building densities should be controlled through physical planning and zoning regulations. Building codes should ensure the safety of all construction throughout the country. To protect reefs, codes of conduct should be drawn up for the diving sector after a consultation process that involves government and stakeholders. Similar codes of conduct could also be drawn up for all other major users of the coastal zone. Explicit regulations about the disposal of sewage and solid waste should be drawn up and widely publicized, with penalties for their nonobservance. Similar regulations can be applied to preserve the banks of lakes and rivers. Tourism development plans for high-value areas should be drafted.

- *National parks* should be designated for all areas of high biodiversity, scarcity, and beauty, with conservation regulations applying to their use. Wildlife can also be protected through well-regulated national parks.

- *Cultural heritage sites* should be identified and preserved. Local communities should be involved in their protection and should obtain economic benefits from their use by tourists.

The financial and technical costs of regulation, preservation, and monitoring can be high for governments. Multilateral and regional agencies, as well as bilateral agencies, NGOs, and foundations, can provide both financial and technical assistance to help governments in Sub-Saharan Africa to manage their environments.

To enhance the country's image and contribute to preserving the natural resource base, accommodation units can apply for "green" accreditation that signifies the successful pursuit of sound environmental management systems. The International Organization for Standardization (ISO) grants the coveted ISO 14001 award. Green Globe, which was initially launched by the WTTC and is now an independent nonprofit organization, provides a framework for assessing an organization's environmental performance, through which it can monitor improvements and achieve certification. Another certification program, the Leadership in Energy and Environmental Design (LEED) of the U.S. Green Building Council, emphasizes the use of recycled and recyclable building materials as well as energy and water conservation. As international concern for the environment intensifies, tourists increasingly seek hotels with "green" accreditation. A growing number of "green" tour operators in developed countries are establishing business relations with hotel and lodge managers that have adopted "green practices"; prime among them are TUI Travel and British Airways Holidays.

Accommodation is considered green if it conserves water and energy, disposes of all waste without polluting, and has recycling and utility monitoring programs, among other requirements. As a result of a "green" accreditation pilot project supported by the U.S. Agency for International Development (USAID) in Jamaica, hotels reported higher profitability, enhanced guest relations, improved ties to local communities, and a sense that they are helping to preserve the island's beauty. Costa Rica has made a concerted effort to implement ecotourism certification effectively after much study and support from organizations such as the Rainforest Alliance. The Costa Rica Tourism Board administers the certificate of sustainable tourism, one of the few certification programs provided free of charge. Well over 200 hotels and tour operators have been certified, and the program now also certifies rental car firms. Maldives has identified development standards and zoning regulations for its many islands, and the Seychelles recently launched its own sustainable tourism label.

Climate change particularly affects the tourism sector through a rise in sea level, threatening islands and coastal areas. Climate change is likely to increase the cost of tourism in the future. The United States already charges airlines $16.50 for each international passenger who lands in or departs from its territory; the United Kingdom charges passengers on the basis of the distance they have flown.[1] Airline transport contributes about 5 percent worldwide to carbon emissions (Wong, Christie, and Al Rowais 2009). While a few planes have been converted to fly on biofuel and cooking oil, public modes of transportation and equipment that use energy, such as air conditioning, still produce high levels of carbon emissions. To counter the industry's contribution to climate change, many tourism operators already offer a carbon calculator and suggest offsetting programs. Meanwhile, Maldives and Costa Rica are competing to be the first "carbon-neutral" destination. Without a doubt, low-carbon or climate-friendly policies must form part of tourism strategies moving forward.

Financing of Tourism and Economic Rents

The government has an important role to play in creating an enabling environment for private sector investment in the tourism sector, maintaining a good credit standing, and abiding by its obligations to attract funding from donors. Other sources of funds for the sector, discussed later in this chapter, include economic rents that require the government to make strategic decisions about ensuring that they benefit the public good and not individual, vested interests.

As demonstrated by destinations across Africa and globally, various sources of funding are available for a viable tourism sector:

- The *government*, through its budgetary resources and capital budget for promotion and marketing, tourism training, regulation of health, prevention of crime, creation of standards and regulations, and monitoring of needed infrastructure
- The *private sector*, through investments in accommodation and tourism services, worldwide promotion and marketing, and infrastructure that the government has failed to provide
- *Local communities and the NGOs that represent them*, through contributions of land and labor in partnership with the private sector, donors, and other NGOs
- *Donors*, through assistance to governments, the private sector, and local communities in the form of myriad supporting services for the sector.

Public-Private Partnerships

Public-private partnerships have long been used to finance hotel developments in Africa but have received particular focus in recent years. Partnerships can be used for dialogue as well as for investment. They are entered into for developing facilities, infrastructure, and, increasingly, national parks. Consultation enables participants to take joint responsibility for policy choices. In Jordan's Aqaba Special Economic Zone, for example, the government is responsible for packaging land, external infrastructure, regulations in the tourism zone, and municipal and local services. The private sector focuses on developing property, building internal infrastructure, and providing shared services for enterprises. The government outsources activities, including planning, infrastructure development, the build-out of real estate, and property management. The private sector can play the role of master developer, owner, builder, or tenant. The mix of sectors makes for a dynamic environment of mutual support between projects and generates activity that is more "lively" than tourism alone.

Concessions and Joint Ventures

Community-based joint-venture partnerships provide an alternative land use arrangement. The communities typically provide the land, and the private sector brings business acumen and capital. These partnerships have been particularly successful in South Africa and Namibia. Wilderness Safaris was the first operator to invest time and resources in negotiated joint-venture agreements with local communities in South Africa and Namibia. A land claim settlement allowed the local community to take ownership in Namibia, and Wilderness Safaris became the lessee. The rental income is used to support education and to supply electricity (Spenceley 2010).

At a national level, the conservancy program in Namibia, enacted in 1996, uses land tenure and responsibility for wildlife as a mechanism for financial and economic growth. This has led to the sustainable use of wildlife resources, stable land tenure by rural Namibians, and improved livelihoods. It has also provided the basis for communities to develop tourism enterprises, either through joint ventures or as community-based operations. Following registration of the first four conservancies, annual income has grown from $87,000 in 1998 to $5.7 million in 2008. More than $19 million has been invested in communal conservancies by the private sector since 1998. There are now 31 formal joint-venture lodges, mostly owned by the private sector, and another 15 in negotiation (Spenceley 2010).

In addition, as discussed in the following section, other sources of financing from tourism and tourists are likely to be available.

Economic Rents

Economic rent is defined as a profit above normal market rates of return obtained from an asset that is in fixed supply and scarce (box 7.1). In the tourism context, an economic rent is created by the value that natural assets add to constructed structures. Mauritius, with its luxury resort tourism, provides a dramatic case study. The coastal zone, including the beaches, lagoon waters, and reefs, creates the added value that has enabled hotels to sell their product to an unusually large slice of the highly competitive international luxury market. Without the coastal assets the number of tourists visiting Mauritius would be greatly reduced, as would their expenditures. The scenarios with and without coastal assets underlines for countries such as Mauritius the negative economic consequences of a significant deterioration of their natural resources, such as national parks and game reserves.

BOX 7.1

Economic Rent

Economic rent is defined as a profit above normal market rates of return obtained from an asset that is in fixed supply and scarce. The public good is served when economic rents are used to ensure the sustainability of the natural asset. There are numerous ways to monetize and capture part of the value added by natural and cultural assets for the public good, including user fees, taxes, and auctions.

The public good is served when the economic rents are used to ensure the sustainability of the natural asset. Sustainability has many definitions, with the simplest being "to maintain the asset's value over the long term." Particularly in the case of national parks and game reserves, sustainability requires that the livelihoods of local communities also be protected and enhanced, since they are critical to preservation of the asset.

There are numerous ways to monetize and capture part of the value added by natural and cultural assets for the public good. Where access to natural parks or marine assets can be controlled, user fees are normally payable. Where enjoyment of the assets is more diffuse, an arrival and departure tax on tourists is efficient, but its purpose should always be explained to visitors. Where hotels are the main beneficiaries of the value added, a tax on their profits may be appropriate. In the case of finite beachfront land, auctions of land for constructing tourist accommodations may be more efficient than the more common leases.

Many tourists visiting Africa pay among the world's highest prices for use of the built and natural facilities that the continent offers. Will they pay more to help to preserve the tourism assets, assuming that the incremental charge goes to the state as rents rather than to the hotels as profit? Market research suggests that the costs of a holiday, even for luxury resorts and safaris, is not completely price elastic, due to the intense competition from other destinations globally for a tiny slice of the market. Moreover, new entrants to tourism markets appear continuously, searching for the same profits that drive investors in existing destinations. Therefore, imposing a blanket tax on tourists that would increase the cost of their visit may not be the best strategy. If one is applied, however, tourists should be made aware of its purpose; given the greater environmental, social, and cultural consciousness of travelers today, many will pay it willingly. Most governments resort to a mix of taxes on both tourists and hotels and user fees on tourists, but changes in the tax system should be evaluated carefully for their possible impact on the demand for tourism.

Tourist User Fees

The most equitable and direct way of taxing tourists for the use of a country's natural resources is to introduce a user fee for each of the natural assets they enjoy. A payment could be charged for using beaches and lagoons, diving and snorkeling on the reefs, visiting marine reserves, viewing big game, and visiting national parks and cultural assets. In these cases, only those who use the resources would be charged. Increasingly conscious about the causes and the impacts of environmental degradation, more governments are earmarking user fees for the protection and maintenance of natural and cultural assets.

Willingness to Pay

A study undertaken in Belize in 1995 by the Harvard Institute for International Development determined that tourists had considerable "willingness to pay" for preserving the Belize barrier reef, over and above the standard costs of their holiday. The majority of tourists interviewed attached two conditions to their willingness to pay: the funds should not enter into general government revenues, and they should be earmarked in a special fund used exclusively for preserving the Belize barrier reef. Other willingness-to-pay studies, as well as those establishing the "existence value" of an asset (such as one conducted by the World Bank for cultural assets in Morocco) confirm that visitors are willing to make special payments to preserve areas of natural beauty and important cultural heritage assets.

Reef Use

The Bonaire Marine Park in the Netherlands Antilles provided an early example of the application of user fees to a marine asset. Most hotels use diving enterprises that are not part of the hotel proper, so guests expect to have to pay for the service. The costs of a visit to a reef on a day's diving expedition could include a user fee that is allocated for reef conservation purposes. If the purpose of the user fee is explained to foreign divers, most, as marine environment enthusiasts, will pay willingly.

The dive entities are normally responsible for collecting the fees and for transferring them to the government. The transaction costs and accounting issues for the divers should be no more complex than keeping track of value added taxes. Most serious dive operations have an established structure behind them—a one-person operation is not recommended in diving. If commercial divers know that the user fee is being used to improve the quality of reefs, most will willingly collect the fee, as it is in their interest to do so.

Beach Fees

Beach fees in the developed world are used as a tool to control beach access. They may not be advisable, however, in a context where they are perceived as a way to preserve the best beaches for foreign visitors, excluding the local people who traditionally have had free access to the beach. In this case, a two-tier system of user fees could be introduced that provides lower-cost access to locals. Only those tourists staying in accommodations that do not have beach frontage would use public beaches, where they would pay the higher user fee. The transaction costs entailed in establishing a system of user fees for public beaches must be offset against the revenues generated. The poor state of public beaches in many countries reduces their recreational value and, consequently, the user fee that can be charged. The justification for a beach user fee would be the improvements to the selected beaches that the charge would make possible—for example, greater cleanliness, more amenities, and the provision of security guards, public toilets, and waste and recycling bins. The choice facing both the foreign tourist and the local individual would be between using the upgraded beach or another that is free but less optimal, providing less of a consumer surplus.

Environmental Taxes

Many examples of environmental taxes exist. The government of Belize found that an increase in the airport departure tax was an effective system for collecting revenue for environmental conservation, given that its purpose was explained to tourists. In Mauritius and increasingly in other countries, hotels now pay an environmental tax as a charge on profits. The funds are allocated for specific environmental purposes and are managed jointly by the hotel and the state. To some extent, resort hotels already pay a levy for use of the beach, in the form of the costs of protecting, reengineering, and managing the beach. In any assessment of economic rents due by hotels, the costs of beach maintenance should be considered as an offset.

Another option is to add an environmental tax to the hotel bill, clearly differentiating it from the value added tax charge. In hotels in U.S. national parks, an environmental charge of 1 percent of the room rate is added to the hotel bill and noted as "a voluntary environmental contribution for the upkeep of the National Park." Tourists have the option of asking for it to be removed but seldom do, having experienced the benefits the parks provide.

Auctions and Leases

Beachfront land for tourism is a finite asset. Beaches everywhere are at best a fragile and at worst a diminishing resource. Therefore, although investors and users should pay a premium for their use and protection, often they do not. In some countries, prices for beachfront properties, particularly when sold or leased to local elites, include only a slight premium over prices for other land. Government efforts to increase both the price of beachfront land and taxes on these properties have been relatively unsuccessful. As a consequence, hotel investors and operators, local elites, and tourists enjoy the value added by coastal assets at the expense of the local community.

Given the scarcity of beachfront land, an auction system for prequalified buyers may help to ensure that economic rents for the land are captured. At an auction, prequalified bidders propose a price and the highest bid wins; in a lease system, competitive bidding takes place, but bids are ranked not by maximum amount but by the quality of the buyer's offer at the highest bid. Unfortunately, leases too often have been allocated without the transparency that competitive bidding should offer. While the government must establish a floor price for the lease value, a system of competitive bidding or auctions would avoid the problem of establishing a price for the lease in advance of knowing the bidders' willingness to pay.

National Parks and Protected Areas

Special considerations apply to national parks and protected areas in which local communities live. When parks are managed by the government, a central agency generally establishes entrance, concession, and other fees either for each park system or for individual parks. The principal objective of this type of eco-tourism is to maintain a healthy ecosystem and to conserve biodiversity. The fees must therefore cover revenues for park management and protection. Local communities that depend on the parks for food and materials for shelter can be trained to become park custodians and guides, earning incomes while partici-pating in the park's management. Consequently, park user fees must be priced to address these objectives. Transparency regarding the collection and use of the fees must be assured. Fees to be distributed according to an agreed share should be distributed promptly to local community representatives under an approved schedule. Only when communities perceive clear benefits from the parks do they contribute to their preservation.

Despite Africa's amazing wildlife resources, very few parks have yet suc-ceeded in recovering sufficient "rents" to pay for operating costs without bud-getary support. Kenya and Tanzania have daily park fees of $40 to $75 per person. The Rwanda Wildlife Authority charges visitors up to $750 per half day to track gorillas. Most other parks, however, charge less than $10 for access. Thus the question of how to maximize positive returns from tourism while protecting national parks and providing equitable returns to the community is central to the development of sustainable tourism in Africa. Kenya uses a tiered pricing system. Lower prices are charged for Kenyan citizens and residents to encourage domestic tourists to visit their own cultural and natural sites of interest.

Because user fees are seldom sufficient to finance the multiple sustainability needs of parks and protected areas and to contribute to the well-being of the surrounding communities, other financial strategies must be devised to raise additional revenues. Typically, these consist of concessions for minimally inva-sive businesses, opportunities for tourists to donate to the park's upkeep or to the local community, and tour operator charges through parks' annual operating license fees.

Case Studies

The case studies in this report illustrate good practice and lessons learned from experience in tourism as a source of growth and poverty alleviation in developing and emerging countries around the world. Some of them also reveal certain failures. The cases range from an overview of Cancun, a very large-scale project with more than 200 hotels, to small ecolodges, such as Nihiwatu in Sumba, Indonesia, which has 14 units. Case activities date from the 1970s to the mid-2000s. The earliest cases have had plenty of time to demonstrate their success or failure and provide a dynamic view of tourism growth over time. Many of the cases cited took much longer than initially expected to reach their "cruising" speed. In a couple, infrastructure works were practically complete before a single hotel was built (Bali and the Dominican Republic). The newer cases reflect more recent policies and trends, such as corporate social responsibility, voluntourism, or charitable tourism. The cases were chosen to illustrate a particular challenge or success and the effects of certain planning decisions. For example, as land acquisition is a frequently encountered problem in tourism, several of the cases address land acquisition. Challenges such as managing growth, access, environmental protection, social inclusion, and charitable support for local communities also find a place in the case studies. They thus illustrate issues and strategic decisions related to the scale of tourism development, the sustainability of the projects, and the financing of tourism.

The geographic scope of the case studies includes both African and non-African destinations. Of the 24 cases, 11 are from African countries, mostly in the *deepening and sustaining tourism* stage of development. These cases provide regional examples of tourism planning and development and highlight key challenges, constraints, and successes in tourism development in Africa. However, since tourism is still an emerging industry in Sub-Saharan Africa, the study also includes cases from outside of the region. These cases are particularly important for countries in the latter two phases of tourism development: *scaling up tourism* and *deepening and sustaining tourism*. The countries with advanced tourism potential need to look beyond their regional borders for examples and lessons from destinations with more experience in tourism development. The cases also provide an opportunity for destinations outside of Africa to learn from experiences in the region. Cases from Asia, for example, provide lessons on the long-term impact of tourism because many destinations there have a more established tourism sector. In Latin America and the Caribbean, countries and destinations have experience balancing both large- and small-scale tourism development and provide lessons on community involvement and donor-government relationships. In the Middle East and North Africa, destinations highlight key challenges for large-scale infrastructure development and the role of government in the success or failure of projects.

Key areas considered in the case studies are outlined in table 7.2 and summarized below. For more information on the main lessons in the cases studies, see part II.

Table 7.2 Case Studies, by Key Areas Considered

Key area	Case study
Access to land	Cabo Verde; Dominican Republic (Puerto Plata); Egypt, Arab Rep. (Sharm El Sheikh); Indonesia (Nihiwatu); Maldives; Morocco (Bay of Agadir); Namibia (Wilderness Travel); South Africa (Wilderness Safaris and &Beyond); Tunisia; Turkey (South Antalya)
Infrastructure development	Dominican Republic (Puerto Plata); Egypt, Arab Rep. (Sharm El Sheikh); Indonesia (Bali); Jordan (Aqaba); Korea, Rep. (Kyongiu); Maldives; Mexico (Cancun); Tunisia; Turkey (South Antalya)
Ecotourism projects	Costa Rica (Lapa Rios); Dominica (Jungle Bay); Indonesia (Nihiwatu); South Africa (Wilderness Safaris and &Beyond); Rwanda (Sabyinya Silverback Lodge); Tanzania (Mt. Kilimanjaro)
Missing middle and certifications	Costa Rica (Lapa Rios); Indonesia (Bali); Maldives; Tunisia; United Arab Emirates (Dubai)
Training and labor development	Cabo Verde; Kenya; Maldives; Singapore (Sentosa); Tanzania (Mt. Kilimanjaro)
Local sourcing	Dominican Republic (expansion); Kenya; Tanzania (Mt. Kilimanjaro); Tunisia
Managing growth and scale	Cabo Verde; Costa Rica (Lapa Rios); Dominica (Jungle Bay); Dominican Republic (future expansion); Indonesia (Bali); Kenya; Mauritius; Singapore (Sentosa); Tanzania (Mt. Kilimanjaro); Tunisia; Turkey (South Antalya)
Air access	Cabo Verde; Costa Rica (Lapa Rios); Indonesia (Bali); Kenya; Maldives; Mauritius; Morocco; Bay of Agadir; Morocco (coastal cities)
Economic returns	Cabo Verde; Dominican Republic (Puerto Plata); Dominican Republic (future expansion); Egypt, Arab Rep. (Sharm El Sheikh); Indonesia (Nihiwatu); Maldives; Mexico (Cancun); Morocco (Bay of Agadir); Turkey (South Antalya); United Arab Emirates (Dubai)
Environmental management	Costa Rica (Lapa Rios); Indonesia (Bali); Indonesia (Nihiwatu); Maldives; Mexico (Cancun); South Africa (Wilderness Safaris &Beyond); Tanzania (Mt. Kilimanjaro)
Public institutions and regulations	Cabo Verde; Costa Rica (Lapa Rio); Dominican Republic (Puerto Plata); Egypt, Arab Rep.; Indonesia (Bali); Jordan (Aqaba); Korea, Rep.; Mauritius; Mexico (Cancun); Morocco (coastal cities); Tunisia; Turkey (South Antalya); United Arab Emirates (Dubai)
Investment promotion and financing	Dominica (Jungle Bay); Dominican Republic (Puerto Plata); Egypt, Arab Rep. (Sharm El Sheikh); Indonesia (Bali); Jordan (Aqaba); Mauritius; Morocco (coastal cities); Namibia; South Africa (Wilderness Safaris and &Beyond); Tunisia; United Arab Emirates (Dubai)
Social inclusion	Costa Rica (Lapa Rios); Dominica (Jungle Bay); Indonesia (Bali); Indonesia (Nihiwatu); Mexico (Cancun); Namibia; South Africa (Wilderness Safaris and &Beyond); Rwanda; Turkey (South Antalya)

Access to Land

Access to land is a reoccurring challenge. In private land markets there must be transparency and low levels of bureaucracy. In countries where the government owns all the land, a negotiated process is needed in which owners receive a fair price for their land, are offered an equivalent plot elsewhere, or are invited to invest in the project. The cases illustrate several models for allocating land for tourism development that have had varying levels of success. These include leasing options, public-private partnerships, and government-selected tourism development plots. Additionally, the cases cover several models for developing tourism on community land. Models for community engagement can be complex to structure and negotiate, but they bring real value to many rural communities.

Infrastructure Development

The development of tourism and the welfare of communities depend on the creation of appropriate infrastructure. Trunk infrastructure is usually provided by the state or public utilities, while on-site infrastructure is usually charged to the project and the end user pays for connections. Cases show alternative scenarios where investors financed and constructed major infrastructure. Throughout the cases, a critical element for all infrastructure development is cost recovery. Investors often complain that they cross-subsidize local communities through the amount they pay for infrastructure services, whether through tariffs or taxation. Yet infrastructure is one of the most potent incentives a government can offer investors. A balance must be found between cost recovery and incentives. The cases also cover other emerging models for infrastructure development, including recovering costs through ground leases and public funding for anchor projects.

Ecotourism Projects

Ecotourism projects tend to be smaller, often with a core objective to conserve nature and extend benefits to communities. This creates benefits for communities through livelihood development and social inclusion, while public agencies value their impact on environmental protection. Often these projects are more complicated to develop and need a variety of stakeholders to reach consensus. The cases demonstrate the commitment, time, and complexity of ecotourism projects as well as the community and environmental benefits.

Missing Middle

Large projects are often perceived as foreign-owned, corporate, impersonal, and "artificial," whereas smaller resort projects are viewed as locally owned, intimate, and authentic. Both of these observations are valid, but both types of projects are needed. There seems to be a "missing middle" of modest-size projects that are large enough to be sustainable but small enough to retain a more individualistic atmosphere. A few cases provide examples of how to develop this missing middle through certification and regulations.

Training and Labor Development

The level of service in tourism establishments is an important part of overall product quality. Tourism training, often overlooked in tourism project work, requires basic education and vocational training and efforts to develop tourism investors, owners, and managers. Training can be delivered by the private or public sector but should focus on creating careers, not just jobs. More attention needs to be paid to training to cover national curricula in the sector; the regulation of hospitality training facilities; the strengthening of partnerships with the private sector on training; and the use of pairing and exchange programs to allow new technology and know-how to enter the hospitality sector. Cases provide examples of training policy and funding, educational institution development, and local communities organizing for better working conditions and training opportunities.

Local Sourcing

An attractive aspect of tourism is the opportunity it offers to enhance links that add value and create jobs. Although in the past links to local production and supplies were overlooked, entrepreneurs are now making an effort to procure goods and services locally. A potential problem in such procurement is a possible spike in prices, shutting local consumers out of the market. Operators must ensure that the supply of locally procured goods is sustainable and remains affordable. Cases illustrate destinations that have either struggled with or overcome these challenges.

Managing Growth and Scale

Managing growth and scale is central. A frequently confronted problem is too much growth, where growth itself threatens the quality of the destination. As that growth explodes, product development and marketing strategies are needed to disperse growth to different areas. Additionally, tourism that relies on community land or attractions must be integrated properly. Cases of successful community involvement rely on ongoing consultations with communities so that decisions regarding growth are made according to local conditions. Growth must also consider the physical conditions of the destination by analyzing carrying capacity. Although these models are useful, projects often overrun their estimates, and better models for forecasting demand are required. The tactics to control growth, such as limiting the number of available rooms or halting new construction in reaction to low occupancy rates, require solid analysis, research, and judgment, which are often in scarce supply. Ultimately, criteria for the successful management of tourism growth must be set and monitoring indicators identified (Bosselman, Peterson, and McCarthy 1999). Many of the cases outline different models for managing growth that are dependent on goals at the national and destination levels.

Air Access

Air access is critical for tourism and was a key area of study in several of the cases. Destinations that have partnered with the private sector to develop air infrastructure and liberalize air transport have realized growth in arrivals and tourism. However, for some of the other cases in this report, air access appears to have been left to chance or to plans cobbled together well after the rest of the resort was under construction. Cases illustrate the importance of public support for liberalizing air access and the attitude of civil aviation authorities.

Economic Returns

The cases review the differences between economic returns in large-scale and small-scale tourism development projects and address key issues with regard to assessing indirect and induced impacts. Large projects provide substantial numbers of jobs as well as tax and foreign exchange revenues and have contributed to a positive national investment climate. Smaller projects may be financially successful and often have valuable community outreach programs, but they may not be economically successful because it is difficult to develop them sufficiently to generate solid economic returns for the country. The economic analysis of tourism projects is evolving quickly, particularly as advances in natural resource economics are made (World Bank 2006, 2011).

Environmental Management

Despite past challenges linking environmental protection with tourism, destinations are now recognizing that tourism and the environment require a sound planning framework and are mutually reinforcing. On a global scale, the key environmental issues in tourism include climate change, environmental management of wildlife and plant diversity, conservation of land resources, and management of coastal zones. Cases reflect planning decisions to mitigate climate change, the use of environmental impact assessments and environmental management plans to diminish the negative impacts of tourism, and the development of environmental certification programs. Overall, the cases provide options for achieving environmental objectives, including physical planning and regulation, incentives, infrastructure, subsidies, and direct management by NGOs.

Public Institutions and Regulation

The public sector is essential in order to stimulate development, whether through policy or investment. Sound institutions are required to promote needed public investment, create the policy framework, and establish regulations. But tourism institutions are frequently weak and appear to be a drag on private investment rather than a catalyst for it—often because there may be no real commitment to tourism as a force in economic development, especially where it is a new sector. Cases reflect destinations where public support created a broad-based working group or agency with the technical skills and decision-making power to cut through bureaucracy and move development forward.

Investment Promotion and Financing

Although not always the case, investment promotion agencies exist in most countries. However, tourism is not always a priority, leaving investors with limited access to finance. The cases illustrate a range of financing options from projects with sole investors (both public and private) to projects mobilizing separate lines of credit from several multilateral institutions. The cases also touch on the limited access to appropriate loans, including long-term credit, smaller loans for small and medium enterprises, or large loans for hotel investment. Finally, the cases offer lessons on investment promotion incentives, including enhancing the risk-reward relationship; direct financial assistance; financing mechanisms, such as bonds or special-purpose taxes; indirect assistance (for example, zoning); and fiscal measures, such as tax holidays.

Social Inclusion

Tourism brings together visitors and locals in a variety of situations. As tourists become more interested in personal stories and authentic experiences, greater contact with local communities is occurring. The smaller projects covered in the cases illustrate community engagement through consultations, ownership, employment, and development funds. The large projects have also contributed immensely to communities through infrastructure development, economic improvement, and job creation. However, the cases also highlight certain failures such as a lack of housing and transport for communities employed in tourism developments.

Note

1. The carbon-trading scheme was introduced in 2005 and now covers large polluters, such as power and cement companies. Airlines are slated to be included in the scheme, which is raising concern in the industry. The program forces companies to pay for permits for each ton of carbon dioxide they emit above a certain level or cap, but some governments have opposed the system. See, for example, http://www .travelmole.com/stories/1148281.php.

References

Bosselman, F., C. Peterson, and C. McCarthy. 1999. *Managing Tourism Growth: Issues and Applications.* Washington, DC: Island Press.

Hawkins, D. E., and S. Mann. 2007. "The World Bank's Role in Tourism Development." *Annals of Tourism Research* 34 (2): 348–63.

Mitchell, J., and C. Ashley. 2009. "Value Chain Analysis and Poverty Reduction at Scale." Briefing Paper 49, Overseas Development Institute, London. http://www.odi.org.uk /sites/odi.org.uk/files/odi-assets/publications-opinion-files/3528.pdf.

National Statistics Office. 2010. "Número de establecimientios y habitaciones de aloja-miento turístico por año, según provincia 2004–2009." Oficina Nacional de Estadística, Santo Domingo. http://www.one.gob.do/index.php?module=articles&func=view &catid=107.

Porter, M. 1998. "Clusters and the New Economics of Competition." *Harvard Business Review* 76 (6): 77–90.

Spenceley, A. 2010. *Tourism Product Development Interventions and Best Practices in Sub-Saharan Africa. Part 1: Synthesis.* World Bank Tourism Industry: Research and Analysis Phase II. Washington, DC: World Bank.

Wong, M., I. T. Christie, and S. Al Rowais. 2009. *Tourism in South Asia: Benefits and Opportunities.* Washington, DC: World Bank, Poverty Reduction and Economic Management Network, Finance and Private Sector Development Unit, South Asia.

World Bank. 1974. "Project Appraisal Document on a Proposed Loan in the Amount of USD 21 Million to the Government of the Dominican Republic for a Puerto Plata Tourism Project." World Bank, Urban Development, Latin America and the Caribbean Region, Washington, DC.

———. 1979. "Project Appraisal Document on a Proposed Loan in the Amount of USD 25 Million to the Government of the Dominican Republic for the Second Tourism Project." World Bank, Urban Development, Latin America and the Caribbean Region, Washington, DC.

———. 2006. "Where Is the Wealth of Nations?" World Bank, Washington, DC. http:// siteresources.worldbank.org/INTEEI/214578-1110886258964/20748034/All.pdf.

———. 2011. "The Changing Wealth of Nations." World Bank, Washington, DC. http://siteresources.worldbank.org/ENVIRONMENT/Resources/ChangingWealth Nations.pdf.

Chapter 8

Recommendations for Tourism Development in Sub-Saharan African Countries

This chapter outlines recommendations for countries in general and for countries at each stage of tourism development. The four stages follow the typology outlined in this report: pre-emerging, potential or initiating tourism, emerging or scaling up tourism, and consolidating or deepening and sustaining success.

Pre-Emerging Countries

In most cases, the 14 pre-emerging countries listed are war-torn, are suffering civil strife, or have recently emerged from these situations but have not yet stabilized. External agencies can do little until responsible democratic governments are empowered to establish stable political regimes and ensure the safety and security of local populations. Such essential requirements must be in place before the country can offer visitors access to its tourism assets, no matter how appealing they may be. The tourism sector cannot grow until these countries emerge from the difficulties that constrain the development not just of tourism but of the macroeconomy as a whole.

Overall Recommendations

Throughout this report, recommendations focus on the following:

- Encouraging tourism managers to focus on the value of their product and be competitive in the international market
- Gaining strong political support for tourism at the highest level of government and encouraging government to take the lead in creating effective

institutions and coordinating mechanisms to maintain a dialogue with all stakeholders

- Ensuring the private sector's vital role, recognizing the need for government to create an enabling environment for investments, and provide supporting infrastructure for those investments
- Recognizing donors and their capacity to assist the tourism sector in many vital areas, such as infrastructure, training, and pro-poor tourism
- Providing investors with needed information and establishing "one-stop" shops
- Acknowledging the critical role of air transport and the need to liberalize air policies
- Improving connectivity within countries and regions and access by road and by air to the region, whether through private sector entrepreneurship, government investments, or a combination
- Resolving the current constraints on tourism and considering other countries' solutions to issues related to the availability of land, lack of access to finance for investment, taxes on tourism investments, low levels of tourism skills, lack of security and safety, high rates of crime, public health issues, visa requirements, and red tape and bureaucracy
- Assessing the scale of development that is appropriate to the country's assets and management resources and determining where and when development will take place
- Recognizing that four pillars of sustainability—financial, economic, social, and environmental—are essential for sustained growth of tourism
- Realizing the potential to finance tourism by appropriating to government the economic rents that tourism generates.

Embracing these strategies consistently is fundamental to developing tourism that is sustainable, economically productive, environmentally sensitive, and protective of cultural heritage.

Recommendations by Stage of Development

This section offers specific recommendations for countries at the remaining three stages of tourism development. The case studies in part II of this report illustrate various ways in which countries have overcome constraints and established themselves either in niche markets or as major players in the international tourism market. An elaboration of some of these recommendations follows.

Countries Initiating Tourism

As in the case of land, improving transport policies and infrastructure in countries at the beginning of their tourism journey requires a practical approach focused on the tourism asset with the highest potential. Countries such as the Dominican Republic, Indonesia, Mexico, and Turkey focused scarce resources on the locations and market segments with highest growth potential. In each location this strategy removed critical constraints pertaining to infrastructure, security, and skills and from the outset attracted world-class investors, who played a critical role in launching the destination. Targeting areas of high potential also enables destinations to focus promotion activities on one or two iconic attractions, to pilot key and delicate policy reforms for land and air transport, and to create appropriate institutions with coordinating mechanisms in a contained setting. The success of these first developments, which had public sector and donor support, encouraged new investors to finance projects in other areas and carried these countries to the next stage of development. Salient issues for countries initiating tourism are discussed in the case studies of Dominica, Indonesia, the Republic of Korea, Namibia, Rwanda, South Africa, and Tanzania.

The strategic recommendations for initiating tourism pertain to building institutional, infrastructural, and policy foundations:

Institutional foundations

- Build and sustain commitment to tourism from leadership in the country
- Focus scarce resources on the tourism segments and locations of highest potential following a fact-based evaluation of assets, discussion of alternatives, and consideration of potential impacts and constraints
- Put in place institutional mechanisms for implementing the strategy, engaging selected local governments, other ministries, the private sector, donors, and local communities
- Put in place independent monitoring to achieve transparency, sustainability, and accountability.

Infrastructural foundations

- Enhance access to infrastructure, utilities, and sanitation in the selected locations.

Policy foundations

- Streamline the processing of visas and work permits for the key tourism segments
- Review and improve land policies in the selected locations, including registration, tenure, and land use, to enable the use of property as collateral

- Review transport policies; consider open-skies policy in selected locations
- Review labor policies in selected locations
- Address critical health and security concerns in selected locations
- Support strategic first movers.

Countries Scaling Up Tourism

Once political support exists, airline access is secure, and land is available for development, investment and destination promotion becomes critical for attracting investors. Destination promotion involves conducting marketing campaigns, building source-market awareness, and enhancing a positive image. Promoting investment involves providing information that will build confidence and streamline the investment process. Some countries have opted to establish a one-stop shop where investors can find a centralized source of information and guidance for investing in a country. Mauritius has become a world leader in this area.

Professional investment conferences are held around the world, at which investors, lenders, insurance companies, real estate agencies, and financial institutions meet, network, and discuss topics of interest. In Tanzania, for example, an investment promotion forum and an outreach program organized by the Multilateral Investment Guarantee Agency, a member of the World Bank Group, was held in 2002, resulting in more than $100 million in investment in the following two years. The main components were an investment forum and a follow-up investor outreach program.

Investors can be attracted by direct financial assistance (such as bonds or special-purpose taxes), indirect assistance (such as zoning), and fiscal measures (such as tax breaks). Although these may not be necessary for viable projects, tourism is replete with incentives, and investors are eager to use them.

The strategic recommendations for scaling up tourism pertain to planning destinations and incremental infrastructure, promoting investments and destinations, ensuring access to land and finance, and managing growth:

Planning destinations and incremental infrastructure

- Scale up and replicate success in other high-potential zones
- Undertake thorough economic, environmental, and social analysis of each project and destination prior to development using tools such as environmental impact assessment and social impact assessment.

Attracting investment and undertaking destinations promotion

- Provide information and support, such as destination research and incentive programs and support for anchor investments

- Promote the destination and products, consider new markets and products, and study the branding of competing destinations
- Engage in ongoing investor promotion and follow-up such as aftercare.

Ensuring access to land and finance

- Generalize policy reforms
- Provide support for small and medium enterprises and microfinance support with a focus on women and young people in tourism development
- Promote and facilitate public-private partnerships.

Managing adaptive growth

- Decentralize responsibilities and build the capacity of local governments
- Monitor destination areas for signs of stress through ongoing consultation.

Countries Maintaining and Deepening Success

As the sector grows, strategies are needed to disperse tourists to different areas and, where possible, to distribute arrivals more evenly during the calendar year. Tanzania's northern circuit is overloaded, and the country is trying to create new areas for tourism growth in the south, in the Pemba and Mafia Islands, the Selous Reserve, and Zanzibar. The Dominican Republic has defined a range of future development areas. Five major developments are located at the extremities of the country, far from the capital. Clearly, sun and sand destinations may be easier to replicate than those involving wildlife or cultural or historic sites. Turkey has been successful in replicating the model of the South Antalya Project in various other destinations around the country.

Inability to manage growth threatens the viability of resorts. The Costa Rican case study best illustrates the successful management of higher numbers of tourists by escalating already high standards and by focusing on its brand image of nature conservation, complemented by the introduction of "green" certification for hoteliers and service providers. Increasing the number of visitor arrivals in the nonpeak seasons can best be achieved by pricing incentives, diversifying the tourism product, and scheduling special events, such as film or music festivals, in the off season. The benefits of nonpeak tourism accrue to the providers of accommodations and their employees, who might otherwise be laid off or work part time, and to the many beneficiaries of tourists' considerable discretionary spending.

Tourism development is always a work in progress. Every destination—whether a single destination within a country or the entire country—has to remain constantly competitive in the world tourism market.

The strategic recommendations for maintaining and deepening success pertain to diversifying, decentralizing, and increasing value added:

Diversifying, decentralizing, and adding value

- Explore options for new markets such as cultural heritage, intraregional travel, and meetings, incentives, conferences, and exhibitions (MICE)
- Add value to existing products and support product innovation to improve economic multipliers and lengthen the tourist season.

Building world-class tourism competencies

- Develop customer awareness and a culture of tourism, for example, through customer service courses
- Provide technical, vocational, and professional capacity building
- Support entrepreneurship with programs to encourage expansion of small and medium enterprises.

Strengthening social inclusiveness

- Build tourism awareness courses into community outreach activities and school curricula
- Enhance community linkages by promoting the local sourcing of goods where possible
- Recognize and support informal tourism services and supply chains.

Managing environmental impacts

- Develop standards to encourage sustainable tourism operations
- Develop policies to anticipate and mitigate the impacts of climate change— for example, by mainstreaming carbon-friendly technologies
- Develop and use sustainable tourism indicators to monitor destination performance.

Part II

Global Perspective: Planning Decisions and Tourism Development around the World

Chapter 9

Learning from Experience

Tourism has been used as a tool for economic development throughout the world. The case studies in this report offer an opportunity to learn from previous experience in Africa as well as in other countries globally. The cases illustrate good practice and lessons learned from experience in tourism as a source of economic growth and poverty alleviation in developing and emerging countries around the world. Some of them also reveal failures. Ultimately, the cases are a tool for Sub-Saharan African countries to use to explore and learn from the experiences of tourism development in Africa and other significant destinations. The cases date from the 1970s to the mid-2000s and were chosen to illustrate a particular challenge or success and the effects of certain planning decisions. The earlier cases provide an extended time frame demonstrating their success or failure. Additionally, they offer perspective on how destinations grow and change over time and how initial decisions affect this potential growth. The newer cases reflect more recent policies and trends, such as corporate social responsibility, voluntourism, and charitable tourism. Together the cases studies are intended to help countries to envisage a dynamic future for tourism in Sub-Saharan Africa.

The cases present key challenges faced by both Sub-Saharan African and global destinations. For example, as land acquisition is a frequently encountered problem in tourism, several of the cases address this issue. Similarly, challenges such as managing growth, access, environmental protection, social inclusion, and charitable support for local communities also find a place in the case studies. They thus highlight issues and strategic decisions related to the scale of tourism development, the sustainability of projects, and the financing of tourism.

The 24 case studies are listed in table 9.1, which includes key features of each case. The geographic location of each study is shown in map 9.1. The cases include (a) large projects based on broad-scale land development (such as Turkey's South Antalya) or citywide programs (such as Cancun or Dubai), (b) specialized cases that focus on specific activities (for example, conservancies in Namibia, mountaineering in Kenya), and (c) smaller cases that are typically individual islands, resorts, or activities (such as Nihiwatu, Indonesia,

Table 9.1 Summary of Case Studies

Country	Project name	Project category	Salient features of tourism development
Cabo Verde	National tourism	Transformation in a small country	Market-oriented policies and democratic processes; quality air transport infrastructure, supportive air policies; scale, form, and type compatible with available resources
Costa Rica	Lapa Rios	Ecotourism	Environmental conservation; tourism certification, including ethics code
Dominica	Jungle Bay	Island ecolodge	Ecotourism integration into world tourism institutions (time-sharing)
Dominican Republic	Puerto Plata	Coastal estate resort	Political support for tourism; transition from public to private investment; model widely replicated in the country; sanitation requirements
Dominican Republic	Future sector growth	Economic and policy analysis	Future dispersion of growth in the country; carrying capacity and diversification of product line
Egypt, Arab Rep.	Sharm El Sheikh	Coastal development	Product diversification; land acquisition; institutional rationalization
Indonesia	Bali	Island, large resort	Protection of cultural heritage; institutional framework; airline access and infrastructure development
Indonesia	Nihiwatu	Island ecolodge	Community partnerships; social inclusion and charitable donations
Jordan	Aqaba	Multisector resort and industrial development	New coastal resort development; integration of multisector investment in economic zone
Kenya	Nairobi	Meetings, incentives, conventions, and exhibitions	Business versus leisure travel, diversification of product line; convention facility investment; targeted marketing
Korea, Rep.	Kyongju	Historic city	Coordination and access; market timing
Maldives	Island resorts	Multi-island, resort development	Transparent evaluation of resort bids; planning framework and environmental controls; business environment; airline access
Mauritius	National tourism	Policy framework	Export and investment promotion; training; control of supply; airline policy
Mexico	Cancun	Coastal resort on uninhabited land	Location and scale; role of public sector developer; all-inclusive tourism
Morocco	Bay of Agadir	Rebuilding of city following earthquake	Mixed-use resort development, residential, commercial, and hotel; business environment, open skies, political support; project stopped because of political difficulties
Morocco	Coastal cities tourism	Preparing city beach sited for private tender	Strengthening ministry's role as tourism planner; regulation and promotion of private investment; parallel measures in support of resort development

(continued next page)

Table 9.1 (continued)

Country	Project name	Project category	Salient features of tourism development
Namibia	Wilderness travel	Public-private partnerships	Concessioning community land to private sector; improved wildlife management through conservancies
Rwanda	Sabyinyo Silverback Lodge	Protection of mountain gorillas	Community partnerships with private sector; biodiversity protection
Singapore	Sentosa Island	Day-trip amusement park and island resort development	Building a resort to appeal to residents and international visitors; importance of training
South Africa	Wilderness Safaris and &Beyond	Public-private partnerships	Land management; concessioning community land to private sector
Tanzania	Mt. Kilimanjaro	Mountaineering packages	Poverty reduction analysis; sanitation and management; trade unions for porters, guides, and cooks
Tunisia	Infrastructure in six zones	Coastal city resort development	Integrated national development; institutional framework, including land bank
Turkey	South Antalya	Large-scale resort	Model widely replicated throughout the country; staff housing problems
United Arab Emirates	Dubai	National transformation	New source of growth in face of depleting oil reserves; how to launch a new sector; investment and promotion

Map 9.1 Geographic Location of Each Case Study

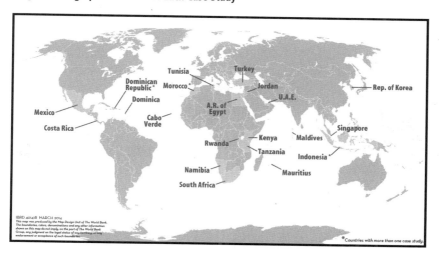

or Jungle Bay, Dominica) with interesting stories to tell. While the cases come from a wide range of destinations, each case was selected to illustrate a specific lesson learned that can be applied to tourism development and planning in Sub-Saharan Africa as well as in other global destinations.

Each case was carefully chosen to be included in this study in order to highlight the different stages of tourism planning, development, and expansion. The case studies from Africa illustrate the successes and challenges of existing destinations and projects in the region. These cases focus on destinations that are in the *deepening and sustaining tourism* stage and are particularly useful for Sub-Saharan African destinations in the first two phases of tourism development: *initiating tourism* and *scaling up tourism*. However, tourism in Sub-Saharan Africa is a relatively young industry for many countries, and broadening the geographic scope of cases to areas outside the region provides a comprehensive set of examples from which Sub-Saharan African destinations at all stages of development can learn.

For example, tourism development in many destinations across Asia is far more advanced than in much of Sub-Saharan Africa. An examination of Asian destinations illustrates the impact of tourism planning and development over an extended period of time. Further, cases from Latin America and the Caribbean illustrate a range of experience with both large- and small-scale tourism development projects. Latin American and Caribbean cases such as Lapa Rios and Jungle Bay demonstrate the importance of community involvement and environmental protection. As a leader in this field, tourism developments from Latin America and the Caribbean can provide widely applicable lessons on livelihood development and environmental protection through tourism. Cases such as Cancun and the Dominican Republic also demonstrate how government and multilateral institutions can work together for long-term tourism development. The Middle East and North African case studies also offer examples of both successful and failed large-scale infrastructure development, providing both caution and guidance for countries focused on large-scale development. Together, the wide range of case studies provides examples and lessons learned that can be applied throughout Sub-Saharan Africa by countries at all three stages of tourism development as well as by other destinations throughout the world. These cases are particularly important for countries in the *deepening and sustaining tourism* stage. As the leaders of Sub-Saharan African tourism, these countries need to look beyond their regional borders to create a vision for tourism development that will help them to develop an even stronger and more dynamic tourism sector.

Each case is organized into five sections as follows:

- *Introduction.* Each case begins with a box summarizing key lessons and a succinct summary of the case and its results.

- *Tourism data.* This section presents standardized data where available, including international arrivals, foreign exchange receipts, contribution to gross national product or gross domestic product, and employment. Additional information may also be included.
- *Sector background and history.* This section varies considerably between cases in order to provide relevant context.
- *The case.* The objectives and scope are presented along with actual experience.
- *Results.* This section summarizes conclusions and lessons from the case.

The following sections present the key areas considered in the cases studies.

Land

One challenge common to most countries is access to land. Where a private land market is functional, the challenge is to increase transparency and reduce the bureaucracy surrounding land transactions. In many countries, however, land is owned by the government, which only it can lease or sell. In others, communities often unwittingly sell their land with vested rights to investors, thus losing their principal source of income. In the past, governments often resorted to expropriating land, but this practice is giving way to negotiated processes where owners receive a fair price for their land, are offered an equivalent plot elsewhere, or are invited to invest in the project. Using land as security for borrowing on the property is a key goal.

To address these issues, governments often try to select the land to be developed for tourism. Most of the large cases in this report preferred this method even if it was the only option open to them (as in the Dominican Republic, Morocco, and Turkey). The government then reviewed the status of the land pertaining to any obligations or encumbrances on it and subsequently rectified them under a legal process before the land was made available for development.

An investor ideally wants to own land outright, but several of the cases show that leasing can be a good alternative. The Arab Republic of Egypt, for example, assembled land in Sharm El Sheik over a 10-year period, with the Tourism Development Authority (TDA) purchasing it from other public agencies. It was an arduous process, as one government agency was negotiating with another. The TDA made land available to investors for a 25-year lease, renewable once. Other countries opt for longer leases. Maldives extends leases for up to 50 years, depending on the framework of the partnership. At the other end of the spectrum, it took Nihiwatu resort 10 years to gain full access to the land it required, negotiating principally with the communities on Sumba.

More generally, all of the leases involve public and private partnerships. A variety of options allow the private sector to partner with government on large projects: (a) at the land development stage, (b) at the infrastructure development stage, and (c) at the build-out phase for tourism facilities. In the first case, the government leases land to a developer or brings it to a partnership as equity; in the second, the government contracts with the private sector for infrastructure, construction, or operation, under various privatization models; and in the third, the private sector comes in at the stage where hotels and facilities are being built. The specific terms depend on market conditions, how active a role the government wishes to play, and how the investor responds to that role.

Many of the earlier programs in tourism fell under the first two options. More recently, a model similar to that used in Morocco is being used. In this model, the government prepares the site plan and contractual documents. It then puts the project out for tender. This model (along with the special economic zone model) appeals to governments because it lets them design the basic regulations on land use and zoning, but gives the private sector sufficient flexibility to respond to market conditions and generate profits. Another type of project involving tourism is that of special economic zones, dedicated to tourism or to multiple industries. Such zones have been used in Asia for many years; closer to Africa, they have been used in Aqaba and Dubai.

Some public sector developers have been instrumental in developing tourism. For example, in Tunisia the Agence Foncière Touristique (AFT), or land bank, has been effective in both purchasing plots for future development and implementing development programs. In Mexico, the National Trust Fund for Tourism Development (FONATUR) has been a partner in five major resorts. The first two were Cancun and Zihuatanejo (Ixtapa), each successful in its own way. Cancun opted for concentrated growth on the island, originally as a hub for the Caribbean coast (the Mayan Riviera), but it now includes intense development extending 100 kilometers south. On the Pacific coast, Zihuatanejo opted for much more decentralized growth (40 hotels compared with more than 200 in Cancun) and, some say, a more human scale. Each has its supporters, and these examples serve to underline the different market niches that complement each other.

A final model, illustrated by the Namibia and South Africa cases, is that of a conservancy. It is well suited for projects, often small, in which communities own the rights to land. Community land is valued as an asset that can provide long-term income for owners. The goals are to make sure that the local owners have a stake in sustainable development. The concession or conservancy can be designed in many ways. In effect, publicly owned landholders (that is, the state directly or an agency of the state, such as national parks) lease land to a community usually for a modest fee (for 50 years or more). The community sets up a community trust or conservancy (for 30–50 years) that invests in retail tourism assets, such as restaurants or lodges. The retail facilities are leased to private operators (for 15–25 years). The model recognizes the interests of each group. Such projects can be complex to structure and negotiate, but they bring real value to many rural communities and families in Africa. In addition, they are sustainable and transparent.

Land development projects are criticized for being planned without room to grow "organically" and for lacking "animation" or "soul." This critique seems to disappear over time, however, and it cannot be said of projects such as Cancun, Punta Cana, or Bali. In many of these resorts, most of the hotels have all-inclusive service, meaning that the projects are enclaves, estates, or in some way cut off from the local community (with various on-site, often local, entertainment). All-inclusive properties have found favor in many market niches, from families to couples. A common feature of these large resorts is that they realize economies of scale and are readily marketed as brands. In some, particularly in the Dominican Republic or Playa del Carmen (close to Cancun), boutique hotels are beginning to appear, adding variety to the product offering.

Infrastructure

Infrastructure is almost as important as land for tourism. The development of tourism and the welfare of communities depend on it. Trunk infrastructure is usually provided by the state or by public utilities; the model adopted by Turkey highlights these relationships. There, for example, the state provided most of the infrastructure in Kemer, which then became a municipality with its own rights and responsibilities for managing the town effectively and locally, taking over the management of certain facilities, such as sanitation. On-site infrastructure is usually charged to the project, and the end user pays for connections.

Variations of this model exist, where, for example, the investor is responsible for all trunk infrastructure. In a project in the Dominican Republic at Punta Cana, investors financed and constructed the airport and water supply facilities; a private power company paid for the costs of generation and transmission. Some elements of infrastructure tend not to be provided, including solid waste and sanitation services (these were canceled in the Dominican Republic's Puerto Plata project, for example), an unacceptable practice in today's world. The Maldives case shows that investors can support the costs of infrastructure and that the resort can still be profitable. The key is to use modern, appropriate technology, such as photovoltaic or wind power, desalinization, small sanitation plants, and roads that are not necessarily black-topped. Effluent from sanitation plants can be used for watering gardens.

A critical element for all infrastructure is cost recovery. Tourism investors often complain that they cross-subsidize local communities through the charges they pay for infrastructure services, whether through tariffs or taxation. Practice varies around the world, but power costs are typically recovered through tariffs or user charges, and sanitation is recovered indirectly through the tax system. Most utility charges are subject to considerable analysis, with lifeline tariffs for residents' minimum consumption and higher tariffs for greater use. Yet infrastructure is one of the most potent incentives a government can offer investors. A balance must be found between cost recovery required for sustainability and incentives required for investment. Other emerging models are based on urban development corporations that recover costs through ground leases. In countries with taxation on improved land (tax on rental value), opportunities exist for cost recovery (Peterson 2006).

Lastly, infrastructure projects often include funding for anchor projects or first movers. Turkey's project included a small hotel and marina, both of which were concessioned out to the private sector after a short period of direct management by the project.

Ecotourism Projects

The smaller projects in the portfolio of cases (Nihiwatu, Jungle Bay, and Lapa Rios) are all leaders in the field of ecotourism. The properties are valued by guests for their uniqueness (and often remoteness), by public agencies for their impact on environmental protection, and by communities for their impact on the social fabric of the area. Their core objective is often to conserve nature and extend benefits to communities. Individuals with a vision and passion often drive these smaller projects.[1] They usually encounter tough conditions at the beginning. As mentioned, Nihiwatu took 10 years to assemble its land package. They must sort out basic challenges before the tourism project itself can emerge, addressing issues like education and social services for local populations. Even at the operational stage, they continue to fund local projects. Several projects from among the case studies (Nihiwatu, Jungle Bay, and, to a certain extent, Maldives) have developed charitable arms that seek to fund community projects from their own resources. They find that their guests are also willing to contribute to a substantial degree.

Missing Middle

Large projects are often perceived as foreign-owned, corporate, impersonal, and "artificial," whereas smaller resort projects are viewed as locally owned, intimate, and authentic. Both of these perceptions are valid, and both types of projects are needed. There seems to be a "missing middle" of more modest projects that are large enough to capture the scale needed to be sustainable and small enough to retain a more individualistic character. Costa Rica, with a clear focus on certification programs for ecotourism lodges, is now building larger hotels on beach sites reserved for larger operations.

Training

The level of service in tourism establishments is an important part of overall product quality. Attention to service is particularly important in Asia, where it has become an art. In Singapore, Sentosa has a local branch of the country's tourism training school (Temasek Polytechnic College). In Maldives, regulations allow the country to import up to 50 percent of staff from South Asia. In Tanzania, workers have organized to ensure good working conditions and the opportunity for training. The country has a multisector training institution offering many fields of study, including tourism, and a two-year associate degree with courses in culinary and catering management, leisure and resort management, and hospitality and tourism management, housed in the business school. It recently opened a culinary academy. More generally, tourism training is fundamental for sector development, although it is often overlooked in tourism project work. Two principal elements generate good service: (a) providing basic education and vocational training and (b) developing tourism investors, owners, and managers. In the case of Singapore, fees cover 20 percent of the costs of training, with the state paying the balance. Alternatively, the private sector and government can cooperate to fund training, with direct inputs from operators on what skills and services are required. The focus should be on creating careers, not just jobs—people need to be assured that long-term employment is an option and that the industry offers an opportunity for personal growth by obtaining a deeper knowledge in specialized fields or by advancing to positions of more responsibility. More attention needs to be paid to offering training that covers national curricula in the sector; to regulating hospitality training facilities; to strengthening partnerships with the private sector on training; and to using pairing and exchange programs to encourage new technology and know-how to enter the hospitality sector.

Outsourcing

An attractive aspect of tourism is the opportunity it offers to enhance linkages that add value and create jobs. In the past, governments put little emphasis on local production and supplies to serve the tourism industry. Today, along with entrepreneurs moved by self-interest and corporate responsibility, they are making an effort to procure goods and services locally. These include consumables (such as dairy products, fish, meats, fruits, and vegetables) and nonconsumables (such as furniture and handicrafts). A potential problem in such procurement is a possible spike in prices, shutting local consumers out of the market. Fish, which in many countries is a staple for the local population, has become scarce and very expensive in Tunisia and Senegal, for example. So operators must ensure that the supply of locally procured goods is sustainable and remains affordable for the local population. A partner with the International Finance Corporation, the Orient Express Monasterio Hotel in Cusco, Peru,[2] reached agreement with a local fish farmer to provide a regular supply of trout to the hotel based on an analysis of the production cycle to ensure its stability and quality. In contrast, most hotel furniture in Tanzania is imported from China, and no trade link exists between local tourism enterprises and the local furniture industry.[3] Such a link would help to supply hotels with local furniture, adding value and extending tourism's impacts. From the case studies, the Dominican Republic is the only island in the Caribbean that produces locally more than 90 percent of supplies needed for its tourism sector, giving it a competitive advantage over other islands.

Managing Growth and Scale

Managing growth and scale is central. Growth often appears to be unmanaged, occurring irregularly depending on economic and global conditions. Boom-and-bust conditions are common. On the Mediterranean coastlines of Italy and Spain, growth has exploded to the point where it is threatening the viability of resorts. Sentosa in Singapore has struggled with managing its size as several investors have departed. However, a frequently confronted problem is too much growth, where growth itself threatens the quality of the resort. As growth explodes, strategies are needed to disperse it to different areas. Tanzania's northern circuit is overloaded, and the country is trying to create new areas for tourism growth in the south, in the Selous Reserve, Zanzibar, Pemba, and Mafia Islands. The Dominican Republic has defined a range of future development areas. Turkey has been successful in replicating the South Antalya project model in other destinations around the country. FONATUR has five major developments located at the extremities of Mexico, far from the capital. Undoubtedly, sun and sand destinations are easier to replicate than those involving wildlife or cultural or historic sites.

Yet criteria for the successful management of tourism growth must be set and monitoring indicators identified.[4] An area that requires initial focus is the marrying of tourism activity with communities. If tourism is not fully integrated into the local economy, it could easily fail. In most of the cases highlighted in this report, consultation with communities, often called a "community character analysis," was part of the process. Lapa Rios, Jungle Bay, and Nihiwatu, to name just three of the case studies, all maintain ongoing consultation with their local communities. These consultations can inform decisions on tourism growth, even as their content varies according to local conditions. In some, the emphasis is on the expected impacts of tourism, whereas in more advanced contexts it is on local communities' expectations from tourism and how much they wish to grow.

Another fundamental element is that certain physical conditions must be present for tourism to take place without harming the environment. These include access to clean drinking water and land for construction. Models to analyze carrying capacity[5] have grown out of wildlife analysis and recreational land use, such as forests and parks, but are still evolving; projects frequently overrun their estimated carrying capacity and design criteria. Better models are required for forecasting demand, as are indicators of growth, such as data on supply and occupancy. Some countries attempt to control growth by limiting the number of rooms available (Bermuda); others rely on occupancy indicators, allowing no new construction as long as occupancies are below a defined level (Mauritius and Tanzania). These tactics require solid analysis, research, and judgment, which are often in short supply.

Air Access

Air access is critical for tourism and is a key area in several of the cases. It was well studied in the Puerto Plata project in the Dominican Republic, which included an airport. That airport is now approved for U.S. carriers,[6] served by American Airlines and US Airways, with direct flights for both narrow- and wide-body planes from Canada, Europe, and the United States. Overall, the Dominican Republic now has six international airports, justified largely by tourism. In Costa Rica, the regional airport in Liberia was planned to handle growing tourist travel to the north of the country and to bypass San José. In Bali, although an airport existed, it was closed to direct international traffic; only when the airport was classified as international did traffic spike and tourism grow. Maldives welcomes all carriers, whereas the Seychelles relies primarily on the national carrier, Air Seychelles, although other airlines now fly there. Another island in the Indian Ocean, Mauritius has a national carrier with extensive pooling arrangements with carriers like British Airways and Air France. Morocco chose an interesting option: in parallel to launching resort development, the government announced plans to partially privatize Royal Air Maroc, the national carrier, and thus facilitate flexible air policy for tourism.[7]

For many of the other cases in this report, air access appears to have been left to chance or to plans cobbled together well after the rest of the resort was under construction. In general, several options can be considered: scheduled service, charter service (which can be transformed into scheduled service), and low-cost carriers, although few cities in Africa outside Johannesburg have markets to support these carriers at the present time. Charters are highly dependent on the attitude of civil aviation authorities, which tend to be quite protectionist (in certain cases, each flight has to be approved, making planning difficult).

Economic Returns

The larger tourism projects have delivered economic returns, albeit quite modest in some cases and barely above the rates needed to stimulate new sources of growth (10–12 percent). However, they generate solid cash flows for investors, managers, and government as a result of generous depreciation allowances. The 10–12 percent rates represent returns to direct inputs; if indirect and induced impacts are included, the rates may be substantially higher. However, it is difficult to generate credible estimates of indirect and induced impact; in their absence, it seems better to rely on direct impacts only. Clearly, the large projects have delivered a substantial number of jobs and tax and foreign exchange revenues, and they have contributed, more intangibly, to a positive national investment climate (for example, in the Dominican Republic). The smaller projects may be financially successful and often have valuable community outreach programs, but it is difficult to develop them sufficiently to generate solid economic returns for the country. The economic analysis of tourism projects is evolving quickly, particularly as advances in natural resource economics are made (World Bank 2006, 2011). Whereas many environmental impacts are measurable, some are difficult to quantify and remain as qualitative inputs.[8]

Environmental Management

The environment and tourism have long been linked; tourism has been the junior partner, often no more than a source of revenue to offset the cost of environmental mitigation plans. More recently, however, tourism and the environment have come to be recognized as requiring a sound planning framework and as being mutually reinforcing. The Bali project, for instance, included a major nursery producing plants suitable for the project area based on research into indigenous varieties; no exotic vegetation was allowed.

The biggest issue related to climate change is global warming, a critical challenge involving rising sea levels and carbon-trading programs. The Maldives resorts project is the case most immediately affected by climate change, as the islands are little more than 1 or 2 meters above sea level.[9] Rising seas are putting many islands and coastal cities, including ports, around the world at risk. Regarding emissions trading,[10] the United States already charges airlines $16.50 for each international passenger who lands in or departs from its territory, the United Kingdom charges passengers on the basis of the distance they have flown. Australia introduced a carbon tax on July 1, 2012. Although no agreement has been reached on climate change internationally, the Copenhagen process continues to seek progress toward an international treaty. Airlines contribute about 5 percent to carbon emissions; other public transport and equipment that use energy, such as air conditioners, also produce high levels of carbon. Tourism is sure to be affected by any Copenhagen deal, although not as a direct negotiator in the process. Regardless of whether the green lobby or global warming skeptics gain the upper hand, the costs for tourism are likely to increase. Car rental companies and airlines are already offering clients the option of paying to offset excess carbon generated by aircraft and cars.

Tourism has a role to play in the environmental management of wildlife and plant diversity, the conservation of land resources, and the management of coastal zones. Environmental impacts can be either positive or negative. The positive impacts include environmental protection, the conservation of historic and archeological sites, the enhancement of the environment, and sound infrastructure design. The negative impacts include water, air, noise, and landscape pollution; excess waste disposal; ecological disruption; and environmental hazards. Today, most projects require an environmental impact assessment and an environmental management plan to mitigate negative impacts.[11]

The tools used to achieve environmental objectives are physical planning and regulation, incentives, infrastructure, subsidies, and direct management by nongovernmental organizations, such as Conservation International or the World Wildlife Fund. In Costa Rica, Lapa Rios is a conservancy of almost 1,000 acres that tries to demonstrate sound environmental practice for the greater Corcovado National Park and Osa Peninsula. More broadly, Costa Rica has set the world standard for certification of ecotourism. In Bali, great care was taken to identify zoning and development standards—regarding building setbacks and access to the beach, for example—as keys to environmental protection. Similarly, Maldives has identified comparable development standards and zoning rules, including one resort per island with a 40 percent coverage maximum and buildings no higher than trees and set back from the high-water mark. TUI Travel, the largest tourism conglomerate in the world, also has an advanced in-house system for measuring its targets for green tourism and awards for recognizing excellence.[12]

Public Institutions and Regulation

The cases presented in this report make one thing clear: in a sector often considered as "private sector driven," public intervention to stimulate development, whether on policy or investment, can be onerous but is essential. In certain cases, some "public investment" may, in fact, be financed by the private sector, but the state typically plays a role in investment as well as in policy areas.

Sound institutions are required to promote needed public investment, create the policy framework, and establish regulations. But tourism institutions are frequently weak and appear to be a drag on private investment rather than a catalyst for it—often because there is no real commitment to tourism as a force in economic development, especially where it is a new sector. Ministries of tourism are commonly the poor cousins of more powerful ministries such as finance and public works, are underfunded, and lack trained personnel. One priority is to communicate to government the full extent and value of tourism to the economy, which can change attitudes significantly. As tourism cuts across all sectors and various ministries, such as public works, that may not understand tourism's role, a second priority is to ensure that the industry is not ignored during the development of work programs. A technical group is needed to cut through bureaucracy. Ideally, a working group should be formed to carry out the analysis needed to make informed decisions. Then decisions must be taken, and be seen to be taken, or problems must be referred back for more discussion. An important weakness in tourism administrations is their inability to enforce key regulations and their tendency to fuss over details. This could be one of the reasons for the boom-and-bust mentality that pervades the sector. The case of Tunisia illustrates the range of agencies, each with its own functions, that are involved in tourism development: a ministry for policy and regulation, a statutory body for marketing and public project development, and a land bank for superstructure construction.

Investment Promotion and Financing

Many of the large projects cited in the cases reported that investors did not rush to snap up options for project sites. Investment promotion was not even included in project design. Today, investment promotion agencies exist in most countries (for example, in Mauritius). Investment promotion is now a professional business, with regular investment promotion conferences held worldwide.

Two of the case studies had ready access to finance, making execution easier. In the Jungle Bay Resort in Dominica, the promoter had been a Wall Street executive and was able to put a full program together. In Dubai, United Arab Emirates, access to finance was not an issue. In several other cases, however, access to finance was quite limited. The Dominican Republic had to mobilize separate projects in which the World Bank and the Inter-American Development Bank provided lines of credit to the central bank, which channeled the funds through commercial banks.

Availability of hotel credit is also often overlooked. Project preparation should include a review of the financial system to evaluate whether long-term credit is likely to be available.[13] In Africa commercial banks fund some tourism projects, but long-term credit is not their specialty; more typically, pension funds or insurance companies fund these projects. Of course, in the larger projects investors often bring in their partner banks and investors who provide credit (often off-shore). Smaller loans may command stronger demand and better returns. Local financial institutions, including commercial banks and specialized institutions, often provide funding for smaller establishments, such as restaurants or gift shops. Such funding through small and medium enterprises or microfinance institutions is vital for tourism.

Lastly, as part of investment promotion, incentives are often offered. These include measures to enhance the risk-reward relationship; direct financial assistance; financing mechanisms, such as bonds or special-purpose taxes; indirect assistance (for example, zoning); and fiscal measures, such as tax holidays.

In the vacuum created by the lack of access to appropriate finance, investors resort to short-term borrowing, which can spell disaster for projects that require heavy up-front funding and only reach stable cash flows after a few years of operation. This is particularly true for small businesses, which often expand incrementally.

Social Inclusion

When people of different cultural backgrounds, language, religion, values, customs, lifestyle, behavior, dress, and attitudes toward time meet, some strain is likely. Tourists and locals typically meet in a variety of environments. Emmanuel de Kadt (1979) mentions three interfaces: purchasing goods and services, experiencing things side by side, and exchanging information and ideas. More recently, as tourists become more interested in personal stories and experiences, greater contact with local communities is occurring, as are volunteer activities. The case studies demonstrate an acute sense of social inclusion and concern for poverty alleviation. The smaller projects are intimately concerned with social conditions, much more so than the larger projects. Small projects reach out to local communities (Lapa Rios, Jungle Bay, Nihiwatu), attempting to employ locals over outsiders. In some cases, local residents are part owners in projects, contributing community land to projects that try to protect the community's assets (Sabyinyo Silverback Lodge in Rwanda).

Some of the cases cited also have a fund or foundation for local projects that benefits the communities in a variety of ways. The large projects—Cancun, Mexico, for example—have also contributed immensely to the community. The state of Quintana Roo had about 40,000 residents when tourism started. Cancun alone now has 500,000 inhabitants. The state has a total population of 750,000, due in large measure to tourism. Its citizens enjoy a higher standard of living than the national average. In Turkey, Kemer was established as a new community of 30,000 people, created with modern infrastructure and good social services. The infrastructure built under the projects, which would not have been a priority for the country in the absence of the projected growth in tourism, also serves local populations.

One area where policy has failed local communities is housing. In the South Antalya project in Turkey, only limited housing was provided for employees, such that workers had difficulty finding accommodation within a reasonable distance at a reasonable cost. Resorts need to provide transport to outlying areas. They could consider small urban areas, with access to housing and availability of urban services that would also be useful in the promotion of small and medium enterprises, or collective housing schemes such as cooperatives and condominiums.

Notes

1. For example, in Lapa Rios, a couple from Minnesota, John and Karen Lewis; in Jungle Bay, Sam Raphael, a Dominican returned from the diaspora; and in Nihiwatu, Claude and Petra Graves.
2. Visit http://www.ifc.org and enter Peru OEH in search box.
3. Amit Sharma, consultant, contributed an unpublished paper as input for a diagnostic trade paper examining several sectors, including furniture.
4. The key ideas in this section originate from Bosselman, Peterson, and McCarthy (1999).
5. Or the negative impact of too much visitation, such as visitor impact studies.
6. U.S. carriers cannot serve an airport if the U.S. Federal Aviation Authority does not approve it.
7. In 2012 the government announced plans to sell 44 precent of shares of Royal Air Maroc to the public. To date, this has not yet occurred.
8. One critical area is to measure the "rents" generated by the natural resources that tourism often relies on, such as national parks and reserves, which seem to be divided unevenly between stakeholders. Another way of looking at this is to suggest that, although tourism is often used to offset the costs of environmental conservation, little evidence shows that this is happening effectively. The costs of maintaining protected areas still weigh heavily on national budgets, and revenues from tourism are unlikely to cover these costs completely.

9. Breakwaters, retaining walls, and polders surround the capital city of Malé.

10. The carbon-trading scheme was introduced in 2005 and now covers large polluters such as power and cement companies. Airlines are slated to be included in the scheme, but some governments have opposed the system. The program forces companies to pay for permits for each ton of carbon dioxide they emit above a certain level or cap. See, for example, http://www.travelmole.com/stories/1148281.php.

11. Environmental impact assessments are becoming more rigorous and provide for strict control and enforcement of the use of natural resources. Increasingly, safeguards on critical issues such as fiduciary responsibility, gender, expropriation, the employment of children, and transmigration are included in project analysis.

12. See http://www.tuitravelplc.com.

13. Several countries have specialized hotel financing institutions that operate like mortgage lenders; others rely on commercial banks or nonbank financial institutions such as insurance companies or pension funds.

References

Bosselman, F., C. Peterson, and C. McCarthy. 1999. *Managing Tourism Growth: Issues and Applications.* Washington, DC: Island Press.

De Kadt, Emmanuel. 1979. *Tourism: Passport to Development.* Washington, DC: Oxford University Press for United Nations Educational, Scientific, and Cultural Organization and the World Bank.

Peterson, George E. 2006. "Leasing Land and Land Sale as an Infrastructure Financing Option." Policy Research Paper 4043, World Bank, Washington, DC.

World Bank. 2006. *Where Is the Wealth of Nations? Measuring Capital for the 21st Century.* Washington, DC: World Bank. http://siteresources.worldbank.org/INTEEI/214578-1110886258964/20748034/All.pdf.

———. 2011. *The Changing Wealth of Nations: Measuring Sustainable Development in the New Millennium.* Washington, DC: World Bank. ChangingWealthNations. http://siteresources.worldbank.org/ENVIRONMENT/Resources/ChangingWealthNations.pdf.

Chapter 10

Case Studies

Cabo Verde: Transformation through Tourism

Key Lessons

- Cabo Verde's government provided strong public leadership for tourism and developed a positive investment climate.
- The government acquired land and provided incentives for investment; this plus a stable economy led to fast tourism growth.
- The fast growth of tourism resulted in gaps in conservation, infrastructure, and links to the local population.
- Currently, the government must address uneven development and high leakage.
- To enjoy the full benefits of tourism, the labor market must be properly prepared for tourism opportunities.
- High-quality airports, good aircraft maintenance facilities, and supportive air policies are crucial to increasing arrivals.

Introduction

In the 1990s Cabo Verde received almost 70,000 tourists.[1] It seemed unlikely that its tourism sector could drive an economy that was growing at a rate of more than 5 percent at that time. And yet Cabo Verde is only the second country in Africa to have graduated from low-income status, changing from a little-known, small island country into a mass tourism destination. Such a complex transition takes time. Tourism growth that occurs too quickly inevitably leads to cutting corners. This has created a challenge for Cabo Verde's authorities, who must now retrace their steps, fill in the gaps, and deepen the connectedness and inclusiveness of tourism.

Tourism Data

Tourist arrivals increased from 67,042 in 1999 to 285,141 in 2008, an average annual growth rate of 14 percent. Tourist receipts grew twice as fast, at a staggering 28 percent a year, resulting in high revenues per tourist. Tourist receipts reached $432 million in 2008, constituting 72 percent of all service exports and 25 percent of gross domestic product (GDP) (Twining-Ward 2010). The tourism sector directly and indirectly employed an estimated 45 percent of the population in 2008 (78,900 people).[2] In 2009, 287,000 tourists arrived in Cabo Verde, but receipts fell to $355 million as a result of the global recession (UNWTO 2011).

Sector Background and History

Cabo Verde is a small island country with big international ambitions. To end its reliance on overseas aid and remittances, Cabo Verde decided to trade on its most ubiquitous commodities: sun, sand, and sea. Attracted by a stable economy, generous incentives, and white-sand beaches, foreign investment in tourism has boomed. In less than two decades, Cabo Verde has overcome significant environmental and geographic barriers and transformed its economy. Tourism has been a key driver of economic growth.

Largely as a result of its extraordinary growth in tourism, Cabo Verde has achieved an average annual GDP growth rate of 6.5 percent over the last decade. It is only the second country in Africa to have graduated from low-income status and the only one in Africa to have negotiated a special partnership agreement with the European Union (EU). A considerable achievement, the EU agreement of November 2007 is likely to lead to enhanced cooperation between Cabo Verde and the EU in trade and in programs such as the European Regional Development Fund.

Cabo Verde has also made considerable progress with regard to social development. The country now ranks fifth in Sub-Saharan Africa on the United Nations Development Programme's Human Development Index. It has been labeled a "fast achiever" in recognition of the progress it has made toward the Millennium Development Goals, particularly in education. Yet many social challenges remain. Development has been uneven; significant rural and urban poverty still exists; and women continue to be underrepresented in employment and in positions of leadership.

The Case

The strong growth of tourism in Cabo Verde is a result of putting the preconditions and enablers for tourism's growth in place. For example, Cabo Verde has succeeded in establishing itself as a "safe haven" for investment. There have been no military coups, no terrorist attacks, and no currency devaluations. Cabo Verde has no malaria and few infectious diseases. Additionally, it has an airport classified as Category 1 by the U.S. government. The peaceful, multiparty democracy has survived changes in leadership, and its government is widely regarded as one of the most democratic in Sub-Saharan Africa. Cabo Verde has also gained international credibility for its sound macroeconomic policies: a stable currency pegged to the euro, low corruption, simplified taxes, and a reformed banking sector.

In addition, realizing that tourism is one of its few economic options, Cabo Verde has aggressively pursued tourism investment. It is one of the few countries in the region to do so. The government put together a generous collection of incentives and purchased large tracts of land on the islands of Sal and Boa Vista. Tempted by fine beaches, good weather, easy air connections, a generous package of investment incentives, and prime coastal sites packaged for sale, European investors have lined up to cash in on tourism and real estate opportunities in Cabo Verde.

Nevertheless, there is more to sustainable tourism than foreign investment. Sustaining growth over the long term also requires a professional private sector, high-quality suppliers, and a large number of "destination services." These include utilities, a skilled labor force, food and materials, garbage collection, sanitation, environmental conservation, and transportation. Seeking growth in foreign investment, Cabo Verde overlooked the importance of these services, leaving gaps in the sequencing of development. As a result, the sector is poorly integrated with the rest of the economy and is not doing as well as it could to alleviate poverty.

Results

Coastal zones are extremely vulnerable to adverse environmental impacts. Tourism development opportunities will be limited if the necessary steps are not taken to conserve this valuable ecosystem. Many of the developments that have been built to date are too close to the water and are not in tune with the scarcity of water, energy, and human resources.

Employment is the primary social benefit of tourism development in Cabo Verde. Unfortunately, the skill level of the workforce has not kept pace with the tourism sector's needs. Given the significant unemployment rate in Cabo Verde, the challenge now is to close the gap between workforce skills and industry needs.

Tourism in Cabo Verde is geographically concentrated. Just two islands—Sal and Boa Vista–have 75 percent of the tourist rooms. These islands together are home to less than 10 percent of the population. The success of tourism in reducing poverty depends on the ability of Cabo Verde to make development more inclusive, to spread the benefits of tourism to a wider area, and to create a fiscal environment that does not disadvantage local entrepreneurs.

Tourism development also puts considerable stress on public infrastructure. In Cabo Verde, the infrastructure was overextended prior to tourism development, and the rapid growth of hotels has made it difficult for municipalities to catch up. The situation has been made worse by revenues lost due to overgenerous tax incentives. If the deterioration in public services goes unchecked, the tourist experience will suffer, crime (already a growing concern) may worsen, and tourism will certainly not reach its potential as an agent for development.

In addition, leakage from the Cabo Verde economy is a considerable problem. Almost 80 percent of all food is imported, and 40 percent of GDP is spent on imported goods and services. Mitchell (2008) estimates that 55 percent of tourism expenditure is used to buy imported goods for tourists. Although Cabo Verde has limited capacity to produce agricultural products, opportunities for creating links between tourism, fishing, agriculture, and other businesses have not been developed well.

Cabo Verde offers various lessons for other countries:

- Market-oriented policies, democratic processes, and investment incentives are a beacon for foreign direct investment, but care should be taken that incentives do not disadvantage local operators.

- High-quality airports, good aircraft maintenance facilities, and supportive government policies are crucial to tourism growth, but domestic transport needs to be improved for tourism to be sustainable.

- To benefit from tourism, the labor market must be properly prepared for tourism opportunities.

- To avoid overstraining local services, investment in public infrastructure is needed before and during the development of hotels; developers should be expected to pay the full price of resources.

- Opportunities for promoting and encouraging domestic investors and small-scale enterprises should not be overlooked in the desire to attract foreign investors.

- Tourism may initially be driven by foreign investment, but its usefulness as a development tool depends on the degree to which it is embedded in the national economy.

- To be sustainable, tourism development needs to be of a scale, form, and type that are compatible with the resources of the destination environment.

- Diversifying tourism products and markets is beneficial for both tourists and tourism destinations.

- Too great a focus on the number of arrivals can lower the quality of the tourist experience. Alternative monitoring strategies, such as indicators of sustainable tourism, can help to determine the ability of the destination to sustain tourism.

Notes

1. This case study is drawn from the executive summary of Twining-Ward (2010).
2. World Travel & Tourism Council, Economic Data Search Tool (http://www.wttc.org /research/).

References

Mitchell, J. 2008. "Tourist Development in Cape Verde: The Policy Challenge of Coping with Success." Overseas Development Institute, London.

Twining-Ward, L. 2010. "Cape Verde's Transformation: Tourism as a Driver of Growth." Report prepared for the Africa Success Stories Project, World Bank, Office of the Chief Economist, Washington, DC.

UNWTO (United Nations World Tourism Organization). 2011. "World Tourism Barometer: Statistical Annex." *UNWTO Barometer* 9 (1).

Costa Rica: Ecotourism Certification in Lapa Rios

Key Lessons

- Costa Rica has proven that tourism and conservation can be developed simultaneously given small-scale development and targeted marketing.
- If sustainability is supported and required by the government through measures such as the adoption of an ethics code, large hotels are responsive.
- Costa Rica's free, voluntary, and comprehensive certification program drives sustainability, but it is costly and time-consuming.

Introduction

Costa Rica has long had a reputation as a stable democratic country in a part of the world where stability has been lacking. Contemporary tourism began in the 1980s with sustainable ecotourism, based on the country's amazing biodiversity, scenic beaches, tropical rain forest, volcanoes, and exotic wildlife (850 species of birds and 200 species of mammals). Its sustainability depends on a responsible tourism sector and visitors who respect the environment and local culture. Costa Rica has been a leader in managing the sector's growth by adopting standards of sustainability through certification programs (such as Green Globe, Blue Flag beaches, and its own Certification for Sustainable Tourism).

Tourism Data

Tourism has grown rapidly, taking off when the government began buying the Papagayo Peninsula one parcel at a time (1970–80) and then developing it for large-scale tourism (table 10.1). Costa Rica received 261,000 tourists in 1986 and 2.3 million in 2009,[1] growing eightfold in less than 25 years. Receipts have grown even faster, 14 times in less than 25 years (UNWTO 2013). This implies that tourist expenditure per person has doubled in the same period. It also suggests that tourism and conservation can go hand in hand. In 2010 tourism (directly and indirectly) contributed about 13 percent to Costa Rica's gross national product and employed about 240,000 people out of a population of 4.6 million.[2]

Table 10.1 Growth of Tourism in Costa Rica, 1986–2009

Indicator	1986	1990	1995	2000	2005	2009
Arrivals[a] (thousands)	261	435	792	1,088	1,959	2,289
Gross receipts (US$, millions)	133	275	718	1,229	1,810	1,985

Source: UNWTO 2013.
a. Includes cruise passengers.

Sector Background and History

Since the beginning, Costa Rica has been recognized for its dedication to small-scale development and conservation. However, it also has large-scale tourism, with high-rise hotels and about a dozen five-star resorts (including the big international chains, such as Allegro, Barceló, Four Seasons, JW Marriott, and Riu). Most guests arrive through a new airport in Liberia, located in the interior of the country, and transfer by ground to the Pacific beaches. The country also has "residential tourism" or retirement living, which was growing rapidly but has stagnated since the recession in the United States. It has also gained a dubious reputation for claiming to be green without actually being so. Approximately half of Costa Rica's tourism can be categorized as small-scale ecotourism,[3] which is laudable. This situation is perfectly reasonable if well managed. Although small lodges cannot be readily "scaled up" or multiplied to create an economic critical mass, hotels can, and together they can create an economic and productive critical mass. However, the focus on ecotourism may be weakened if large-scale tourism increases its influence in an unsustainable manner. For example, since 2002, Costa Rica has been fighting a reputation as a sex tourism destination, which is not compatible with sustainability, particularly when it involves the commercial sexual exploitation of children. However, evidence shows that large hotels are now taking corporate social responsibility, the protection of children, and the country's image seriously, and they are developing these angles as part of their ongoing business strategies. The real problem is to avoid the danger of "commoditizing" biodiversity. Not only should tourism enterprises be certified, but certification should be extended to guides, service providers, artisans, hawkers, and others engaged in helping tourists to access natural resources.

The Case

The Costa Rica Tourism Board (ICT) administers the Certificate of Sustainable Tourism.[4] It categorizes and certifies tourism companies according to their impact on the natural, cultural, and social resources of the country and thus

Table 10.2 Hotels and Tour Operators in Costa Rica, by Level of Certification, June 2011

Number of leaves	Hotels	Tour operators	Total
Five	15	7	22
Four	33	8	41
Three	59	19	78
Two	39	15	54
One	22	7	29
Total	168	56	224

Source: Costa Rica Tourism Board (http://www.visitcostarica.com/ict/paginas/TourismBoard.asp).

on sustainability. The ICT defines sustainable tourism "as the balanced interaction of three basic factors within the tourism industry: (a) proper stewardship of natural and cultural resources, (b) improvement of local communities' quality of life, and (c) economic success that can contribute to national development."[5] The ICT's concept of sustainable tourism is broader than simply ecotourism: it includes respect for human rights, particularly the rights of children. The program has a set of performance-based standards that constitute guidelines for sustainable tourism and measure "the degree to which they comply with a sustainable model of natural, cultural, and social resource management." The process is free, voluntary, and open to hotels, lodges, and cabins as well as to tour operators and travel agencies. The enterprise submits an application received from the ICT. A site visit and evaluation by the ICT's National Accreditation Commission follow, and the property is awarded one of five levels (or "leaves") for sustainability.[6] The total number of approved organizations is shown in table 10.2.

Results

What is in it for the actors? The Lapa Rios project (box 10.1), among many others, attests to the value of a sustainability ranking and maintains that visitors buy into the concept. Studies show that many tourists are willing to pay for the experience. In fact, many visitors come to see how the system works. Numerous other countries have expressed interest in the system, and all of the other Central American countries intend to adopt it. However, the process of certification is time-consuming, and the program is costly to staff and maintain (especially if the goal is to move from one leaf to five).

For several years, efforts have been afoot to reach agreement on global criteria for sustainable tourism. The tempo quickened after the World Conservation Congress in October 2008. The Global Sustainable Tourism Council (GSTC), a global membership council created in 2009, emerged as the leading proponent

BOX 10.1

Lapa Rios

Set in a private nature reserve spread over 1,000 acres of Central America's last remaining lowland tropical rain forest, Lapa Rios Ecolodge overlooks the pristine point where the Golfo Dulce meets the wild Pacific Ocean. The 930-acre Lapa Rios Reserve helps to buffer the Osa Peninsula's Corcovado National Park from the ocean and serves as a wildlife corridor. Lapa Rios Ecolodge is more than just a beautiful rain forest hotel or an ecoresort near the beach. Lapa Rios is a model ecotourism project: it has attained Costa Rica's highest sustainable tourism certification, the Certificate of Sustainable Tourism, represented by five "leaves."

Source: Lapa Rios Ecolodge (http://www.laparioa.com/).

of certification. The GSTC offers a common understanding of sustainable tourism and helps enterprises to adopt universal sustainable tourism principles and criteria. The GSTC began by tentatively identifying 37 such criteria,[7] based on what is needed to protect and sustain the world's natural and cultural resources, while ensuring that tourism supports local communities and helps to alleviate poverty.

Support for certification can be sought from member organizations, such as Sustainable Travel International and the Rainforest Alliance, which offer training and the verification of standards.[8]

Costa Rica has built a respected ecotourism industry that helps to protect its environment and opens up opportunities for local communities, whatever the size of the operation. It provides lessons for both emerging and maturing destinations.

Notes

1. The data include cruise ship passengers, which accounted for 366,000 visitors in 2009. The Center for Responsible Travel estimates that cruise ship passengers spend $55 per night, while terrestrial tourists spend $1,000 per trip. See http://www.responsibletravel.org.
2. World Travel & Tourism Council, Economic Data Search Tool (http://www.wttc.org/research/).
3. The jewel in the crown is the Oro Peninsula, but Costa Rica also has protected 24 national parks and reserves.
4. The Instituto Costarricense de Turismo. The ICT has had the support of the International Union for Conservation of Nature and several academic institutions

in the region. It also works closely with nongovernmental organizations such as the Rainforest Alliance.

5. See http://www.turismo-sostenible.co.cr/en/.

6. As of 2008, all applicants must also be signatories to the code of conduct against the sexual exploitation of children and adolescents. See http://www.thecode.org.

7. The initial criteria were organized around four main themes: planning for sustainability, maximizing social and economic benefits for the local community, enhancing cultural heritage, and reducing negative impacts on the environment. See http://www.sustainabletourismcriteria.org.

8. For Sustainable Travel International, see http://www.sustainabletravel.com. For the Rainforest Alliance, see http://www.Rainforest-Alliance.org.

Reference

UNWTO (United Nations World Tourism Organization). 2013. "Tourism Factbook." UNWTO, Madrid. http://www.e-unwto.org/content/v486k6/?v=search.

Dominica: Community Involvement and Training in Jungle Bay

Key Lessons

- The Jungle Bay Resort and Spa took five years to develop and was successful due to the close links with the community and the availability of sufficient capital for its business plan.
- Sustainability is achieved through a balance of backward linkages to the community, strong marketing, and constant product innovation (for example, time-share development).
- Jungle Bay's nongovernmental organization, South East Tourism Development Committee, provides long-term training, mentorship, and small loans to help local enterprises to integrate into the tourism industry.
- Jungle Bay's success can be attributed to in-depth community involvement and a long-term commitment to improving the community through training and projects.

Introduction

Dominica's claim to tourism fame is largely due to its homegrown ecotourism. The country was a trail blazer in the development of ecotourism, integrating it into the global industry. The leading example is Jungle Bay Resort and Spa, a small resort in the coastal forest, set on 55 acres (25 hectares) along Dominica's southeast coast (map 10.1). Opened to travelers in 2005, Jungle Bay demonstrates what ecotourism is likely to become. It strives for environmental and socially responsible tourism with a high level of luxury and is wired into the world's travel market. Ecotourism is a relatively new concept in the Caribbean (although resorts like to promote "green" tourism), and Dominica has been branded as the first Green Globe country. Jungle Bay has succeeded in operating a resort that respects both environmental and social concerns. It is becoming a model for the Caribbean and perhaps beyond.

Tourism Data

In 2009 Dominica hosted about 85,000 tourists a year, slightly more than its population of 73,500 at the time. Tourist arrivals are spread fairly evenly

Map 10.1 Dominica

throughout the year, as the sun shines a great deal even during the wettest period, from July to November (UNWTO 2011). Tourism directly and indirectly contributed almost 28 percent to the island's gross domestic product in 2009 and is expected to grow over the next 10 years; the sector employed about 8,800 people, directly and indirectly, in 2009.[1]

Sector Background and History

Dominica, in the Eastern Caribbean, between Guadeloupe and Martinique, is the largest of the Windward Islands. It is about 30 miles long and 15 miles wide, extending 289 square miles, with 91 miles of coastline. Of the 71,000 residents,

30,000 Caribs (the original inhabitants of the islands) live in community-owned reserves. Dominica is noted for its extensive rain forest, diving, and mountainous terrain, offering different options for a Caribbean vacation than the usual model. It has the only United Nations Educational, Scientific, and Cultural Organization (UNESCO) world heritage site in the eastern Caribbean, the Morne Trois Pitons National Park. Dominica has 365 rivers and streams, waterfalls, hot sulfur springs, a "boiling" lake, and four freshwater lakes, two of which are situated more than 2,500 feet in the highlands. The island's altitude and rainfall have given rise to a wide variety of vegetation. Native flora include more than 1,000 species of flowering plants (including 74 species of orchids and 200 ferns). To date, 172 bird species have been recorded, including two endemic parrot species. Among its long list of awards, Dominica is the first country to be benchmarked as a Green Globe 21 Eco Destination.[2] The island has few beaches, but its coral is relatively close to the shore and easily accessible.[3]

The Case

The Jungle Bay Resort and Spa broke ground in 2000, just as Dominica's agricultural crisis struck due to a loss of market share in the fiercely competitive banana market. The resulting unemployment made it easy to hire workers. Most of the resort's employees, including those who work in construction and in operations, come from three villages. The resort worked closely with the village councils of the three communities and finally opened in 2005. Management and staff give 10 percent of total tips to fund local projects, ranging from school rehabilitation to care for the elderly. The resort now employs close to 60 people.

Jungle Bay has 35 wooden cottages elevated on wooden stilts, nestled beneath jungle and accessed through a network of footpaths and stone staircases. It was built from discarded rocks and reclaimed timber. The main building has two large yoga studios, a gift shop, a recreation complex, a business center, and conference facilities. A large open-air restaurant overlooks the volcanic stone swimming pool. The resort offers a mix of jungle adventure and spa and wellness treatments.

Jungle Bay initially faced several challenges: it was on a previously unknown rainforest island with above-average rainfall, it had few beaches on its inhospitable (but beautiful) coastline and often heavy seas, and it had no direct flights from major destinations. However, it was able to mobilize enough capital ($7 million) to execute its business plan efficiently, not intermittently as money became available.[4] Jungle Bay's model advocated operating a luxury hotel with minimal disturbance to the natural environment (box 10.2). It functions as a tool to further the economic and social welfare of the local population

BOX 10.2

Jungle Bay Resort Mission Statement

According to Sam Raphael, president, Jungle Bay Resort's mission is "to enhance the natural environment and improve the livelihood of surrounding communities so that the region is improved in a sustainable way, while providing quality, comfortable, nature-based experiences for our guests."

Source: Jungle Bay (http://www.junglebaydominica.com/)

---

through backward linkages to the population and forward linkages to the worldwide travel industry. Few ecoresorts are able to do this effectively; this advantage ensures a positive, long-term impact on local communities, a fact that is not lost on the resort's promoters.

Since Jungle Bay opened in 2005, it has sought to develop backward linkages to industry. Small farmers and fishermen from Dominica's southeast have gained a new market for their fresh organic produce, and handicraft producers and heritage dancers have gained a venue for their trade. Sixty villagers have been trained to host visitors as tour guides, spa attendants, cooks, room attendants, maintenance people, and managers.

Jungle Bay also created a local nongovernmental organization, the South East Tourism Development Committee, to help residents of the area to prepare for the advantages and opportunities that tourism offers. Over the past 10 years, the South East Tourism Development Committee has developed a network of natural sites and trails, trained farmers, small entrepreneurs, and tour guides, and promoted environmental concerns and the overall welfare of the rural community. At the same time, farmers are given incentives to increase their productivity.[5] To date, Jungle Bay, its staff, and clients have contributed about $405,000 to the charity. In January 2006, Jungle Bay Resort and Spa launched the Southeast Entrepreneur Loan Fund, which allows 10 to 15 local entrepreneurs to borrow up to $32,400 for business activities, such as producing organic fruits and vegetables, seafood, and local arts and crafts[6] and providing guides for local tours and hikes, that can contribute to Jungle Bay's operations.

Results

Jungle Bay's Ecovillage Vacation Program is the Caribbean's first vacation ownership club (time-share) targeting eco-adventure travelers. The program allows investors to share investment costs and maintenance and to enjoy a vacation hideaway with luxury accommodation and breakfast in a Jungle Bay cottage for one week a year for 30 years. A unique feature of Jungle Bay's Ecovillage Vacation Program is that it operates on a floating-week basis, so clients are not locked into a specific week of the year and can "bank" their week and enjoy a two-week stay every other year. The investment can also be transferred or resold. Jungle Bay is affiliated with Interval International, a vacation ownership membership organization with a pool of 2,700 affiliated properties in 80 countries.[7]

Jungle Bay is always looking for better environmental solutions. It is currently investigating wind power, which could reduce its dependence on fossil fuels and gas. Its cabins are built on stilts to minimize impact on the ground below. Ninety-five percent of the food served in the restaurant is local and organically grown, and food waste is composted. All furnishings in the resort are built from locally produced renewable timber. All water on the resort is from spring-fed streams on the property, and reusable water bottles are distributed to guests.

Jungle Bay has won multiple awards for excellence in ecotourism, for example, by the *Los Angeles Times* (United States), the *Guardian* (United Kingdom), and the *Daily Telegraph* (United Kingdom), as noted on its website.

Notes

1. World Travel & Tourism Council, Economic Data Search Tool (http://www.wttc.org /research/).
2. Dominica has reserves of subterranean thermal power.
3. Climate and temperatures vary depending on the season and altitude. Average daytime temperatures range from 75°F to 85°F. Rainfall in the interior can be as high as 300 inches a year; the wettest months are July to November, and the driest are February to May. See http://www.caribbeantravelweb.com/dominica/about _dominica.htm.
4. Jungle Bay's promoter, Sam Raphael, a Dominican trained in finance in the U.S. Virgin Islands and Wall Street, had access to funding through his contacts.
5. Jungle Bay has financed two demonstration greenhouses and encourages farmers to generate additional income, for example, by opening up their farms to visitors and explaining their organic farming methods.
6. More than half of the handicrafts sold in the Caribbean are made in Asia.
7. See http://www.intervalworld.com.

Reference

UNWTO (United Nations World Tourism Organization). 2011. "World Tourism Barometer: Statistical Annex." *UNWTO Barometer* 9 (1).

The Dominican Republic: Political Commitment to Tourism in Puerto Plata

Key Lessons

- Transforming the tourism industry in the Dominican Republic required strong and consistent political support over an extended period of time.
- The public sector invested in large-scale anchor projects in Puerto Plata, which the private sector then replicated in other zones.
- Centralized coordination of all project activities through the Tourism Infrastructure Department (INFRATUR) during the first project facilitated its success despite delays and challenges.
- A lack of financial systems and knowledge by the government led to delays in project implementation.
- Infrastructure was developed by both the public and, later, the private sectors.
- Employee housing and sanitation systems were abandoned during the first project and have threatened sustainability in some cases. Sanitation is now being addressed.
- The all-inclusive resort model was supported by Spanish hotel chains and tour operators looking for a high-volume alternative in the Caribbean. Although all-inclusive resorts procure supplies and labor locally, they inhibit interactions between tourists and communities and restrict the flow of tourists to local businesses outside the resort.

Introduction

In 1972 no more than 1,600 hotel rooms existed in the Dominican Republic, compared to 9,000 in Puerto Rico and 6,600 in Jamaica at the time, and the country had only one international airport. Now, it has more than 66,000 hotel rooms and six international airports. The Dominican Republic currently hosts more tourists than any other destination in the Caribbean, and tourism is an integral part of the economy, having overtaken sugar as the most important product.

Tourism Data

From the time the two tourism projects outlined in this case study were conceived in 1971 until they were completed in 1989, arrivals in the Dominican

Republic rose from 137,000 in 1971 to 1.4 million in 1989; Puerto Plata alone hosted 360,000 tourists in 1989 (World Bank 2005).[1] In 1979 tourism receipts amounted to $124 million, growing to $0.9 billion by 1989. Hotel capacity rose to 18,500 in 1989, overtaking the Bahamas, with 14,800 rooms at that time, and Jamaica, with 13,000 rooms. The project was designed for 1,900 rooms, although at its completion it provided 3,292 rooms.[2] This occurred despite the fact that Playa Grande remained undeveloped, with only one hotel. Tourism has further added to the national budget: a per capita arrival tax of $10 collected at the point of entry and a departure tax (originally $10, but now $20) generate a buoyant stream of revenue for the government. An 8 percent value added tax is also levied on tourism.[3] Overall, according to the United Nations World Tourism Organization (UNWTO 2013), the Dominican Republic received almost 4.5 million international arrivals in 2009; total international tourist receipts amounted to $4.1 billion. According to the World Travel & Tourism Council (WTTC), tourism's total contribution to gross domestic product was 16.5 percent in 2009, with total direct and indirect employment in the sector equivalent to 566,800 jobs.[4]

Sector Background and History

In the early 1970s, contrary to advice he received from a Spanish technical assistance team to promote other sites (notably the capital, Santo Domingo), President Joaquín Balaguer chose Puerto Plata as the first publicly supported site for tourism in the Dominican Republic. His idea was to support the regions rather than the capital. The World Bank partnered with the government to fund the proposed development as two separate projects.

The Puerto Plata region is strategic for trade in produce from the country's fertile Cibao Valley (map 10.2). It is a thriving community, with a preserved colonial urban core and one of the earliest forts in the Caribbean, the Fortaleza de San Felipe. At that time, it was a market town with a protected port that had little or no tourism. The area chosen for development included the city and two potential resort areas along the northern coast's beaches, Playa Dorada (2 kilometers from Puerto Plata) and Playa Grande (80 kilometers to the east). The countryside is diverse, with mountains in the background, extensive sugar plantations, sandy Caribbean beaches, and clear waters along the Atlantic coast, protected by reefs and fringed by palm trees.

The Case

The Puerto Plata project was implemented in two phases.

Map 10.2 Dominican Republic

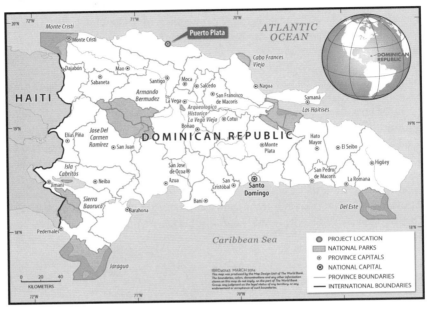

Project I

The Puerto Plata project (World Bank 1974) was designed by Shankland Cox and funded by the United Nations Development Programme (UNDP), with the World Bank as executing agency and ultimately as lender. A department of the central bank, the Tourism Infrastructure Department (INFRATUR) supervised the project.[5] INFRATUR was modeled after a similar organization in Mexico called FONATUR, a fund under the Ministry of Finance that was largely responsible for launching tourism in Mexico. As implementing agency, the central bank was a powerful, well-managed organization. (Later, when tourism was well launched, it withdrew from its role of promoting tourism.) For the Puerto Plata project, INFRATUR supervised the acquisition of land and the execution of the works; it also marketed serviced plots to investors.

The project's objective was to provide infrastructure for an integrated resort at an international destination in the north of the Dominican Republic. Project components included land acquisition[6] in Playa Dorada and Playa Grande and land use plans to create critical mass to support 1,900 hotel rooms and 375 apartments (box 10.3). Investment costs and a financial plan are outlined in table 10.3. Serviced land was to be sold or leased to hotel investors to recover investment costs, and the completed infrastructure was to be handed over to a local authority (the municipality) or an appropriate utility.

BOX 10.3

Components of the Puerto Plata Project

- Site works and network infrastructure
- Solid waste disposal facilities
- Two golf courses
- Riding stables
- Commercial center
- Low-cost housing in Playa Dorada
- Separate water supply and sewerage for the town of Río San Juan (near Playa Grande)
- Puerto Plata Airport, including an access road, terminal building, and navigational equipment
- Hotel training facilities
- Technical assistance for project implementation.

Table 10.3 Costs of Puerto Plata Tourism Project I in the Dominican Republic
US$, thousands

Component	Appraisal			Actual		
	Local costs	Foreign exchange	Total	Local costs	Foreign exchange	Total
Playa Dorada	5,355	6,447	11,802	16,368	4,136	20,504
Playa Grande	3,255	2,110	5,365	3,326	281	3,607
Airport	1,665	3,016	4,681	6,223	3,603	9,826
Hotel school	179	287	466	925	190	1,115
Investment promotion	54	479	533	428	372	800
Professional services	—	—	—	1,827	1,710	3,537
Project administration	149	25	174	—	—	—
Technical assistance	525	1,075	1,600	1,392	1,223	2,615
Contingencies						
Physical	930	1,571	2,501	—	—	—
Price	3,055	5,816	8,871	—	—	—
Land acquisition	—	—	—	7,528	—	7,528
Total	15,167	20,826	35,993	38,017	11,515	49,532

Source: World Bank 1991.
Note: — = not available.

The utilities provided technical standards and approved the project works, but INFRATUR managed procurement and construction. The fact that all works were managed by a single agency greatly facilitated project coordination (box 10.4). The private sector Hotel and Restaurant Association (ASONAHORES)[7] was kept apprised of progress.

After completion, INFRATUR kept an office in Puerto Plata to ensure the provision of certain services in the resort (landscaping and maintenance, street lighting, upkeep of communal space, and administration). Finally, rather than being retained by the government, these services were sold to an association of hotel companies operating in Playa Dorada (in contrast, Playa Grande remained the property of INFRATUR until recently, when it was sold to a private developer). Map 10.3 shows the project area and land use.

BOX 10.4

Agencies Responsible for Managing Puerto Plata Infrastructure

- *Airport:* Comisión Administrativa Aeropuertuaria
- *Electricity:* Corporación Dominica de Electricidad
- *Roads:* Secretaría de Estado de Obras Públicas
- *Solid waste:* Municipalities
- *Telecommunications:* Compañía Dominica de Teléfonos
- *Water and sanitation:* Instituto Nacional de Aguas Potables y Alcantarillado.

Map 10.3 Puerto Plata Region, Dominican Republic

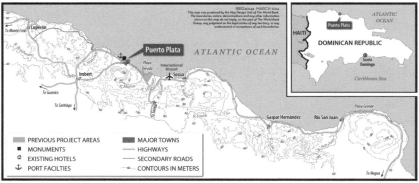

The project faced various physical, contractual, and import delays, which is not unusual for a complex tourism development that must adapt to unforeseeable changes on-site, but has survived to become a lasting destination, benefiting from direct flights (more than 50 scheduled and charter carriers) from Europe, North America, and Latin America. Because of the nonperformance of several contractors, construction periods and costs doubled those estimated initially. Another major concern was that, by 1983, six years after the project was launched, in spite of incentives (Law 153 of 1971), only 300 of the planned 1,900 rooms had been constructed.

Large-scale resort complexes typically require long lead times, a phenomenon noted in several projects of the time, so funding for an initial anchor hotel is useful to overcome the hesitation of prospective first movers. Adding weight to the project, a hotel school was opened in 1983, which eventually was transferred to the Catholic University in Puerto Plata. It continues to provide a range of training courses for the industry. Other adjustments were also made. Despite having 240 hectares, a superior beach, and an upscale Robert Trent Jones golf course, Playa Grande attracted only one hotel, and most project funding was diverted to Playa Dorada. Employee housing requirements proved difficult to estimate, and that component was dropped. The contract for sewerage at Río San Juan was judged too costly and also subsequently dropped. These amendments had significant environmental and social repercussions, as explained below.

In the final planning stages, the central bank itself considered building some hotels (to be managed or leased by professionals and ultimately sold) and making loans to investors. In the end, a sufficient number of private investors contributed, and the central bank only invested in the first hotel (a Jack Tar Hotel).[8]

Project II

Slow progress in hotel investment was due in part to the absence of long-term mortgage finance in the Dominican Republic. To address this constraint, a line of credit was considered and granted for a second tourism project (World Bank 1979). This project included an apex line of credit to INFRATUR to be on-lent through 12 prequalified commercial banks to finance the debt portion of hotel projects, improvements in Puerto Plata harbor to receive cruise ships, support for handicrafts, and the strengthening of sector policies and administration. Of funds under the line of credit, 96 percent were disbursed for hotel investments in Playa Dorada. Costs are shown in table 10.4.

Some problems arose pertaining to this project as well as several changes. The commitment of funds was delayed for three years, as the government was unfamiliar with both apex lines of credit and hotel lending terms (box 10.5). The economic situation was deteriorating, and key products, such as cement, were

Table 10.4 Costs of Puerto Plata Tourism Project II in the Dominican Republic
US$, millions

Component	Original forecast	Revised forecast[a]	Actual
Line of credit	23.6	23.9	20.4
Handicraft center	0.3	0.2	0.1
Technical assistance	0.5	0.3	0.3
Urban works	0.6	0.6	0.7
Total	25.0	25.0	21.5

Sources: World Bank 1974, 1991.
a. The Bank approved a reallocation of funds.

BOX 10.5

Hotel Finance

- INFRATUR's role was to manage World Bank funds.
- A review of commercial banks and their eligibility to make and service loans was conducted: 12 were prequalified.
- Commercial banks were required to blend their own resources with World Bank funds.
- Loans were denominated in U.S. dollars.
- Lending terms and processes for credit approval—on-lending margins and rates for borrowers—were determined.
- The ceiling of 12 percent interest was augmented by up-front closing costs of 3–4 percent to enhance returns for the banks.
- Financial conditions for subloans and model feasibility studies were established.
- Credit procedures were approved, and implementation was supervised.
- Subloan identification was processed.
- Contract negotiations and conditions were defined.
- Technical supervision took place.

Source: World Bank 1991.

in short supply. In addition, with rising inflation, the subloans, whose interest was capped at 12 percent,[9] became highly concessionary, as commercial rates rose to 24 percent, and the central bank became reluctant to on-lend. Although initial interest was lukewarm, reflecting the lack of experience in planned tourism development, several investors came forward.

Results

As noted, the two Puerto Plata projects underwent substantial changes. The political and economic environment changed every four years following the presidential election. As most of the investors in Playa Dorada were wealthy landowners and industrialists, not hotel management experts, they made mistakes along the way, especially by slashing prices and contracting with unstable operators when business turned down. The projects could have taken much longer to develop had there not been interest on the part of Spanish hotel groups to invest in the Caribbean, especially in Cuba and Mexico (Barceló, Mélia, Occidental, and Riu, among others).

In the 1990s, room rates barely covered salaries and food requirements, and there was no spare cash for rehabilitation or promotion, much less for profits. It was then that a new resort, Punta Cana, materialized, threatening the very survival of Puerto Plata. Occupancy rates slipped below 60 percent in the mid-1990s but have recovered in spite of the increase in capacity.

Critical for Puerto Plata was the support of tour operators, who were looking for a new market niche for the Caribbean, one of high volume rather than the traditional high-end, high-price tourism in the region. Moreover, due to knock-on effects from Playa Dorada, the north coast market from Puerto Plata, via Sosúa, to Cabarete and Samaná Peninsula strengthened, helping to expand tourism in the region. In addition, the Dominican Republic invested heavily in infrastructure and roads in the 1990s, and access to many tourism areas is now much improved. Early on, the hotels were not all-inclusive, so restaurants and bars flourished in Puerto Plata. When hotels switched to the all-inclusive operating model as a result of the economic downturn, local restaurants suffered and some closed, transforming the resorts into enclaves. The move to all-inclusive resorts is a project legacy that has both advantages and disadvantages. All-inclusive resorts procure a great many supplies locally, and many of their employees come from local towns and villages.[10] They remain a strong market force, popular with middle-income families, which explains how Playa Dorada was able to build a market from zero and weather the stringent economic conditions of the mid-1990s. Now, however, individual travel is growing rapidly again, and boutique hotels are emerging in Sosúa and other northern coast locations.

By 1991, there were 14 hotels in Playa Dorada, 4 owned by Spanish interests and 10 by Dominican companies. The handicrafts center was closed, as it failed to achieve popularity after six years of experimentation. The balance of funding was used to upgrade the port park and Puerto Plata's export-processing zone. The government estimated that 40,000[11] jobs were created by the first project alone, 12,000 of them direct. In Puerto Plata itself, 8,800 jobs were created. With completion of the second project, these figures increased at least 50 percent, with about 4,300 jobs in hotels alone.

Notwithstanding the move to an all-inclusive model, the projects had a profound impact on the economy of Puerto Plata, where tourist service outlets now line the streets (car and equipment rentals, food establishments, and so forth). The workers are 30 percent women and 97 percent Dominican. The combined economic rate of return on the two projects ex post is estimated to be 12 percent, compared to an ex ante evaluation of 17.5 percent. This comparatively low rate of return is explained by the slow build-up of hotels and cost increases. However, the estimation is based on direct inputs only—it includes neither indirect nor induced effects. With direct and indirect activities, the internal rate of return exceeds 20 percent.

Despite delays, cost overruns, and institutional difficulties, the combined results of the two projects were considered "a substantial and important success" by the World Bank's independent audit. By 1999, 10 years after the projects were completed, international arrivals to the Dominican Republic reached 2.7 million and by 2009, just under 4 million. By 1999, expenditures reached $2.8 billion and by 2009, $4.05 billion. Average daily expenditure is about $100 per tourist, and the length of stay is between 9 and 10 days. By 1999, overall hotel capacity had grown to about 50,000 rooms and by 2009, to 67,197 rooms (with about 17,000 in the Puerto Plata zone, almost 30 percent of the country's total). The average national hotel occupancy rate reached 67 percent in 1999 and is at about that level today (after increasing to more than 70 percent in 2000 and 2003 and then falling back during the recent recession and slowdown in international travel). Occupancies in Puerto Plata hotels tend to be several points lower than the national average.

More recently, another major development was launched, putting the Dominican Republic in its premier position in the Caribbean today. Punta Cana is a major resort complex of more than 40 hotels and several real estate developments in Altagracia Province in the east of the country. It drew heavily on the experience of Puerto Plata. It began with two purchases of land in the Bavaro and Punta Cana areas, the former by Barceló Hotels (Mallorca, Spain) and the latter by investors who had participated in Playa Dorada as well as well-known personalities like Julio Iglesias and Oscar de la Renta (the latter had originally been associated with Casa de Campo). In this case, the government and private owners sold land to the investing companies on a negotiated basis. These investors built the trunk and network infrastructure, including a private international airport, brought in water by aqueduct, constructed sewerage and sanitation systems, and built a private power plant (serving tourists and local communities and connecting with the national power distributor). They also promoted hotel investment and attracted numerous companies, many of them Spanish with similar operations in Cuba and Mexico,[12] that constructed more than 40 hotels for a total of 23,000 rooms in the province. A new real estate company, Cap Cana, is anchored by a Jack Niklaus golf resort.[13]

The projects also had important spin-off effects: there are now more than 16,000 rooms along the north coast in Cofresi Beach, Sosúa, and Cabarete, as well as Playa Dorada. Sosúa, a small town by a protected bay with a beautiful curved beach, has developed up-market hotels. Cabarete, a rough and tumble development built on surfing and kite surfing, has also expanded rapidly. In spite of tourism expansion, the project areas still have vast fields of sugarcane, and their essential character has been maintained. They have served as a model for replication and for responsible expansion in other areas.

As the completion report points out, "In reality, it can be safely assumed that little or none of the tourism development at Puerto Plata would have occurred in the absence of the infrastructure investments, hotel credit, and demonstration effects of the two projects." The World Bank judged the project to be sustainable based on evidence that the sector had expanded from a minor industry to a growth sector in 20 years and on evidence that it was continuing to grow, in budgetary impact, foreign exchange earnings, and employment created. Despite the problems encountered during construction, the Puerto Plata projects created the base for the Dominican Republic's tourism industry and secured its place as an integral part of the economy.

But there is no place for complacency. Tastes change, and new competition is always on the horizon. Customers are looking for activities and experiences that cut across demographic groups. Sun and sand are commodities, traded irrespective of location, often at rock-bottom prices. Unlike many Caribbean islands, the Dominican Republic has the elements to support change. It has valuable natural resources and cultural assets for tourism and a diversified economy. The rich agricultural area of Cibao supplies tourism resorts nationwide, and the country has a well-trained workforce. The country embraces entrepreneurship and a willingness to test new ideas.

The lessons from the Dominican Republic projects are summarized in the following points:

- None of the tourism development at Puerto Plata would have occurred in the absence of the infrastructure investments, hotel credit, and demonstration effects of the two projects. In many ways, the projects helped to launch a new industry.

- The government stepped in to launch a new industry but stood aside when it was apparent that the private sector could take the lead. While the government promoted the Puerto Plata project, it was fully privatized with the purchase of INFRATUR's management unit by the local association of hotel owners. It now resembles the Punta Cana resort as a private, independent resort facility. The government still has an important role in formulating policy and setting strategic direction to lead the sector to the next level.

- The projects improved the Dominican Republic's image as a destination for foreign direct investment as well as its overall investment climate, beyond tourism.
- ASONAHORES and the ministry have adopted a code of ethics.
- It is unfortunate that the sanitation and employee housing components were dropped from the projects, as they are both critical services for an environmentally sound tourism sector. For sanitation, in the north coast the government is now implementing a World Bank–funded program to connect Sosúa and Cabarete to the sewerage system and provide an ocean outfall. Regarding employee housing, the opportunity to create an urban environment and urban services close to the main resort areas was missed. However, several hotel companies are working to solve this problem. One option is to build cooperatives of low-cost condominiums for Dominican families working in resort areas.
- The all-inclusive operating model is a subject of debate everywhere. The service inside these resorts is of high quality, but tourists experience an enclave environment that prevents practically any informal contact with the local people; it is almost impossible to gain access to them. The idea of *mine host*, "open to the public," is lost here, and even beaches are the private domain of the resorts. The all-inclusive formula has put Dominican resorts in a fiercely competitive market that exerts downward pressure on prices. One or two groups (Victoria hotels in Playa Dorada and Starz hotels in Sosúa) are establishing boutique hotels that attract a much higher room rate. Moreover, Casa de Campo (La Romana) and hotels in real estate developments have always relied on individual clients. Cap Cana appears to be relying on an individual market as well.
- The region and the country are now establishing a brand image that should distinguish between the country's different regions. The government and ASONAHORES are cooperating on this through the Tourism Promotion Council.

Playa Dorada remains a sound model for planning and replication in other areas. As tourism continues to grow, the government should devise a planning framework with clear regulations to ensure that carrying capacities are not overstretched.

Notes

1. See http://www.asonahores.com/.
2. See http://www.asonahores.com/.
3. ITBIS (*Impuesto a las Transferencias de Bienes Industrializados y Servicios*) is a value added tax on the transfer of industrialized goods and services.
4. WTTC, Economic Data Search Tool (http://www.wttc.org/research/).

5. Departamento para el Desarrollo de la Infraestructura Turística.

6. The land was acquired through negotiation, not expropriation.

7. ASONAHORES is the Asociación de Hoteles y Turismo de la República Dominicana. See http://www.asonahores.com/.

8. Jack Tar Hotels, a Texas company, is now defunct. The hotel was sold to Allegro Hotels, a Dominican company, and subsequently to Spain's Occidental Hotels, one of four the company owns in the Playa Dorada complex.

9. In addition, closing costs of 3–4 percent were also charged to offset low interest rates.

10. In a study of eight all-inclusive resorts in the Caribbean in 2004, GTZ (2006) found that the average wage bill was $1.7 million per establishment (the resorts ranged from 100 to 300 rooms), and the procurement of local goods and services averaged $1.6 million a year. Three-star hotels created jobs for 1 employee per room, and five-star hotels created jobs for 1.5 to 2 employees per room; in addition, each direct job created 3–5 indirect jobs. More than 96 percent of employees were nationals of the country. In the Dominican Republic, it found that, compared with the basic national salary of $110 a month, a hotel employee earned a basic wage of $180 plus benefits (social security plus a mandated 10 percent tipping policy), which raised the total to $182; with meals and transport, the total reached $282. What is more, employees were permanent, had a contract, had social security coverage, and received 30 days paid vacation annually. Employees and suppliers seem to win with all-inclusive resorts, but taxi drivers and local businesses suffer.

11. ASONAHORES estimates that the hotel sector employs about 0.8 employee per room.

12. Only Mexico, Spain, and the República Bolivariana de Venezuela had diplomatic relations with Cuba at the time.

13. See http://www.capcana.com.

References

GTZ (German Organisation for Technical Cooperation). 2006. "CSR beyond Charity: How the Core Business of All-Inclusive Resorts Contributes to Poverty Alleviation and Local Development in the Caribbean and Central America." GTZ, Eschborn.

UNWTO (United Nations World Tourism Organization). 2013. "Tourism Factbook." UNWTO, Madrid. http://www.e-unwto.org/content/v486k6/?v=search.

World Bank. 1974. "Dominican Republic: Puerto Plata Tourism Project." World Bank, Washington, DC. http://documents.worldbank.org/curated/en/1974/10/725561 /dominican-republic-puerto-plata-tourism-project.

———. 1979. "Dominican Republic: Second Puerto Plata Tourism Project." World Bank, Washington, DC. http://documents.worldbank.org/curated/en/1979/04/726598 /dominican-republic-second-puerto-plata-tourism-project.

———. 1991. "Dominican Republic: First and Second Puerto Plata Tourism Projects." World Bank, Washington, DC. http://documents.worldbank.org/curated /en/1991/04/724560/dominican-republic-first-second-puerto-plata-tourism-projects.

———. 2005. "Dominican Republic Mission Report." Unpublished report, World Bank, Washington, DC.

The Dominican Republic: Planning Future Sector Growth

Key Lessons

- The Dominican Republic has developed a mature tourism industry but must balance a desire to expand tourism with limited capacity in existing tourism zones.

- Expanding tourism in new zones will involve more effort and investment, but investors have been quick to respond due to the country's proven track record in tourism development.

- Without the Tourism Infrastructure Department, the Department of Tourism must improve its capacity to mobilize the private sector for new development.

- The Dominican Republic must choose between expanding the existing high-volume, low-value market or initiating a low-volume, high-value market.

Introduction

The Dominican Republic has solidly launched tourism with Puerto Plata, Punta Cana, Cap Cana, La Romana, and Boca Chica. The latter two, smaller, projects were conceived in parallel with the Puerto Plata development: (a) the exclusive La Romana resort (Casa de Campo) on the southeastern shore, promoted by the Gulf and Western Corporation, with major interests in sugar on the south coast, and (b) Boca Chica, near the capital.[1] Casa de Campo has grown into a resort and real estate development, drawing on its famous Teeth of the Dog golf course designed by Pete Dye. The town of La Romana has also grown beyond recognition. Boca Chica has been developed somewhat, but Caribbean storms have undermined its sand base, which has led to the deterioration of its beaches. Puerto Plata has also grown, to encompass Sosúa, Cofresi Beach, and Cabarete along the coastal road. The Dominican Republic is already a mature tourist destination.

Tourism Data

Overall, according to the United Nations World Tourism Organization (UNWTO 2013), the Dominican Republic received almost 4.5 million international arrivals in 2009; total international tourist receipts amounted to

$4.1 billion. According to the World Travel & Tourism Council (WTTC), tourism's total contribution to the Dominican Republic's gross national product was 16.5 percent in 2009, with total direct and indirect employment in the sector equivalent to 566,800 jobs.[2]

Sector Background and History

As mentioned in the previous case study, in the early 1970s President Joaquín Balaguer chose Puerto Plata as the first publicly supported site for tourism in the Dominican Republic. The region is diverse, with mountains in the background, extensive sugar plantations, sandy Caribbean beaches, and clear waters along the Atlantic coast, protected by reefs and fringed by palm trees. The site proved perfect for the development of tourism. The World Bank partnered with the government to fund the proposed development as two separate projects.

The Case

Tourism in the Dominican Republic is at a crossroads. Under consideration is whether the country should limit further expansion and concentrate on improving current capacity or launch new zones. Too much development in the existing zones could threaten already overloaded infrastructure systems, although some gaps could still be filled if managed conservatively. But if development moves too fast, tourism could outstrip the government's ability to provide a comprehensive regulatory framework.

In reality, the Dominican Republic has ambitious plans for expansion. Strong leadership will be needed to navigate the next phase of development. The overall program, shown on map 10.4, is as follows:

- Amber coast (Puerto Plata and Sosúa)
- Santo Domingo to La Romana
- Constanza and Jarabacoa
- San Cristóbal, Palenque, Peravia, and Azúa de Compostela
- Macao-Bavaro
- The south, including Barahona, Bahoruca, Independencia, and Pedernales
- The northwest, including Montecristi, Dajabón, Santiago Rodríguez, and Valverde
- Samaná Peninsula
- Nagua and Cabrera.

Map 10.4 Current and Projected Tourism Development Programs in the Dominican Republic

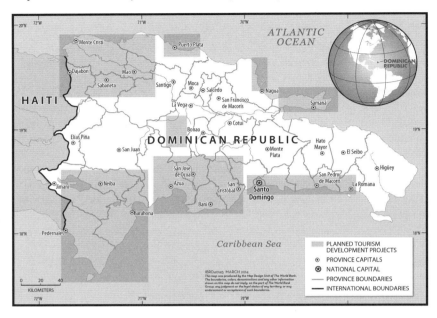

The country could easily double the size of its already large tourism market. But in addition to the country's physical carrying capacity, the population's desire to accommodate more tourism should be considered. Signs of stress already exist. The average daily expenditure of tourists has stagnated at about $100 a day for the last few years, and hotel occupancies have fallen.

So the question remains whether the Dominican Republic should continue the high-volume, low-mark-up strategy that has served it well or explore other options. Those options include securing a better return on existing assets (via higher expenditures and a longer season, for example); diversifying the product offering by bringing in the country's many historical, cultural, and natural attractions; promoting several parallel markets (different expenditure profiles); or concentrating on niche markets (adventure, ecotourism, or birding, for example) or on regional markets to capitalize on the assets of neighboring countries and islands. Central to that discussion are the country's overall economic, poverty reduction, social inclusion, and environmental concerns.

Results

One clear strategy would be to connect the various regions and promote more open tourism that is not dependent on the all-inclusive market. For years, travel in the Dominican Republic was hampered by bad roads that have now been considerably improved. The north coast is connected by a four-lane road from Puerto Plata to Río San Juan and beyond. Nevertheless, travel to Samaná is still difficult. A new highway from La Romana to Punta Cana cuts travel time from Santo Domingo almost in half. Indeed, the road network has been expanded considerably, and most resorts are connected to modern two-lane roads or highways.

Assuming that the Department of Tourism can improve its planning capacity and enable the private sector to bid on new projects, there is every reason to believe that the Dominican Republic can increase its tourism, broaden its range of products, and capture new market segments.

Notes

1. Boca Chica, located around a public beach 30 kilometers from Santo Domingo, received support from the Inter-American Development Bank (the loan was subsequently canceled). The Bank later helped to facilitate hotel credit once the climate for investment had improved.
2. WTTC, Economic Data Search Tool (http://www.wttc.org/research/).

Reference

UNWTO (United Nations World Tourism Organization). 2013. "Tourism Factbook." UNWTO, Madrid. http://www.e-unwto.org/content/v486k6/?v=search.

United Arab Emirates: Dubai's Transformation from Oil to Tourism

Key Lessons

- Strong political support, a commitment to quality, and a professional attitude drove the development of the tourism industry in Dubai.
- The public sector recognizes the importance of the private sector and supports it by offering incentives, setting standards for classifying tourism businesses, and enforcing contracts.
- Dubai continues to plan for the future, with support from external experts.
- Dubai's airport and its national carrier, Emirates Airlines, have played a major role in tourism development.

Introduction

Dubai has modernized rapidly. It began as an arid desert with light trading activity around the Creek, a small sea inlet that forms a natural harbor. It was remote, undeveloped, and unremarkable in the 1950s and 1960s. By 2010 Dubai boasted 560 hotels, a leading national airline with a worldwide network, and a position as a tourism and trade hub that extends from the Arab Republic of Egypt to India and South Africa. It has some of the most productive hotels in the world, with occupancy rates in the range of 80 percent, and is a sought-after location for most of the world's best-known hotel brands. Dubai is also a distribution and transport hub between East and West and is a popular vacation destination with Western Europeans. It is a remarkable success story.

Tourism Data

Already in 1993, Dubai had 167 hotels with 9,383 rooms; by 2010, it had an estimated 560 hotels and 67,369 rooms (table 10.5). Another two dozen hotels were under construction. Dubai hosted 4.7 million guests in 2002 and almost doubled that number to 8.6 million by 2010. The Arab market has been stable at about 1.9 million visitors since 2002, as shown in table 10.6. Europe is the second most important market, rising from 1.2 million in 2002 to 2.2 million guests in 2009, and Asia is the third, with 1.6 million in 2009.[1]

Table 10.5 Hotel Capacity in Dubai, 1993–2010

Year	Hotels	Hotel rooms	Hotel guests (millions)
1993	167	9,383	—
2002	272	23,170	4.7
2008	566	43,419	6.1
2009	530	58,188	7.5
2010[a]	560	67,369	8.6

Source: Government of Dubai, Department of Tourism and Commerce Marketing (http://www.dubaitourism.ae/).
Note: — = not available.
a. Estimated.

Table 10.6 Hotel Guests in Dubai, by Source Region, 2002 and 2009
millions

Source region	2002	2009
Arab	1.9	1.9
European	1.2	2.2
Asian	1.0	1.6
Russian Federation	0.3	0.5
African	0.3	0.4
Other	0.0	0.9
Total	4.7	7.5

Source: Government of Dubai Department of Tourism and Commerce Marketing (http://www.dubaitourism.ae/).

Sector Background and History

Modern Dubai grew around the Creek, which was dredged in the 1950s to enlarge its capacity. This excavation helped to develop trade, real estate, and tourism by opening up trading and transit facilities. In the 1960s oil was discovered, and in the early 1970s the United Arab Emirates were formed.[2] Led by the emir's family, Dubai seized the opportunity made possible by oil money to develop infrastructure, including the largest man-made port and distribution center in the world and an airport that can handle planes of any size.[3] Mindful that oil is a finite resource, the city leaders sought to secure the future by investing in nontraditional sources of growth, including tourism. Dubai took these efforts seriously and hired the best talent it could find to reach its goal. It was a high-risk, high-reward strategy that turned profitable. The recent world recession put a brake on growth in the city, but only for a short while, as the other emirates stepped in to help Dubai to restructure its debt.

The Department of Tourism and Commerce Marketing has been effective, and indeed the entire government has backed growth from tourism.[4] Dubai sees tourism as a planned and integrated sector that extends from the port to the two Palms—Palm Jumeirah and Palm Jebel Ali. The quality of hotels, restaurants, and services associated with tourism is promoted aggressively through some of the world's highest-profile celebrities, such as Colin Montgomerie, Andre Agassi, Tiger Woods, and Rory McIlroy, the golf champion from Northern Ireland. Although success is inspired by the emir and the royal family, who themselves have huge investments in Dubai, the rulers recognize the importance of the private sector and promote the strict enforcement of contractual engagements. The country sets standards for classifying hotels and furnished apartments, which extend to shops, restaurants, transport, and all first-contact points for tourists.

Results

Dubai has witnessed spectacular real estate expansion, having constructed the tallest building in the world and offshore, man-made sites, such as the Palm Jumeirah and the Palm Jebel Ali, built on reclaimed land in the ocean. Exclusive, high-end residential areas attract an affluent market. The Burj Al Arab, a self-styled seven-star hotel, and the Jumeirah Beach Hotel have rapidly become world landmarks, both for their architecture and for their quality of service. The parent chain is further diversifying by acquiring properties around the world, such as London's Dorchester and New York's Essex House. Subletting houses and apartments is also popular. Dubai set about planning for tourism in a highly professional manner and with total commitment to high quality. The effort included a 10-year vision of Dubai as "a high-class destination with world-class facilities," with support from experts in logistics and distribution, real estate development, and tourism operations as well as economic policies that support foreign direct investment (FDI).

Tourism is based on shopping, whether in the traditional markets (*souks*) near the docks (where traders from the Indian Ocean unload their wares), in modern malls, or at the airport, reputed to be the best such facility in the world. But Dubai also has superb facilities for beach tourism, water sports, golf, equestrian activities, desert tours, and other entertainment—in one of the hottest, most arid countries in the world. Temperatures are frequently very high. The weather is best from December to March, during the peak tourist season, with average temperatures amounting to 24°C (75°F) during the day; the hottest period is from June to September, when temperatures are over 40°C (104°F). Dubai is also famous for its indoor ski center and water parks.

For the most part, there are no impediments to visiting Dubai, although visa requirements could be simpler. Travelers from many countries require a visa, but many can obtain a visa for up to 90 days on arrival at the airport; citizens of a few countries (for example, the United Kingdom) do not require a visa. Dubai has a dress code that is consistent with the requirements of a conservative nation, but, if the rules are respected, they do not represent a hindrance to tourism.

No destination is more dependent on guest workers than Dubai, but they live in poor conditions, work in very difficult circumstances, pay high fees to obtain jobs, and have no prospect of becoming citizens.[5] Of Dubai's population of 1.9 million people, 85 percent are guest workers, principally from India and Pakistan.[6] Conditions are slowly getting better as the government works to improve the situation in response to the poor image the policies cast on the country.

Dubai's success has been to create new sectors funded by depleting oil assets, but what stands out are the seriousness and dedication with which the city addressed its future growth—the government believed in it, when many did not. The city has shown what is possible with vision, clear thinking, and hard work.

Notes

1. See the Government of Dubai, Department of Tourism and Commerce Marketing website (http://www.dubaitourism.ae/).
2. The seven emirates are Abu Dhabi, Ajman, Dubai, Fujairah, Ras al-Khaimah, Sharjah, and Umm al-Quwain. Abu Dhabi is the capital, and Dubai is the most populated.
3. Dubai International Airport has flights from more than 120 carriers and 260 destinations. Emirates Airlines itself flies to more than 100 destinations.
4. See http://www.dubaitourism.ae/.
5. "Emirates Making Peace with Migrant Workers," *New York Times*, August 6, 2007.
6. The female population is 400,000, and the male population is 1.5 million.

Arab Republic of Egypt: Tourism Diversification in Sharm El Sheikh

Key Lessons

- Diversification from its traditional cultural and historical tourism to Red Sea tourism led the Arab Republic of Egypt to emerge as a leader in world tourism.
- The creation and empowerment of the Tourism Development Authority (TDA) as a one-stop shop for investors encouraged investment by well-known investors.
- Political support for the development of a tourism master plan resolved many issues surrounding access to land and increased investment.
- Prompt responses to security threats helped to stabilize tourism in the country.

Introduction

For as long as people have traveled, Egypt has been a destination for tourists. Yet its emergence as a powerhouse of modern tourism is quite recent. Since the 1980s, the Arab Republic of Egypt has become a fully mature, large-volume destination, with 15 million tourist arrivals annually and foreign exchange revenues of $12.5 billion. Leading to that surge in growth was recognition that the government's role was to promote private investment in tourism rather than to acquire those investments, as might have been expected from a one-party state. In parallel, an effort to resolve the many bureaucratic issues surrounding access to land regulation was critical. The creation of the Tourism Development Authority (TDA) in 1991 as an agency of the Ministry of Tourism was a determining factor, producing the "champion" the sector had long been lacking.

Egypt was at the core of the "Arab Spring" during which its people overthrew the regime that had ruled for more than 30 years.[1] Although this may augur well for the country in the long term, the revolution halted tourism early in 2011. Nevertheless, the overall prospects for tourism in the country remain strong.

Tourism Data

In 1970 Egypt attracted fewer than 400,000 tourists,[2] but, by 1980, the number had reached 1 million. From 1990 to 2005, visitor arrivals grew from 2.9 million to 8.6 million, and by 2010 total international arrivals amounted to just under 15 million (UNWTO 2013). By 2010, tourist expenditures reached $12.5 billion (UNWTO 2013). The same year tourism contributed 8.1 percent to Egypt's gross domestic product (GDP) and remained the country's largest foreign exchange earner, ahead of worker remittances and petroleum products.[3] According to the World Travel & Tourism Council (WTTC), in 2010 total direct and indirect employment in the sector was equivalent to 3.7 million jobs.[4]

Sector Background and History

Egypt has an impressive array of tourism resources. Its archeological sites date from the 27th century B.C. and include unparalleled temples and tombs of the pharaonic dynasties, scattered along the Nile River from Aswan/Abu Simbel to Luxor, Karnak, and Cairo. The region has been important in the Arab world as a cultural, religious, and political center for centuries; Alexandria was a central city in the Roman and Christian eras. The Library of Alexandria and the Cairo Museum are renowned worldwide, and Egypt is known as a destination of "cultural and historic" significance for the Western and Arab cultures. Until very recently, the Sinai and Red Sea areas were of little interest as tourist attractions. Yet the opening to the Red Sea and its marine ecology led to Egypt's emergence as a leader in world tourism. The country is now a multiproduct destination with sun and sand, culture, and history that competes effectively with many other destinations in the Mediterranean, including Italy, Morocco, Spain, and Turkey. It is now experimenting with desert tourism, linking oases with the great trade routes and many of Egypt's smaller destinations. Its Nile River cruises (Cairo to Luxor) still hold a fascination for many tourists, especially first-time visitors to Egypt.

Although Egypt has been the victim of several terrorist attacks, notably on the country's cruise ships on the Nile River, it has responded promptly to these attacks.

Until the 1980s, when the motivation for traveling to Egypt was focused principally on its history under the pharaohs, the Ministry of Culture's Supreme Council of Antiquities was the dominant agency. It is still very powerful. At the same time, realizing that the country's northern coastline had no particular competitive advantage over other countries in the Mediterranean basin, the Ministry of Tourism gradually supported the development of beach tourism, specifically on the Red Sea.[5] The largest community is Sharm El Sheikh, a city of 35,000 that has become a well-known center for international conferences and beach tourism. The choice of the Red Sea was a game changer because, by 1988, tourism had become the country's leading source of foreign exchange earnings, with about a quarter coming from the Red Sea.

Many partners have supported Egypt in its quest to develop its tourism. The World Bank has funded both urban and tourism projects. The latter included infrastructure improvement in Luxor and Abu Simbel as well as support for the Cairo Museum. The U.S. Agency for International Development supported certain sectors. In particular, its work on the Red Sea helped to orient Egypt's decision to diversify into tourism. These and others agencies helped the government to focus on promoting private investment (rather than on providing public funding for hotels and other tourism establishments) and to complement the cultural offerings with beach tourism. The World Bank, along with the United Nations Development Programme and the United Nations Environment Programme, helped the government to prepare a Red Sea regional framework plan in the 1990s to protect biodiversity and prevent pollution (Global Environment Trust Fund 1992; World Bank 1979, 1990).

Results

Of the issues Egypt faced when diversifying its tourism near the Red Sea and on the Sinai Peninsula, access to land was the key concern that required urgent resolution. For the government to support private development, access to land under favorable conditions within the context of a master plan was critical for investors.[6] From the 1970s to the 1990s, the evolution of Egypt's institutional and regulatory framework for tourism lurched toward a solution that allowed a catalytic approach to tourism growth. While many changes were made to the legal and regulatory framework, there was also inertia in the system, an unwillingness to change, and, above all, interests that fought jealously to maintain traditional rights, such as those of the petroleum industry, the military, the ministries of the interior and of agriculture, and the Egyptian Environmental Affairs Agency. Finally, the Ministry of Tourism and the TDA were able to establish sites for tourism development, cleared of impediments and easements. The TDA is in effect a one-stop shop for tourism development, and it has developed capacity in evaluating investment proposals and assisting investors to prepare their projects for approval.[7] It also helps investors to obtain the approvals they need to move their projects forward. As a result of these investment promotion services, private investment has surged, with well-known names such as Hyatt Regency, Accor, Marriott, Le Méridien, Four Seasons, and Ritz Carlton becoming active players in Egypt's tourism sector (Abou Ali n.d.).

As noted, Egypt has had several terrorist attacks but has responded to them responsibly, well aware that they affect not only Egyptians but also visitors. These events have not dissuaded the government from its goal of attracting and retaining cultural visitors.

Egypt has gained a new appreciation for tourism and is respected in the world of cultural travel. But addressing the land issue on the Red Sea has forced the country to address broader institutional questions as well. Over time, its agencies have become more responsive to market requirements such that, with the possibility of greater democracy on the horizon, Egypt is well placed to position itself as a competitive destination offering an even wider variety of tourism products than in the past.

Notes

1. Following 18 days of popular protests, President Hosni Mubarak stepped down on February 11, 2011. The Supreme Council of the Armed Forces assumed the president's responsibilities and vowed to oversee a peaceful transition leading to free and fair presidential elections. As the Egyptian people grapple with their newfound freedom, the broader economic and social impact of these events, both in Egypt and across the region, will continue to unfold over an undetermined period of time. Prior to these events, the global economic slowdown had affected Egypt's real GDP growth, fiscal balances, inflation, and poverty levels. Real GDP grew 5.3 percent in fiscal 2010, up from 4.7 percent in fiscal 2009 (but still below the 7 percent average of fiscal 2006–08). Robust activity was evident in sectors such as construction, tourism, and communication, yet the recovery was too slow to have a significant effect on the rising unemployment rate. See http://data.worldbank.org/country/egypt-arab-republic.
2. These data are assembled from data published by the United Nations World Tourism Organization and the World Travel & Tourism Council as well as sources such as press releases and speeches by the minister of tourism.
3. WTTC, Economic Data Search Tool (http://www.wttc.org/research/).
4. WTTC, Economic Data Search Tool (http://www.wttc.org/research/).
5. The Red Sea is unique. Djibouti, Egypt, Eritrea, Israel, Jordan, Saudi Arabia, Sudan, and the Republic of Yemen all have shores on the Red Sea, which is 1,930 kilometers long and covers 270,000 square kilometers. It is connected to the Mediterranean Sea by the man-made Suez Canal and to the Indian Ocean by the Bab el-Mandeb Strait, making it the most saline body of water connected to the world's oceans. It has an abundance of coral and sea grass communities and extensive wetlands and mangrove forests (250 different coral reefs and 1,000 species of fish). Water temperatures range between 18°C and 21°C in winter and between 21°C and 26.5°C in summer. Underwater visibility is more than 30 meters, and diving is possible down to 45 meters. The climate is equatorial, with temperatures between 35°C and 41°C. All of this occurs in a zone far north of where it occurs naturally in other parts of the world. Critical for tourism, the land around the Red Sea has remained rural and largely undeveloped, although it is now threatened by oil prospecting as well as by the risk of excessive growth in tourism.
6. Land for tourism is leased for 25 years, renewable (but under a new contract).

7. The minister of tourism chairs the TDA; the board is made up of public officials from related ministries. It consults widely with the Egyptian Federation of Touristic Chambers, which has been quite active in proposing reforms that have become public policy. Broadly, the TDA has the mandate to execute national tourism strategies, including prioritizing areas for development and management, deciding on the disposition of public lands for tourism development, preparing infrastructure projects, and promoting private investment. It can also borrow internationally and locally.

References

Abou Ali, Ahmed M. G. n.d. "Egypt: Simplifying Procedures for Tourism Development in the Red Sea Area." Unpublished paper prepared for Foreign Investment Advisory Service, World Bank, Washington, DC.

Global Environment Trust Fund. 1992. "Arab Republic of Egypt: Red Sea Coastal and Marine Resource Management Project." World Bank, Washington, DC.

UNWTO (United Nations World Tourism Organization). 2013. "Tourism Factbook." UNWTO, Madrid. http://www.e-unwto.org/content/v486k6/?v=search.

World Bank. 1979. "Egypt: Tourism Project." World Bank, Washington, DC. http://documents.worldbank.org/curated/en/1979/04/726701/egypt-tourism-project.

———. 1990. "Egypt: Tourism Project." World Bank, Washington, DC. http://documents.worldbank.org/curated/en/1990/12/737863/egypt-tourism-project.

Indonesia: Protecting Cultural Heritage through International Tourism in Bali

Key Lessons

- Donor and external experts supported the development and implementation of a tourism master plan commissioned by the government.
- The master plan laid out a holistic development strategy that included investment promotion, infrastructure development, and the opening of a training institution.
- The master plan provided detailed regulations to protect the island's unique social and cultural assets and its environment.
- The Bali Tourism Development Corporation and the Bali Tourism Development Board provided strong public leadership, which made it easier to coordinate investments and enforce regulations.
- Successful resort development often needs to establish the first hotel as an anchor project and to include an aggressive investment promotion program.
- Modern and upgraded airports and liberalized air access policies drastically increased the flow of arrivals to Bali.
- Increasing internal migration and new tourism developments are overextending infrastructure and threatening the sustainability established through the first Nusa Dua project.

Introduction

Bali is a small island in the Indonesian archipelago with a big name as a world-class resort. It has a population of about 3 million, more than 90 percent of whom are Hindu, in the heart of the largest Muslim country in the world. Tourism in Bali dates to the 1930s, when Bali had a couple of renowned hotels, but modern tourism did not begin until the late 1950s or early 1960s, when a few young adventurers sought out new surfing destinations in the northern part of the island and in Kuta in the south, close to the capital. Today surfing tourists still go to the beach in droves. In 1969, as Bali began to attract more tourists, the government promoted large-scale tourism with a five-year plan. Nusa Dua, a large, secluded complex with numerous hotels that attract international visitors from around the world, grew out of this plan. Bali accounts for no more than

1 percent of Indonesia's territory, yet it attracts more than 30 percent of Indonesia's tourism. The island has become a giant among the world's large resorts, predominantly managing to preserve its traditional Hindu culture, while adapting to its evolving economy.

Tourism Data

According to the United Nations World Tourism Organization (UNWTO 2013), Indonesia had 6.3 million international arrivals in 2009. Total international tourist receipts were more than $6 billion. According to the World Travel & Tourism Council (WTTC), in 2009 Indonesia's total tourism contribution to gross domestic product was 10 percent, and total direct and indirect employment in the sector was equivalent to 9.3 million jobs.[1]

In 1973, 95,000 tourist arrivals were registered in Bali, at a time when the three major destinations in Asia—Singapore; Bangkok; and Hong Kong SAR, China—together generated about 1 million tourists. By 1978, however, arrivals in Bali had tripled to 278,000, and by 1991 they had reached half a million (World Bank 1985; UNWTO 2013). There were 1.4 million arrivals in 2000 and 1.96 million by 2010. The number of foreign passenger arrivals grew at an overall rate of 8 percent from 1990 to 2008, well above the international rate of about 5 percent. The surge in tourism survived terrorist bombings in 2002 and 2005—twice in Kuta and once in Jimbaran—both of which cut into Bali's growth.[2] Although tiny, Bali accounts for one-third of Indonesian tourism. It benefits from a regional market, including Australasia and Japan, while the number of tourists from China is increasing. It also appeals to small segments of the European and North American population. About two-thirds of visitors travel to Bali for pleasure, whereas one-third travel on business, either for conferences and for incentive trips (Bali Tourism Board 2013).

Sector Background and History

Bali has a dazzling array of tourism resources, including its sea, sand, and myriad water sports. Its handicrafts serve religious and secular purposes; statues and masks portray the island's Hindu deities, and wooden sculptures and pottery are handmade. Bali is also famous for its silks and batik textiles. Ubud is the cultural heartland of Bali and the center of its arts. Set in an area of ravines and terraced hillsides, it houses many of the island's leading artists and shrines. The hinterland includes inland lakes, terraced mountainsides, and agriculture that relies on bovine rather than mechanized power. Produce includes exotic fruits, spices, and fresh vegetables. Bali's culture permeates the island and draws tourists.

Map 10.5 Bali, Indonesia

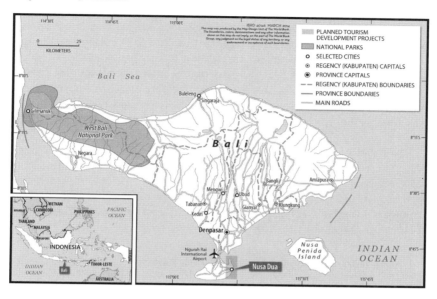

The Indonesian government's initial five-year national master plan (1969) identified six main areas for the development of tourism in the country. Bali was identified as a top site, as part of a grouping that also included Java and Lombok. The master plan for Bali, commissioned in 1970, was carried out by the French consulting group, Société Centrale pour l'Equipement Touristique d'Outre-Mer. It called for extensive investment to restore the temples and ruins and to protect the fine arts and handicrafts. Pacific Consultants, a Japanese firm, carried out the feasibility study, which was funded by the United Nations Development Programme and supervised by the World Bank. The chosen site was south of Denpasar, the capital, and close to the airport (map 10.5). Called Nusa Dua, or the second island, it gave its name to the project. The project took a long time to develop but survived to become a sustainable destination within an extraordinary culture.

The Case

The Bali tourism development project was launched in 1972. The site for the development of a major resort complex was chosen after exhaustive analysis. Criteria included the existence of economic activities other than tourism, the physical conditions of the site, and its proximity to access points. Two suitable locations emerged, with Bukit Peninsula on Nusa Dua chosen over the other setting located to the northwest of the island and remote from any airport. Proximity to the international airport and to Denpasar (as well as to Kuta and Sanur) gave Nusa Dua the advantage. In addition, the land on the site was unproductive scrubland with few alternative uses and inhabitants.

The objectives of the project were to promote international tourism in Bali, while increasing foreign exchange earnings, creating employment, improving income generation, and supporting regional development. The tourism plan was designed to protect the island's unique social and cultural life as well as its physical environment.

The project consisted of infrastructure and facilities for a self-contained Nusa Dua tourism estate (310 hectares) capable of supporting a minimum of 2,500 rooms; a hotel training school; an access road to the estate, improvements for 11 streets in central Bali, and a Denpasar bypass road; a 10-hectare demonstration farm and nursery; and technical assistance for implementation. Project costs before and after construction are shown on table 10.7.

Table 10.7 Costs of the Nusa Dua Project in Bali, Indonesia
US$, millions

Component	Appraisal	Actual	Change (%)
Tourism estate			
Water and sewerage	7.55	5.05	−14
Core amenities	2.32	4.32	139
Hotel training	1.14	3.85	334
Land	1.01	1.85	133
Other	9.49	12.05	62
Subtotal	21.51	27.12	61
Roads and bridges			
Nusa Dua access	0.16	0.75	—
Denpasar bypass	3.42	9.15	303
Other roads	8.16	—	—
Subtotal	12.74	9.90	17
Other components			
Telecommunications	1.26	0.06	−19
Pilot farm	0.27	0.03	−82
Technical assistance[a]	0.32	0.22	−31
Subtotal	1.85	0.31	−81
Total	36.10	37.33	3.8

Source: World Bank 1985.
Note: — = not available.
a. Provided by the Bali Tourism Development Board.

Development guidelines for the project stated that similar activities should be grouped in clusters (for example, hotels), with a centrally located tourist service center (and commercial area) and hotel training school. Conditions also stated that all hotels were to face the sea, with construction to be phased over a 10-year period. To the extent possible, all infrastructure was to be buried underground or integrated into the landscaping. A network of paths and access routes (including to the beaches) was to be accessible to tourists and to the Balinese public. The estate also used specific zoning rules to achieve low-rise, low-density buildings in harmony with Bali's traditional architectural standards. The regulations sought to protect the environment and to ensure against overcrowding, including

- Setbacks from the high-water mark of 30 meters
- Maximum building height of 15 meters
- Room density not to exceed 8 rooms per hectare
- A distance between buildings of at least 30 meters
- A project manager who exercises control of all exterior signage.

The government recognized Nusa Dua as a path-breaking, integrated resort project whose success would determine the future of tourism on Bali. A public agency operating under private law, the Bali Tourism Development Corporation, was set up in 1973 as the principal agency[3] to create and manage the tourism estate at Nusa Dua. It still manages investment promotion and landscaping at the site. The approach made coordination easier and cost control more effective, and it advocated strong policies to protect the local culture and environment, to enforce quality standards, and to ensure a coherent design. At about the same time, the government set up the Bali Tourism Development Board, staffed with senior government officials and chaired by the governor, to supervise the implementation of urban and tourism plans for the rest of Bali, including zoning, land use plans, and building regulations.

In the private sector, the Bali Hotel Association was the primary professional association, although several other groups ran their own associations—for example, the restaurant association. In addition, a private group, the Hindu Dharma Parishad, monitored religious practices. Along similar lines, but with both public and private participation, the Consultative and Promotional Council for Cultural Affairs was charged with preserving artistic standards. Citizens also played an active role in the daily life of the community and were represented by traditional village groups, which the Indonesian government wisely kept after independence (the Banjar and Desa Adat system). This structure continues today.

Results

The increase in tourism may have outstripped the government's capacity to manage growth. Part of the initial concept included the idea of Nusa Dua as a hub-and-spoke development, with tourists staying in Nusa Dua and fanning out for excursions. This idea has since been overtaken by events, with construction all over the island. In fact, the government supported the development of new resorts, although the results have not been successful. The private sector is pressuring for expansion, as is the case in many other countries. Nusa Dua's principles must be reestablished in terms of development guidelines and land use standards or excessive growth will destroy the very assets that made Bali such a desirable destination. In effect, the government was unable to regulate growth and the gradual sale of land for tourism development. The government did stop the expansion of hotel capacity in the early 1990s but relented shortly thereafter. One consequence is that infrastructure systems, particularly sanitation and solid waste management, are overextended, and proposed new hotels and resorts will result in increasing environmental degradation and possibly submerge Bali's traditional culture.

Table 10.8 shows the build-up of hotel capacity projected during the appraisal phase and at actual realization. The reasons for the delays were mostly economic in nature, although there were project delays and the investment promotion effort seems to have faded early on.[4] A clear lesson to be drawn for future projects is the need to establish the first hotel as an anchor within the project and to

Table 10.8 Build-up of Hotel Capacity in Bali, Indonesia, 1978–89

Year	Projections at appraisal	Actual build-up	Projections at project completion (May 1984)
1978	800	n.a.	n.a.
1979	1,300	n.a.	n.a.
1980	1,700	n.a.	n.a.
1981	2,000	n.a.	n.a.
1982	2,300	n.a.	n.a.
1983	2,500	450	450
1984	n.a.	n.a.	450
1985	n.a.	n.a.	850
1986	n.a.	n.a.	1,700
1987	n.a.	n.a.	1,975
1988	n.a.	n.a.	2,325
1989	n.a.	n.a.	3,000

Source: Calculations based on World Bank 1985.
Note: n.a. = not applicable.

include an aggressive investment promotion program as an explicit component of development. The anchor hotel provides a focal point for the resort that can subsequently be leased or sold.

When the project started in 1973, there were approximately 1,000 hotel rooms in Bali.[5] As infrastructure was built in Nusa Dua itself, 1,700 rooms were to be built by the private sector by 1980. But with the economic downturn, investors were slow to come forward, and it was 1983 before the first new hotel was opened, which was sponsored by the state-owned airlines, Garuda. Although the support was welcome, the delay underlined the difficulty of attracting private investors to a new resort. Subsequently, however, private investment picked up dramatically, and, by 1989, approximately 3,000 rooms were available.[6] By the turn of the century, there were 104 hotels and 17,000 rooms in Bali. Hotel capacity reached 19,522 classified rooms in 142 properties in 2009.[7]

Air Transport

The airport at Denpasar, built in 1969, was upgraded to accommodate jet airliners in the early 1970s. By 1972, Bali was receiving 73 flights a week, 42 purely domestic and only 6 directly from overseas. But there was a binding constraint: foreign scheduled flights to Bali could not use Bali as their final destination in Indonesia, although charter flights were not bound by this restriction. At the same time, the government was open to the possibility of joint ventures or pooling arrangements between Garuda and foreign carriers. These measures were intended to protect Garuda but were a real hindrance to the destination's development. Finally, the government conceded and declared Denpasar an international entry point, allowing foreign air carriers to terminate flights there. The effect on tourism was immediate and positive: growth was dramatic. Indeed, as in so many of the other cases, lack of access had been a major bottleneck to development.

Culture

Over many years, the Hindu religion found its way from Orissa in India down through Malaysia and Indonesia to the small island of Bali. The Balinese are fiercely proud of their traditions, culture, and distinctive architecture. The island has a Balinese architectural code known as Asta Kosala Kosali that protects its traditional style. The culture survives largely because it has the capacity to evolve and change. The most familiar sight is women carrying offerings to the gods on their heads. Every hotel has a sanctuary supervised by Balinese over which the hotel managers have no influence. The Monkey Dance, formerly a secular Ramayana performance, has gradually taken on religious meaning. Supervision by traditional Hindu Dharma Parishad and the Banjar and Desa Adat village management groups has been effective in protecting religious ethics and standards. However, greater interaction with non-Balinese has weakened their influence. Dance and Balinese Gamelan music are central aspects of the culture, accompanied by recognizable masks. Unlike dance in the west, many rituals take place in both secular and religious sites, including in the inner sanctums of temples, in their middle or outer courtyards, and even in locations away from the temple. Thus tourists and residents often find themselves in close proximity.

Change is in sight. The inhabitants of Bali have accepted new forms and styles of art introduced by outsiders. Although certain ancient dances and crafts such as tortoiseshell work, bone and horn carvings, and terracotta figures are dying out, new art objects and designs are being adopted, such as batik from Java, furniture styles, woodcarvings, and masks. At the same time, increasing numbers of Indonesians are attracted to Bali, and there are signs of stress. The government sensibly allowed the island to return to the traditional forms of Banjar and Desa Adat management, which helped to resolve cultural problems between the Balinese themselves, but the arrival of other Indonesians has caused the system to break down, and problems between the groups are rife. Moreover, the Balinese have limited influence in the national government.

Notes

1. WTTC, Economic Data Search Tool (http://www.wttc.org/research/).
2. The United States lifted its travel warning in 2008, but Australia, which suffered great loss of human life in the bombings, still retains a danger warning of level four on a scale of eight.
3. Telecommunications were implemented by the National Telecoms Corporation (Permutel) of the Ministry of Communications, and roads were the responsibility of the Ministry of Public Works and Power.
4. At the time of the project's development, today's international hotel investment conferences, which are attended by hotel companies, investors, real estate companies, and financing intermediaries, did not exist, which made connecting with principals a much more arduous task.
5. The Pacific Asia Tourism Association provided incentives to build several new hotels, giving Bali the critical mass needed to promote the island intensively. An additional three hotels with about 500 rooms were also completed in 1974.
6. Much of the investment in hotels was Balinese or Indonesian. Many investors appointed managers or concessionaires who marketed them under international brand names, such as Club Méditerranée, Conrad, Hilton, Sheraton, and Sol Mélia.
7. Added to these figures are an additional 19,682 in nonclassified establishments, representing 1,323 properties, such as bed and breakfasts and small lodges.

References

Bali Tourism Board. 2013. "Data Statistics." http://www.balitourismboard.org/stat _arrival.html.

UNWTO (United Nations World Tourism Organization). 2013. "Tourism Factbook." UNWTO, Madrid. http://www.e-unwto.org/content/v486k6/?v=search.

World Bank. 1985. "Indonesia: Bali Tourism Project." World Bank, Washington, DC. http://documents.worldbank.org/curated/en/1985/06/18489761/indonesia-bali -tourism-project.

Indonesia: Nihiwatu on Sumba

Key Lessons

- Strong leadership was needed to launch a profitable business that is attractive to clients and also supports environmentally and socially sound policies.

- The project took 10 years to launch due to the investors' desire to acquire land with full community consent.

- Development of the local community was set as a goal from the start of the project.

- Guests receive a high-quality tourism experience and are willing to donate to community development.

- Donations are channeled through the Sumba Foundation, a charitable foundation with a community plan that helps it to implement projects with guest donations.

Introduction

Small ecolodges often thrive on the passion and drive of their founders, and Nihiwatu is no exception. Nonetheless, the economic impact of ecolodges may be limited, and they cannot increase in size to any significant extent. If, however, they reach out to the local community and forge links of mutual advantage, they can pack much greater economic punch, pay more attention to conserving the environment, and enhance community welfare. Nihiwatu, on the island of Sumba in eastern Indonesia, is among the recent tropical resorts around the world that have embraced their responsibility as good corporate citizens and given back to local communities, while running a responsible tourism operation.

Tourism Data

According to the United Nations World Tourism Organization (UNWTO 2013), Indonesia had 6.3 million international arrivals in 2009. Total international tourist receipts were over $6 billion. According to the World Travel & Tourism Council (WTTC), in 2009 Indonesia's total tourism contribution to gross domestic product was 10 percent, and total direct and indirect employment in the sector was equivalent to 9.3 million jobs.[1]

Sector Background and History

The sponsors of Nihiwatu set out to find a site from which to launch a profitable business attractive to their clients, while supporting environmentally and socially sound policies that help to conserve the regional biodiversity and improve the lives of the local people. It took the sponsors 10 years to acquire full rights to access the land on which to build the 14-unit, high-end resort. Local tradesmen built the entire project using local materials where possible. The result is stunning: a resort that offers activities such as world-class fishing, surfing, and diving, not to mention spectacular scenery and a vivid local culture. They have also succeeded in support- ing the community through efforts "to ease the oppressive impacts of poverty for our neighbors," via ideas that are passed on to guests at the resort. The investors sought "to provide at least the basic needs everyone deserves to have, like clean water, functioning health facilities, and opportunities for education."[2]

The island of Sumba, in the Indonesian archipelago (about three hours east of Bali by air), is a remote island known for its ancestral traditions and culture, which are of great interest to visitors (map 10.6). The traditional Marapu religion still dictates (secular) daily life on the island, although somewhat fewer than half of the 600,000 inhabitants still practice it. In recent years, however, many citizens have converted to one of the five faiths recognized in Indonesia (Buddhism, Catholicism, Hinduism, Islam, and Protestantism).[3] Of Sumba's many rituals, the most spectacular are the Pasola ceremonies—martial arts events in which horsemen charge at each other with spears on a large

Map 10.6 Sumba Island, Indonesia

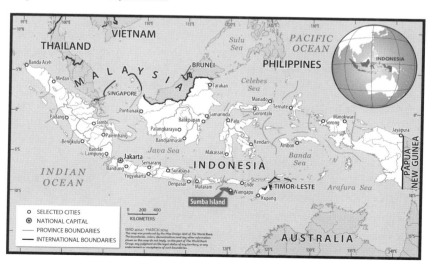

playing field. Serious injuries are common, and there are occasional deaths. The ceremonies are performed to set the right conditions for the rice harvest, as the local tradition asserts that blood on the ground is necessary to fertilize the land.

The Case

It used to take two and half days to reach Sumba from Bali when the Nihiwatu resort first opened. Its motto was "Nihiwatu is far from everywhere, that's the beauty of it!" Honeymooners and surfers are attracted to the site, but it also caters to families and offers multiple recreational activities. It can now be reached by air from Bali twice a week via a charter flight (Sumba used to be served by Indonesian domestic carriers, but many went out of business due to increased fuel prices). Nihiwatu maintains an office in Bali.

Despite many difficulties, Nihiwatu is successful and is known as one of the remotest sites in the world. Its owners have mastered the logistics of getting there, and guests are seldom disappointed.

In the early years of the project in the 1990s, Nihiwatu started working with its neighbors in nearby villages and found that the resort's guests were willing to support its efforts.[4] More than 500 guests at Nihiwatu have contributed funds for local projects, with donations amounting to roughly $400,000 annually. But the scale of need was overwhelming, even for modest improvements in poverty and overall health. Over time the owners wrote a community plan to provide drinking water and health care. With support from Nihiwatu's clients, this led to the establishment in 2001 of the Sumba Foundation, dedicated to alleviating poverty on the island.[5] About 90 percent of donations go directly to beneficiaries. Humanitarian aid is provided through village-based projects, and the underlying concept is to help the Sumbanese to help themselves. The result is a small but powerful operation that has improved the lives of local communities and families in ways that were unimaginable a few years ago. The resort has helped more than 20,000 people living in 147 villages in a 110-square-kilometer area of West Sumba, by

- Introducing nontraditional agriculture products and training health care workers
- Reducing malaria by 85 percent
- Building five new clinics treating 18,000 people
- Supporting 13 primary schools with water and toilets, tables and chairs, library books, and supplies
- Supplying clean water via 40 wells and 141 water stations
- Bringing in specialists who have contributed life-changing surgery to more than 200 patients (eye, burn, and cleft palate surgeries)

- Promoting a project to combat malnutrition that has helped hundreds of children.

Results

In 2010 Nihiwatu was awarded the top prize at the Responsible Tourism Awards as well as the award for reducing poverty most effectively. The judges stated that they "were impressed by the unquestionable scale of change achieved by this comparatively small resort. Nihiwatu has been able to leverage the income from what is a very luxurious tourism experience to alleviate poverty among the Sumbanese, and they have done so without compromising the comfort of that experience."[6] One of the judges, Justin Francis said, "This year, I have been heartened by the depth of commitment and connection our winners have shown to the local communities in their destinations. Their successes and pioneering spirits are remarkable, and the very real and authentic experiences they have created set responsible tourism apart. They also remind us that holidays can be both luxurious for visitors and enhancing for local people—helping build schools, water pumps, [and] clinics and conserving cultural and natural heritage."

The combined resources of Nihiwatu and the Sumba Foundation have resulted in a powerful mechanism for delivering local utility and health care services. It is a model that can be usefully implemented elsewhere.

Notes

1. WTTC, Economic Data Search Tool (http://www.wttc.org/research/).
2. For Nihiwatu's website, see http://www.nihiwatu.com/index.php?id=35.
3. Since 1965, under a policy enacted by President Suharto, to qualify for a public sector job, Indonesians must belong to one of the five recognized religions. Of Sumba's 600,000 inhabitants, 65 percent are registered Christians. The rest practice Marapu—a unique mix of faiths in the world's largest Muslim country. Sumbanese Christians respect the authority of the traditional Marapu leaders in matters related to traditional culture.
4. See also Turtle Island, Fiji, for a similar operation. Many safari lodges in Africa also provide outreach to local communities.
5. For the foundation's website, see http://www.sumbafoundation.org.
6. See http://www.responsibletravel.com/.

Reference

UNWTO (United Nations World Tourism Organization). 2013. "Tourism Factbook." UNWTO, Madrid. http://www.e-unwto.org/content/v486k6/?v=search.

Jordan: Integrating Tourism, Transit, and Industry in Aqaba

Key Lessons

- Integrated development has been key for generating interest in the zone and for creating a synergy between the sectors toward the goal of economic and community development.
- Leadership through the Aqaba Development Corporation and the Jordan Tourism Promotion Board and services provided by a one-stop shop encouraged investment.
- Clear roles exist for both the government and the private sector, with room for partnerships, creating a dynamic investment environment.
- Jordan used integrated development to create beach tourism on the Red Sea, diversifying its overall tourism offerings.

Introduction

Aqaba is at the heart of the Middle East, at the head of the Gulf of Aqaba, where Israel, Saudi Arabia, and Jordan meet (map 10.7). Through the Red Sea, the Gulf of Aqaba provides access to the world's great ocean trading routes. All of Jordan's trade passes through Aqaba, which is Jordan's only access to the sea, as does much trade to and from Iraq. It has built a reputation as a diving and beach resort, transportation hub, and special economic zone, which mutually support each other, despite a tumultuous political environment. This cooperation has been achieved through integrated tourism and industrial activity in the Aqaba Special Economic Zone (ASEZA), which has attracted billions of dollars in foreign direct investment (FDI) in industry, transit, and tourism. The goal was to attract $6 billion by 2020. The project had already attracted more than $7 billion by 2006, and the population of Aqaba had doubled to 100,000. Integrated development has been key for generating interest in the zone and for creating synergy between the sectors toward a goal of economic and community development.

Tourism Data

According to the United Nations World Tourism Organization (UNWTO 2013), Jordan received more than 7 million international arrivals in 2009, and

Map 10.7 Aqaba, Jordan

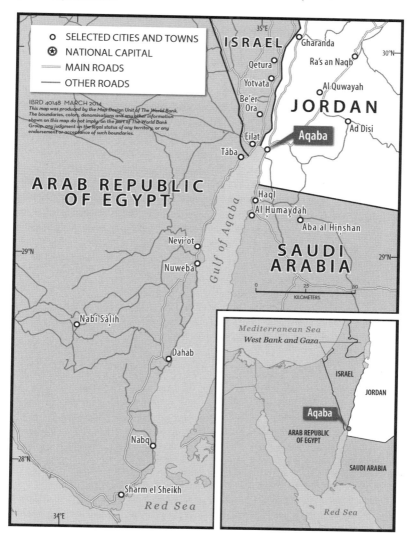

total international tourist receipts were \$3.4 billion. According to the World Travel & Tourism Council (WTTC), in 2009 Jordan's total tourism contribution to gross domestic product (GDP) was 22 percent, and total direct and indirect employment in the sector was equivalent to 309,000 jobs for a population of 5 million.[1]

Sector Background and History

Jordan has a successful tourism industry, based on its location in the heart of an area steeped in history and successive cultures. Additionally, it has generally pleasant weather, with temperatures ranging from a reasonable 20°C (68°F) in winter (November to March) to 30°C (86°F) and higher in summer. In addition to its 7 million international arrivals in 2009, it has a large middle-income domestic population that takes vacations, mostly northerners visiting the southern part of the country. Jordan's museums are popular destinations, attracting more than 3 million visitors a year.[2] The country had 204 hotels in 2009, with 15,000 rooms and 30,000 beds. As mentioned, tourism contributes about 20 percent to GDP and is expected to maintain that share over the next 10 years. In addition, employment in tourism is expected to grow to about 400,000 jobs over the next 10 years. Located in the regional administrative city or the south of Jordan, Aqaba has 54 hotels with more than 3,800 rooms that constitute more than 25 percent of national capacity. Visitors to Aqaba also visit Wadi Rum and Petra, two of Jordan's best cultural attractions.

Jordan has partnered with the World Bank on several tourism-related projects. The first, completed in 1983, focused on enhancing Jordan's cultural offerings in Jerash, Petra, and Wadi Rum; a second project deepened the reforms set up under the first (World Bank 1985, 2005). Two other Bank-supported activities were environmental: the Dana Wildlands Project, Phase I, and the Gulf of Aqaba Environmental Action Plan (World Bank 1996).[3]

The Aqaba Special Economic Zone was set up in 2001, with 375 square kilometers and 27 kilometers of coast bordering the Arab Republic of Egypt, Israel, and Saudi Arabia.[4] It was part of Jordan's economic decentralization program. It has an international container terminal, an open-skies airport, and outstanding tourism assets on the Red Sea. ASEZA has autonomous powers, including on land use, building regulations, and environmental and health issues, and it offers economic incentives.[5] As noted in its vision statement (box 10.6), it explicitly seeks to integrate tourism and industry.

BOX 10.6

Aqaba Special Economic Zone Vision Statement

ASEZA is a world-class Red Sea business hub and leisure destination enhancing the quality of life and prosperity of the community through sustainable development and a driving force for the economic growth of Jordan.

This is a powerful message for other countries that is often forgotten as tourism struggles to integrate into national economies. A sister organization, the Aqaba Development Corporation (ADC), is responsible for industrial and tourism promotion, working in cooperation with the Jordan Tourism Promotion Board. Together, they provide a one-stop shop for investment and aftercare. Although the government owns shares in ASEZA and ADC, they operate separately under private law and outsource many activities to the private sector, including consultants. Jordan has received large amounts of foreign investment in Aqaba, and donors support the program via training, planning, and policy reform.

The ASEZA model is based on a partnership in which the government is responsible for packaging land, providing external infrastructure, regulating the tourism zone, as well as providing municipal and local services. The private sector focuses on property development, internal infrastructure, the provision of shared services for enterprises, and the outsourcing of activities on behalf of the government, including planning, infrastructure development, the build-out of real estate, and property management. The private sector can play the role of master developer, owner-builder, or tenant. The mix of sectors makes for a dynamic environment of mutual support between projects of a very different nature and generates activity that is more "lively" than tourism alone.

Results

Aqaba is one example of a type of project that blends activities around trade and transport of goods and people. Other examples include Dubai and Abu Dhabi, which, in many ways, are similar ventures on a grander scale. The overall goal is to promote regional growth and job creation through diversification. The common threads include the focus on a sound transport base, with economies of scale in the provision of all transport infrastructure; environmental conservation within the zone as well as around it; the mitigation of harmful effects (for example, from the export of phosphates); and community development.

Initial problems in setting up the project were related to financing, physical planning, and regulations. Sovereignty issues in dealing with multiple parties also had to be overcome, and it took a long time to educate the people on the ASEZA's law and regulations. With the resolution of these problems, the zone is now operating well as an industrial area, and Aqaba is competitive with the Eilat and Egyptian resorts on the Red Sea.

Notes

1. WTTC, Economic Data Search Tool (http://www.wttc.org/research/).
2. Data from Jordan's Department of Statistics (http://www.dos.gov.jo/dos_home_e /main/index.htm).

3. For information on the Dana Wildlands Project, Phase I, see http://www.thegef
.org/gef/project_detail?projID=355. For information on the Gulf of Aqaba
Environmental Action Plan, see http://projects.csg.uwaterloo.ca/inweh/report
.php?ListType=ProjectDocument&ID=7&MenuItemID=35.

4. See http://www.aqabazone.com. Some of the land was acquired in a trade with
Saudi Arabia.

5. For example, no customs duties, 100 percent foreign ownership, and flexible labor
policies (up to 70 percent is foreign labor). It applies a 7 percent sales tax, 5 percent
corporate tax, and 6 percent tax on land purchases. Capital and profits are
transferable.

References

UNWTO (United Nations World Tourism Organization). 2013. "Tourism Factbook."
UNWTO, Madrid. http://www.e-unwto.org/content/v486k6/?v=search.

World Bank. 1985. "Jordan: Tourism Project." Project Completion Report 5729, World
Bank, Washington, DC. http://documents.worldbank.org/curated/en/1985/06
/741958/jordan-tourism-project.

———. 1996. "Hashemite Kingdom of Jordan: Gulf of Aqaba Environmental
Action Plan Project." Project Document 15290 JO, World Bank, Global Environment
Facility, Washington, DC. http://documents.worldbank.org/curated/en/1996/05/696557
/jordan-gulf-aqaba-environmental-action-plan-project.

———. 2005. "Jordan: Second Tourism Development Project." Project Completion
Report 34554, World Bank, Washington, DC. http://documents.worldbank.org
/curated/en/2005/12/6538687/jordan-second-tourism-development-project.

Kenya: Business and Conference Tourism in Nairobi

Key Lessons

- Public leadership simplified tourism policies and refined the development, marketing, and regulation of tourism to encourage growth.
- Product diversification in the meetings, incentives, conferences, and exhibitions (MICE) market mitigated the decline in tourism brought on by the 2007 violence.
- Development of the MICE market was successful due to a focus on improved facilities, services, and training institutions and collaboration between the public and private sectors.
- High-quality training, competitive salaries, and career opportunities supported by legislation have retained staff in Kenya.

Introduction

Kenya is renowned for its leisure products, but the country has adapted its marketing and promotion to strengthen another segment, business tourism, to recover from a dip in its leisure business. It serves as an example of how market segments can be diversified and yet compete with each other in international markets. This case underlines the importance of high-quality training for the meetings, incentives, conferences, and exhibitions (MICE) sector. Kenya is considered the originator of wildlife safaris and is also noted for its white-sand beaches. It is the perfect "bush-beach" destination. However, outbreaks of violence following the 2007 elections sent international arrivals tumbling 40 percent to 1.2 million visitors and trips to national parks dropping 36 percent to 1.6 million visitors in 2008 (Kenya Ministry of Tourism 2010b). These events served as a wake-up call. Kenya responded by engineering a dramatic turnaround led by the minister of tourism, who adopted an aggressive marketing campaign coupled with investments in conference and business facilities and in the MICE environment (Tribe Hotel 2010). Conference tourism became the fastest-growing segment in tourism, with a higher financial return than leisure tourism (Mwalya 2009). A great deal of effort went into exploring new markets in China, India, the Netherlands, the Russian Federation, South Africa, Tanzania, Uganda, and the United Arab Emirates (Maina 2010), putting Nairobi's airport to good use.[1]

Tourism Data

According to the United Nations World Tourism Organization (UNWTO 2013), Kenya received 1.49 million international arrivals in 2009, and total international tourist receipts amounted to $1.1 billion. Tourism directly and indirectly accounts for 11.5 percent of gross national product, with the MICE market playing an enhanced role. Total direct and indirect employment in the sector is equivalent to 504,300 jobs.[2]

Of travelers to Kenya, 12 percent are on business. The country is now ranked fourth in Africa after South Africa, the Arab Republic of Egypt, and Morocco for business meetings (Oyuke 2010). The government aims to triple the MICE segment to $73 million by 2013 (Miima 2009).

Nairobi hotels operate at full capacity in peak season, and, even during the low season, occupancy reaches 85 percent (World Bank 2010). These figures reflect the high demand and the shortage of premium accommodation. In 2010 prices rose 31 percent over an 18-month period to an average of $205. The sharp increase in prices is attributed by some to the heavy discounting that the industry had to make in 2008 following the slump in bookings (Maina 2010).

Sector Background and History

A key feature of Kenya's tourism program was the partnership between sector agencies and the private sector.[3] The need for this partnership was recognized and organized to drive the MICE tourism sector in Nairobi. In 2008 Kenya passed a comprehensive law introducing new policy and addressing bureaucratic constraints, including an overwhelming 44 different legislative instruments used to regulate tourism (World Bank 2010), overlapping functions in 15 public organizations that regulated the sector, and 11 associations and civic organizations that represented the different markets (World Bank, IFC, and MIGA 2009). The legislation focused on product quality, accommodation capacity, infrastructure, marketing, safety and security, and travel advisories. In 2010 a tourism bill was proposed as a single piece of legislation to refine the development, marketing, and regulation of sustainable tourism, including upgrades of the Kenyatta International Conference Center and Kenya Utalii College, Kenya's well-known hotel school (Kenya Ministry of Tourism 2010a).

The Case

Business and conference tourism is highly dependent on the investment climate and operating environment. Nairobi offers good opportunities for add-ons,

Figure 10.1 Typical Overall Hotel Expenditure in Nairobi, Kenya

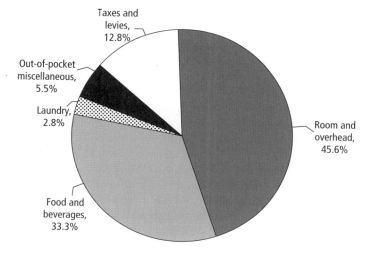

Source: Global Development Solutions, cited in World Bank 2010.

such as safari trips over the weekend or day trips to Nairobi's national park. In 2010 the price of a room in a five-star hotel in Nairobi ranged from $165 to $266. For a five-day conference, the average daily expenditure is approximately $180 or more than $900 a week (World Bank 2010). Overall expenditure in a typical hotel is shown in figure 10.1.

As shown in the figure, room sales account for nearly 46 percent, food and beverages for 33 percent, laundry for almost 3 percent, and out-of-pocket expenses for 5.5 percent. Taxes and levies constitute almost 13 percent of the value chain in Nairobi, with value added tax topping the bill (at 57 percent of taxation), followed by a service charge (35.7 percent) and training levy (7.5 percent). Most are taxes on tourists, which push up prices and eventually may contribute to a softening of demand, especially as new hotels open. Hotels in Nairobi are increasingly sourcing many supplies in the local market, of which many are locally produced (World Bank 2010). Over the last decade, the quality of food and services has improved markedly (World Bank 2010). One of Nairobi's hotels, the Tribe Hotel, was recently chosen as Condé Nast's top 100 for its blend of style, service, and technology (Tribe Hotel 2010).

Regarding the operating costs of hotel rooms, variable costs account for 37 percent of departmental sales (rooms, food and beverages, and other hotel departments), and the wage bill accounts for 41 percent (Tribe Hotel 2010). In the food and beverage department, costs consist of departmental sales of 30 percent and a wage bill of 57 percent (World Bank 2010). These wages are much higher than in many hotels in Africa, reflecting efforts to enhance the quality of service and retain staff (Tribe Hotel 2010).

Results

Investment in marketing and promoting MICE tourism since 2008 has clearly stimulated demand in Nairobi and catalyzed the refurbishment of hotel and conference facilities in the city. The shift from a purely leisure market rippled through the sector, with very positive results. It also provoked greater effort not only to train staff but also to retain them in Kenya by paying competitive salaries and providing career opportunities, as was intended by the 2008 legislation. The constraints include a shortage of premium conference facilities, a limited number of high-quality restaurants, unreliable communications, and the high cost of electricity (World Bank 2010). A critical factor is corruption, with 75 percent of firms in Kenya reporting that they have made informal payments to "get things done," often paying as much as 12 percent of a contract's value (World Bank 2010). Transparency International ranks Kenya as one of the world's 10 most corrupt countries (U.S. Department of State 2008).

This case study offers three key takeaways for other mature destinations: avoid relying on one product line (although it may pay to focus on one product in the initial stage of a recovery), diversify, and, particularly following a crisis, invest in positive marketing and promotion (Okech 2009).

Notes

1. This case study is adapted from Spenceley (2010).
2. WTTC, Economic Data Search Tool (http://www.wttc.org/research/).
3. These included the Kenya Tourist Development Corporation, the Kenya Tourist Board, Kenya Utalii College, Kenya Tourism Federation, the Hotel and Restaurant Authority of Kenya, the Kenya Investment Authority, the Kenya Association of Tour Operators, and Ecotourism Kenya.

References

Kenya Ministry of Tourism. 2010a. "Tourism Bill Published." Ministry of Tourism, Nairobi. http://www.tourism.go.ke/ministry.nsf/pages/news_25_11_10?opendocument.

———. 2010b. "Visitor Arrivals and Departures by Purpose of Visit." Ministry of Tourism, Nairobi. http://www.tourism.go.ke/ministry.nsf/pages/facts_figures.

Maina, W. 2010. "Nairobi Hotels Ranked Most Expensive." *Business Daily,* September 21. http://www.businessdailyafrica.com/Corporate%20News/Nairobi%20hotels%20ranked %20most%20expensive/-/539550/1014872/-/1121442/-/index.html.

Miima, E. 2009. "Launch of Kenyatta International Conference Centre (KICC) Strategic Plan." Speech presented at the official launch of the KICC Strategic Plan (2008–12), Nairobi, October 14. http://www.kicc.co.ke/index.php?kicc=speeches2.

Mwalya, K. 2009. "What It Takes to Reap from Emerging Conference Tourism." *Business Daily,* June 22. http://www.businessdailyafrica.com/-/539444/613550/-/view /printVersion/-/ci2sy6/-/index.html.

Okech, R. N. 2009. "Managing Sustainable Events: Using Kenya as a Case Study." In *Event Management and Sustainability,* edited by R. Raj and J. Musgrave, 232–51. Oxfordshire, U.K.: CABI International.

Oyuke, J. 2010. "Kenya Bags Top Global Ranking in Tourism." *Standard,* June 14. http:// www.standardmedia.co.ke/InsidePage.php?id=2000011636&cid=4.

Spenceley, A. 2010. *Tourism Industry: Research and Analysis Phase II: Tourism Product Development, Interventions, and Best Practices in Sub-Saharan Africa, Part 2: Case Studies.* Washington, DC: World Bank.

Tribe Hotel. 2010. "Tribe Puts Kenya on World." Press release, May 6. http://tribehotel .wordpress.com/2010/05/06/press-release-tribe-puts-kenya-on-world/.

UNWTO (United Nations Tourism Organization). 2013. "Tourism Factbook." UNWTO, Madrid. http://www.e-unwto.org/content/v486k6/?v=search.

U.S. Department of State. 2008. "2008 Investment Climate Statement: Kenya." Department of State, Washington, DC. http://www.state.gov/e/eeb/ifd/2008/100889 .htm.

World Bank. 2010. *Kenya's Tourism: Polishing the Jewel.* Washington, DC: World Bank, Finance and Private Sector Development, Africa Region.

World Bank, IFC (International Finance Corporation), and MIGA (Multilateral Investment Guarantee Agency). 2009. "Licensing Case Studies: Tourism Sector." Foreign Investment Advisory Service, Washington, DC.

Republic of Korea: Tourism in Kyongju

Key Lessons

- The government did not wait for the results of a national tourism plan to begin construction of the Kyongju project, assuming that the project had every chance of succeeding.

- Making reliable market projections for new development on greenfield sites is challenging.

- A lack of market research and marketing resulted in lower-than-expected demand and led to the project's failure.

- Large tourism projects are complex and require coordination among multiple agencies, which were new and untested in the Republic of Korea.

Introduction

In the early 1970s, the government of the Republic of Korea sought new sources of growth and diversification and concluded that tourism offered the right prospects. Accordingly, it pressed ahead with the Kyongju project, judged to be a sure-starter, without waiting for the results of a national master plan that was under way. Unfortunately, the project proved premature and folded as the anticipated market failed to materialize. At that time, Korea hosted fewer than 40,000 foreign tourists nationally, and Kyongju failed to create a tourism product that could attract more.

Tourism Data

In the 1970s, international tourism in Korea was negligible.[1] Visitors averaged about 42,000 annually in the mid-1960s; approximately half were Americans, mainly on business or official duty. Of the remainder, most were expatriate Koreans visiting their families. The number of foreigners taking vacations in the country rose from 19,000 in 1966 to 210,000 by 1972, growing at an average annual rate of 50 percent during the period. The following two years saw a deepening of this trend. More than twice as many foreigners visited Korea on vacation in 1973 as in 1971, spurred by the doubling of the Japanese market to 80,000 visitors, the potential core market for Kyongju. Travel receipts increased from $7.7 million in 1965 to $31.2 million in 1971 or 6.5 percent of total receipts from invisible exports (World Bank 1973).[2] By the end of 1975, capacity in international hotels increased more than 40 percent to 5,000 rooms, due to higher demand as well as to liberal investment incentives (five-year income tax holidays, exemption of customs duties on imported materials, and public provision of basic infrastructure).

According to the United Nations World Trade Organization (UNWTO 2013), Korea received 7.8 million international arrivals in 2009, with $13.3 billion in tourism receipts. According to the World Trade & Tourism Council (WTTC), in 2009 tourism's total contribution to gross domestic product (GDP) was 6.3 percent, and total direct and indirect employment in the sector was equivalent to more than 1.5 million jobs.[3]

Sector Background and History

Located north of Busan on Korea's southeastern coast, Kyongju is the ancient capital of Korea and its preeminent cultural and historic center. Kyongju has unique archeological monuments, including an observatory built in 634 A.D. that is the oldest of its kind in Asia, a 25-foot-high golden Buddha dating to the eighth century, and many other buildings and shrines of the Silla Dynasty (58 B.C. to 935 A.D.). Many of these cultural relics had fallen into decay, and the government decided to focus on major restoration work to attract touristic and cultural interest. Although it is several hours away, Kyongju is easily accessible by road and rail from Busan and Seoul, the two main entry points into Korea for foreign visitors.[4]

The Case

In 1971 the government asked the World Bank to assist it in assessing the potential for tourism in Korea. A sector survey mission visited the country and, on the basis of its findings, agreed with the Korean authorities that the Kyongju area offered excellent prospects for attracting greater numbers of foreign visitors. The World Bank was actively involved in the evaluation and in the subsequent refinement of the master plan for the urban and touristic development of the area. Access was mostly by air through Busan and Seoul airports, each about two hours away from Kyongju.

A comprehensive national tourism study was also under way within the Korean presidency, supported by the U.S. Agency for International Development, to provide the framework for the long-term development of tourism. The government's preliminary review of opportunities for tourism development led to the conclusion, supported by the Bank, that prospects for a tourist resort at

Kyongju were so promising that the proposed project could be implemented without waiting for completion of the long-range study.

The Kyongju project was to upgrade urban and tourism facilities in Kyongju, Bomun Lake, and surrounding areas, including

- Construction of a dam and a small irrigation system
- Expansion of the water supply, sewerage, and solid waste disposal systems
- Supply of electrical and telecommunication facilities
- Realignment of 57 kilometers of access roads to historical monuments and to Bomun Lake and construction of secondary roads within the resort
- Establishment of a hotel school for 250 to 300 students
- Improvements in nearby picturesque and traditional villages
- Initiation of a feasibility study for another potential tourist area, Cheju Island.

The total project cost was an estimated $50 million, and a World Bank loan of $25 million was made, representing the project's foreign exchange cost. The economic rate of return on the investments was estimated at 16.5 percent.

The project was expected to be fully operational in 1984. By that time, it would provide direct employment for about 5,400 workers in hotels and 1,500 workers in other facilities. Indirect employment generated in construction, agriculture, handicrafts, transportation, and other services is difficult to compute but could have amounted to between 10,000 and 15,000 persons.

A site at Bomun Lake, some 6 kilometers from Kyongju, was selected for construction of the resort. The government acquired approximately 1,000 hectares of land. Its plan for developing the area envisaged the construction of 6,000 hotel rooms, condominiums, apartment buildings, youth hostels, and camping sites over a 20-year period. The first phase consisted of several hotels with total capacity of 3,000 rooms and the provision of utilities, services, and recreational facilities. This phase was to be completed by 1982, corresponding to the proposed project. Its principal components were the construction of a ring road around an existing artificial lake; the street network; hotel sites parallel to the shore; sites for traditional restaurants; an amenity core, including shops, theaters, and community facilities such as a fire station and health clinic; and recreational facilities such as a sports ground, a marina, and a golf course.

Results

Ultimately, however, the project did not achieve its objectives and was abandoned. Infrastructure was not completed and hotels were not built.

The government and the Bank perhaps should have waited for the national tourism study to be completed, although the study would most likely not have offered reservations concerning the Kyongju project.

Kyongju highlights the difficulty of making market projections for greenfield sites. Although the restoration work has been remarkable and good recreational facilities are available in the area (for golf, swimming, and other sports), the information was not disseminated. This case also highlights the complexity of tourism projects that require coordination among many agencies. In this case, many of the agencies were new and untested. Also, the ground transportation required to reach Kyongju added several hours to the journey to Korea by air.

Notes

1. However, tourism eventually did grow, and international arrivals reached 7.8 million in 2009.
2. Tourism is often described as an invisible export since it is a service that is performed within the country but contributes to foreign exchange.
3. WTTC, Economic Data Search Tool (http://www.wttc.org/research/).
4. In 1972 about 1.2 million Koreans and more than 76,000 foreigners visited the city. Of the latter group, only half stayed overnight, reflecting the shortage of hotel rooms.

References

UNWTO (United Nations World Tourism Organization). 2013. "Tourism Factbook." UNWTO, Madrid. http://www.e-unwto.org/content/v486k6/?v=search.

World Bank. 1973. "Appraisal of the Kyongju Tourism Project, Korea." World Bank, Washington, DC.

Maldives: Incremental Expansion of Tourism and Environmental Management on Island Resorts

Key Lessons

- Maldives has developed a superior planning framework and environmental controls: policy dictates one resort per island and strict environmental and design standards.

- To lessen the burden of development, the government requires investors to establish infrastructure.

- The transparent and objective evaluation of bids to lease islands built confidence in the system.

- The government's use of master plans balanced growth and quality of investments, putting in place many regulations to ensure incremental growth and environmental management.

- The country's open policy pertaining to airline access has benefited the expansion of tourism. Nonetheless, air access poses constraints, as planes cannot stay on the ground for long due to lack of space.

- Maldives has an impressive record of growth and rapid expansion of its lodging capacity, achieving this success by managing its land effectively through the leasing of islands and by improving access to the island resorts.

Introduction

Tourism in Maldives has been a hard-won victory. The island nation is far from its markets in Europe, Asia, and North America; many of the islands are only 2 meters above sea level and thus subject to the ravages of climate change and rising seas; fresh drinking water is in short supply; the country is on the fringe of the two annual Indian Ocean monsoons (southwest and northeast); most goods used in the manufacture of tourism projects are imported; transportation between the islands is expensive, and the airports require land reclamation and complex engineering; and about half of the staff in hotels are foreign (in the 1970s when tourism started, the country had no specialized expertise). Not the least of its problems is the political situation, which has been tense.[1]

Nonetheless, Maldives has overcome these obstacles to build a world-class industry, often considered one of the most coveted destinations in the world.[2] It started quietly with adventurers seeking out surfing and diving opportunities as well as new destinations in a fast-growing industry (Maldives is now on the calendar of international surfing competitions). Subsequently, traders in Maldives began investing in tourism, using their skills in trading to fashion resort investments. As interest in the country rose, the government decided on a policy of one resort per uninhabited island, with infrastructure provided by the investors. After initial difficulties pertaining to private investment in the first master plan, this decision led to the development of a well-organized sector, and an emphasis on sound environmental conditions (recommended in the master plan) resulted in "green" solutions that have helped to strengthen the area's image as a custodian of the environment. With more than 700 uninhabited islands and considerable room for expansion, the country is fostering a sound environmental image. Several resorts have received "green" endorsements, including the Green Globe, ISO 14001, or a similar standard. Maldives has attracted many of the world's top operators as well as built a homegrown industry. The country received 683,000 arrivals in 2008, more than double the national population (UNWTO 2013).

Tourism Data

According to the United Nations World Tourism Organization (UNWTO 2013), in 2009 Maldives received 659,000 international arrivals, and total international tourist receipts amounted to $1.4 billion. According to the World Travel & Tourism Council (WTTC), in 2009 tourism's total contribution to gross domestic product (GDP) was 48 percent, and total direct and indirect employment in the sector was equivalent to 74,100 jobs.[3] Tourism growth rates have been impressive, often well above regional or global growth rates, at about 10 percent since 1972. As a consequence of the world recession, growth slowed in 2007, but by 2008 Maldives had recovered, receiving more visitors than it had received in 2005. The country attained 5 million bednights for the first time in 2004, although the number dropped for a few years before rising again, reaching the current 5.5 million bednights. Tourism to Maldives was less affected by the economic recession than tourism to other countries and rebounded in 2009. In the first seven months of 2010, tourism increased 29 percent month on month compared with 2009. The three key markets are Germany, Italy, and the United Kingdom. The United Kingdom has traditionally been the largest market, although, in 2009, it was overtaken by China, which became the largest market for Maldives. Arrivals from the Russian Federation, Japan, and Australasia also increased. Typically, Maldives is a winter destination, with a peak season from November through March-April. In recent years, however, the summer season, June to September, has also been promoted. In fact, since 2004, there has been little marked seasonality, with resorts busy year-round, possibly due to lower prices during the off-season (UNWTO 2013).

Sector Background and History

Maldives lies about 500 kilometers to the west-southwest of India and Sri Lanka (map 10.8). It has a unique geological formation of 1,190 coral islands grouped into 26 atolls (with 200 inhabited islands and approximately 100 islands with tourist resorts). The archipelago, 1,000 kilometers long and 100 wide, is located strategically along major sea-lanes in the Indian Ocean. Taken together, the islands have a landmass of no more than 300 square kilometers. Its coral reefs host the densest mass of tropical fish in the world. The temperature ranges from 26°C to 31°C, with humidity between 78 and 82 percent. Officially, the months of May to October are "sunny-rainy" and November to April are "sunny-dry." Even in the rainy season, there are long spells of sunshine.

The interaction between tourism and the environment is important both for conserving the environment and for maintaining the quality of tourism. The overriding environmental issue is that of rising seas, a result of climate change, which expose the islands to flooding, as most are no more than 1 or 2 meters above sea level. Considerable effort has been expended in Malé, for example, to protect its coastline, including significant land reclamation and the construction of substantial retaining walls. Maldives has 25 officially designated marine protected areas, with one combining marine and terrestrial biodiversity protection measures. Lagoons and reefs make up 21,300 square kilometers of Maldives, and the reefs contain more than 200 coral species. Coral bleaching killed as much as 90 percent of the coral in 1998 (as a result of El Niño winds). The coral was showing signs of recovery when the tsunami hit in 2004, covering it with sand, which retards coral growth. However, the harsher forms of degradation due to coral and sand mining, dragnet fishing and poisoning, and dynamite fishing have been outlawed in Maldives, and protection measures are in place for the resort islands.

Tourism in Maldives is the responsibility of the Ministry of Tourism and Civil Aviation, under Law 2/99.[4] The ministry is responsible for setting policy and for planning and implementing certain functions, such as marketing, through the Maldives Tourism Promotion Board and the Government Tourism Information Office in Germany. The ministry has acted astutely as tourism has grown and matured. It has relied on advice from two tourism master plans. The first covered the period 1983–90 and set a ceiling of 12,000 beds. The plan was successful in that it "captured the entrepreneurial spirit of the Maldives private sector quite succinctly" and simultaneously channeled growth away from a laissez-faire model that was threatening tourism's future. It also developed Malé as a hub at the center of the industry, with growth poles to be selected where needed in the archipelago. The plan also recommended that the Department of Tourism become a ministry, which occurred in 1988. The second tourism master plan covered the period 1995–2005. It recognized the preeminent role of the private sector in resort development and underscored the government's role as being "to facilitate the business

Map 10.8 Maldives

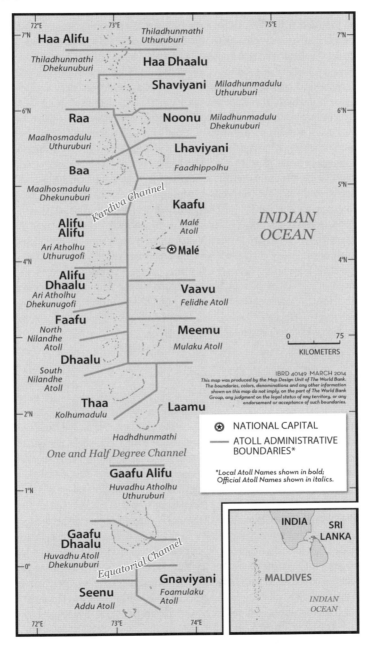

environment whereby the private sector can operate efficiently" rather than to provide infrastructure. Indeed, a key success factor is facilitating the private provision of infrastructure. This formula has worked remarkably well, with resorts providing their own infrastructure under guidelines from government. In summary, while the first tourism master plan focused on growth, the second one emphasized the quality of growth—its distribution, human resource development, the environment, institutions, as well as marketing and promotion. The government has been particularly efficient in putting in place design standards to protect the environment, as discussed below. The ministry works closely with the ministries of planning and finance and the central bank on tourism matters.[5]

The services sector in Maldives has one of the highest ratios of international tourism receipts to GDP in the world.[6] Until recently, the country had no corporate tax revenue from tourism, and taxation was based on long-term resort leases negotiated on a per bed basis for each individual resort island. A value added tax on tourism of 3.1 percent, introduced in January 2010 (the tourist goods and services tax, TGST), has been raised to 12 percent, and a second amendment to the Tourism Act seeks to replace resort leases with land rents.[7] In addition, a business profit tax was signed into law in January 2011, after it twice failed to pass in parliament. By July 2013, the bednight tax of $8 that each tourist pays will be phased out, replaced by the higher TGST, but tourists pay a one-time airport tax (or user charge) of $12 (included in the airline ticket). The other major source of taxation is a duty on all imports (except for initial construction, which is exempt as an incentive).

The Case

Accommodation capacity has grown rapidly in recent years to a total of 10,485 rooms in 2009, about 21,000 beds (UNWTO 2013). Malé has 8 hotels, 28 guest inns, and 113 vessels (used as lodging and for touring). Approximately 100 islands have resorts on them, with between 20 and 400 rooms; about 30 have 100 or more rooms. Occupancies have historically been high, peaking in 2004 at 84 percent. Following political unrest in 2005, occupancies dropped to 64 percent, but have since risen to over 80 percent again. The average length of stay is about eight days, reflecting a blend of one-, two-, and three-week stays that are typical for Europeans in Maldives; Asians typically stay three to five days. The newer resorts are geared increasingly toward individual clients at the upscale level, and international chain operators are entering the market with their own in-house marketing capability. Most lessee-owners are Maldivians, and the industry remains largely in Maldivian hands, mostly multisector trading companies. Well-known international brands have established themselves recently (for example, Four Seasons, Hilton, and One and Only). A survey carried out in 2005 on the investment climate

(World Bank 2006) concluded that the lodging industry is predominantly owned by citizens, which confirms a trend seen in many countries where ownership is often local, but management (or leasehold) is in the hands of foreigners.

Some resorts in Maldives offer their own activities for snorkeling, fishing, and speedboat excursions. They also tend to outsource certain services (for example, submarine reef trips). The larger hotels outsource these activities by permitting tour operators to offer excursions outlined in their brochures for presales and to main desks in resort lobbies for on-the-spot sales.[8] In fact, these constitute a significant aspect of the business of many resorts.

Maldives has developed about 100 intermediaries over the past 30 years. Most of the world's key tour operators and travel agents offer Maldives in their brochures. They have their own local offices or agents who provide ground-handling and transfer services.

Leasing of Islands

While managing growth and avoiding a boom-and-bust environment, Maldives benefits from its land structure of hundreds of uninhabited islands, which lends itself to incremental expansion. Generally, the government advertises that a few islands are being opened for tourism and invites bids to lease the island and develop a resort. The preconditions include rigorous environmental conditions.

The land lease process is political and a matter of hot debate in government and private circles.[9] Nonetheless, the government has tried to make the process transparent and objective, which offers lessons that may be useful for tourism projects in other countries. Several underlying conditions must exist before an island is offered for lease (World Bank 2006). The island must

- Be uninhabited
- Demonstrate the carrying capacity to support a resort
- Be within reasonable distance from an international airport (by sea or air) to ensure manageable transfer times.

Some 100 islands have already been leased for tourism; several hundred more could conceivably be leased over a long period. In addition, the original leases, negotiated between 1975 and 1985, are coming to term and must be renegotiated.

The leasing procedure consists of auctioning uninhabited islands in a bidding process after the specifics have been published and evaluated by independent and disinterested persons. Standardized bids facilitate comparisons. In 2005, 200 proposals bidding on 11 island opportunities were evaluated on the following basis (World Bank 2006):

- *Concept plan:* 20 percent
- *Business plan:* 10 percent

- *Human resources:* 10 percent
- *Environment plan:* 10 percent
- *Resort lease value:* 50 percent.

The terms of the lease were standardized so that bids would be more directly comparable. They now include

- 25 years as the norm
- 35 years, if the investment is over $10 million
- 50 years, if some shares are sold on the Maldives stock market
- No more than 25 years, if the lease is awarded to foreign investors.

In addition, the rules set standards for environmental impact management and infrastructure, including

- An environmental impact assessment and mitigation plan
- Setbacks of at least 40 meters from the high-water mark
- Ground coverage ratios of no more than 20 percent
- Building heights limited to treetop level
- Infrastructure that is environmentally conscious
- Close attention to beach and sand erosion or accretion.

Investors must provide the necessary infrastructure networks and services as part of the transaction, which explains the government's modest outlay for tourism of only 1 percent of the national capital budget. The islands have introduced desalination (Malé's water supply consists of desalinated water, as the water table is polluted), septic tanks (with soak pits or ocean outfalls), or mechanized small-scale treatment plants. Most resorts use generators; some are experimenting with renewable energy generation. It is explicitly prohibited to introduce exotic, nonindigenous plants, to dynamite fish and coral, and to mine sand. Investors are also impelled to protect marine environments (shorelines, beaches, and coastal vegetation).

This model has worked well, although it puts a premium on the resort lease payment and appears to favor local investors. The TGST and substitution of resort rentals by land rents should help to soften the intense bidding war that has raised resort leases to untenable levels as investors fight for access to the new island opportunities. These regulations should put land rents in line with those of other countries, representing approximately 5–10 percent of total investment. Twenty-five years is a suitable time frame to generate a profitable investment and gives the country an exit if the lessee does not perform to Maldivian standards. In contrast, many countries use 99-year land leases, such as francophone

West Africa's *bail amphythéotique*. Nonetheless, the industry would welcome having the option of an additional 10 years at the end of the lease. One disincentive is a clause requiring the residual value to be determined at book, rather than market, value (present value of future earnings).

With the new land rent proposals, less focus will fall on the value of the lease and more attention will be paid to the technical aspects of the deals to achieve desirable policy outcomes, including infrastructure options to harness new technologies in water, sanitation and solid waste, and energy. Such improvements must be specified when the contract is negotiated or the government loses the opportunity to require them for at least 25 years. Maldives is already a leader in remote-area technologies such as the use of reverse osmosis for water treatment, the treatment of sewerage effluents for watering gardens, and the use of renewable energy. In addition, its septic tanks could eventually be replaced by mechanical sewerage treatment via mini-plants, for example. The use of local materials for building or food supply could also be emphasized, including products for thatching, coir, agricultural, and horticultural produce. Additionally, the government could revise the model to emphasize job creation for Maldivians. At present, about 50 percent of personnel in the industry is foreign; that number could be reduced (and local unemployment addressed) by taking a proactive stance to increase the proportion of Maldivians, with a quid pro quo to address training and career development.

Only the lease's extension to 99 years (and uniform application to all investors) would silence private sector complaints of bias, although this is unlikely to occur, as the land lease is an important instrument of government policy. In the longer term, a process of more modest land rents could prove more efficient. A potential property tax might better reflect the value of the business. A new corporate tax was introduced in 2011, helping to reveal profitability based on actual results, not estimated projections designed to win bids without reflecting operating realities. Another option could be for the government to seek bids by category of resort, with land leases established by category. (The hotels in Maldives are rated by tour operators such that a common understanding of the country's hotel categories exists.)

Lastly, the survey on the investor climate indicated that a secondary market is developing for the sale of leases. The government may wish to reinforce the secondary market system to ensure sound regulation and conditions of sale by legislating in favor of a framework to manage the resale of resort property leases.

Access

The main entry point for tourists in Maldives is the Ibrahim Nasir International Airport on Hulhulé Island, a 10-minute ferry ride from Malé. The airport was privatized in 2010.[10] It has a blacktop 3,200-meter runway, which can accept most planes, and a water runway, which handles seaplane transfers directly to resorts. The country opened a second international airport in Gan (with a 2,600-meter runway) at a converted military site. Approximately 80 percent of all leisure visitors arrive via tour operators on a package tour that includes a charter flight.

International and domestic access is simultaneously a bottleneck and a means of managing access throughout the country. Maldives has always had an open attitude to both charter and scheduled international airlines; more than 30 airlines currently serve the country. The national carrier is Maldivian, which was formed in 2008 from Island Aviation. Before Gan Airport was built, many potential island destinations were simply too far to be reached from Hulhulé in a reasonable amount of time, and most resorts were located within a couple of hours of Malé. The transformation of Gan Airport into an international civil airport (with an adjacent Shangri-La Hotel) has eased the pressure on Hulhulé and made the southern islands more accessible. Plans are also being considered for a new airport in the northern section of the country that will open the northern islands to investment. Transfers between these airports are provided. Service to the islands is either by boat or by seaplane. By boat, the choice is between traditional *dhonis,* which are slow and unsuited for long trips but very typical of Maldives and add local color (the shipyards where they are built from palm wood are an interesting tourist attraction), and power boats, most of which are owned by the resorts, although some passengers find them unattractive and a most uncomfortable ride. In addition, sea taxi services operate (Trans Maldivian and Maldian Air Taxi) with a total of 31 Twin Otter aircraft. Only clients with reservations can visit an island, and the resort management confirms each reservation (or provides service on its own boat).

Results

Maldives has an impressive record of growth and rapid expansion of its lodging capacity, having achieved this success by managing its land effectively through the leasing of islands and by improving access to the island resorts.

In sum, Maldives has effectively promoted an economically productive tourism model. One successful ingredient has been its willingness to experiment and innovate. It privatized its main airport and had no direct corporate income tax for an extended period of time. It also introduced land rents to defang the resort lease model and a value added tax to replace the bednight tax. The revised lease model, as well as improved access to the country, helped to facilitate the expansion of tourism in a managed, incremental way. The country's geography also aided the process.

Notes

1. The presidential elections in 2008 produced unrest, followed by demonstrations against the government's austerity program. However, President Mohamed Nasheed was credited with trying to introduce reforms.
2. See http://www.maldives.com/.
3. WTTC, Economic Data Search Tool (http://www.wttc.org/research/).
4. See http://www.themaldives.com/government/.
5. Much of the information in this section was derived from Maldives Association of Tourism Industry (2005).
6. Although per capita income in Maldives is not as high as in the Seychelles ($6,000), it clearly has achieved more through tourism than any of its South Asian neighbors in improving the welfare of its citizens. Maldivians have shown remarkable capacity to adapt since tourism began in the 1970s, perhaps reflecting their long exposure to trade routes.
7. For properties of 200,000 square feet or less, the rate will be $1 million; for areas between 200,000 and 400,000 square feet, the rate will be $1.5 million; and for areas larger than 400,000 square feet, the rate will be $2 million a year. No estimates are available of the expected revenues from this new tax, but revenues are projected to be somewhat lower than at present, but more predictable.
8. Excursions include arrival and departure from the airport ($75–$200 per trip); a day or half-day trip to Malé for sight-seeing and shopping; fishing, snorkeling, scuba diving, and surfing trips, picnics to uninhabited islands, island-hopping tours, and other tours by water. Spa operations are also offered by concessions, affiliated companies, and independent concessionaires (for example, Clarins).
9. Tourism generates about 30 percent of total government revenues, and land rents are equivalent to approximately 30 percent of tourism revenue. Land leases therefore generate roughly 9–10 percent of total government revenue, a significant figure. This is changing due to the increased TGST and the introduction of the new corporate tax system.
10. The tour operator is GMR-Malaysian Airlines, which won over two other bidders, with a total package of $511 million. It is to build a new passenger and VIP terminal (47,400 square feet), together with landside development and land reclamation. The government will receive an initial up-front fee of $78 million and a fixed annual concession fee of $1.5 million.

References

Maldives Association of Tourism Industry. 2005. "Strategic Directions for the Maldives Tourism Industry." MATI, Malé, Maldives.

UNWTO (United Nations World Tourism Organization). 2013. "Tourism Factbook." UNWTO, Madrid. http://www.e-unwto.org/content/v486k6/?v=search.

World Bank. 2006. "The Maldives: Sustaining Growth and Improving the Investment Climate." World Bank, Washington, DC. http://documents.worldbank.org/curated /en/2006/04/7887430/maldives-sustaining-growth-improving-investment-climate.

Mauritius: Managing the Environment and Creating a Competitive Tourism Sector

---

Key Lessons

- Mauritius targeted tourism for growth and exercised close control over its coastline to ensure environmental management.
- Strategic partnerships with European airlines were critical for success because Mauritius is located far from source markets.
- Explicit emphasis was placed on training and high-quality service, with adequate government support and policies.
- Expansion is controlled by stopping new hotel construction when occupancy rates drop below a certain level.
- Leadership for investments and promotion is coordinated through the Mauritius Export Development and Investment Authority.

Introduction

The travel industry in Mauritius presents the image of a successful destination with the world's best hotels catering to a high-income market.[1] With a population of about 1 million, Mauritius received close to 1 million (930,456) international tourists in 2008, representing a total expenditure of $1.4 billion. Tourism contributes 13 percent to gross domestic product (GDP), and Mauritius has a remarkable visitor repeat rate of 30 percent. The island nation also controls expansion of capacity to ensure a sound operating environment.

Tourism Data

According to the United Nations World Tourism Organization (UNWTO 2013), Mauritius received 890,000 international arrivals in 2009. Total international tourist receipts amounted to $1.39 billion. According to the World Travel & Tourism Council (WTTC), in 2009 tourism's total (direct and indirect) contribution to GDP was 28.1 percent, and total direct and indirect employment in the sector was 145,400 jobs.[2]

Sector Background and History

Mauritius became a single-sector economy (based on sugar production) after independence in 1968 (map 10.9). Few countries have set about economic diversification and export-led growth with as much drive and commitment as Mauritius. It began by making sugar production into a large-scale industry rather than a cottage industry. Although the island had no sheep, it became a world leader in woolen knitwear and is the world's biggest exporter of canned

Map 10.9 Mauritius

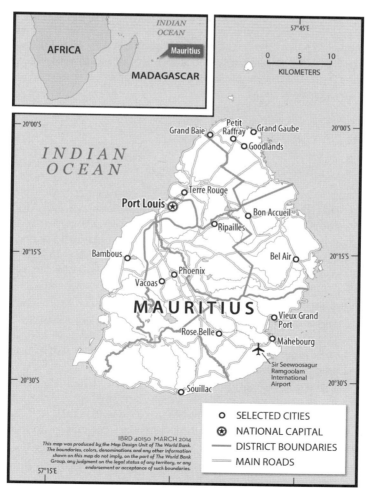

corned beef, squeezing out Argentina. It started with export-processing zones in the mid-1980s (and perfected the idea of a one-stop shop for investors). The development of tourism followed, with the government exercising close control over the entire coastline and ensuring that new properties conformed to environmental standards.

As a result, Mauritius is now a superior sun and sand destination, with 90 percent of its hotels on tropical beaches. To avoid the pitfalls of overexpansion, the government declares a moratorium on the construction of hotels when it judges that occupancies have dipped too low. According to the Mauritius Chamber of Commerce and Industry, the room occupancy rate was 68 percent in 2008 and 63 percent in 2010, with robust revenues.[3] Mauritius has 104 large hotels of more than 80 rooms, and the bed and breakfast market is burgeoning. In support, local entrepreneurs have opened taxi and small bus companies and handicraft and sports activity enterprises; they also supply food for the hotels. Mauritius has a well-developed financial sector, with incentives for qualifying operations in tourism, such that economic development has reached even the poorest areas of the island.

Results

Mauritius credits its growth in tourism to three factors:

- As Mauritius is far from its main markets in Europe, it needs good air access to succeed (60 percent of its market comes from France, South Africa, and the United Kingdom). Although it created its own airline, Air Mauritius, it sought to partner with others as a core strategy. Through pooling agreements, it has sound relationships with major carriers, such as British Airways and Air France, and actively discourages charter flights. It has thus turned its distance from originating markets into an advantage, using its remoteness as an indication of exclusivity.

- While embarking on export-led growth, the government promoted human rights—Mauritius has one of the best human rights records in Africa. It also boasts a fine hotel school. Many hotels are staffed entirely by Mauritanians, including at the managerial level, although Mauritius is a net importer of labor. A passion for high-quality personal service is high on the government's list of priorities, and Mauritius markets high quality as part of its brand. It provides incentives for entrepreneurs to release their staff for training. Students in the general education system are encouraged to learn four languages.

- Tourism in Mauritius relies heavily on partnerships between the public and private sectors, with the help of international strategic partners.

Responsibility for tourism is entrusted to the Ministry of Tourism, Leisure, and External Communications, which works closely with a dynamic private sector, represented at the highest level by an apex organization, the Joint Economic Council. Private sector associations are active in policy dialogue and advocacy with government. The Mauritius Export Development and Investment Authority aids in every aspect of developing exports and attracting foreign direct investment.[4]

Notes

1. This case study is based on the case study of Mauritius in Christie and Crompton (2001), with updates. It also draws on Craig (n.d.).
2. WTTC, Economic Data Search Tool (http://www.wttc.org/research/).
3. See the Mauritius Chamber of Commerce and Industry website (http://www.mcci .org/).
4. See http://www.gov.mu/portal/site/GovtHomePagesite/menuitem.ea8cbf04ae2 aa1de12c7c910e2b521ca/.

References

Christie, I., and D. Crompton. 2001. "Tourism in Africa." Africa Region Working Paper Series 12, World Bank, Washington, DC.

Craig, Peter. n.d. "Comparison between Niger and Mauritius." Unpublished paper, World Bank, Washington, DC.

UNWTO (United Nations World Tourism Organization) 2013. "Tourism Factbook." UNWTO, Madrid. http://www.e-unwto.org/content/v486k6/?v=search.

Mexico: Building a Resort City in Cancun

Key Lessons

- Cancun's success can be linked to a comprehensive master plan that included development of tourism, residential zones, and a world-class airport.

- The Ministry of Finance developed the National Trust Fund for Tourism Development (FONATUR) to lead the Cancun project. FONATUR created the anchor project by assembling land, constructing the integrated resorts, and managing their development. The FONATUR model has been replicated throughout the world.

- Cancun reaches its target markets in North America by offering diverse accommodation, conference facilities, year-round activities, and other appropriate, market-oriented products.

- Although environmental regulations were in the plan for Cancun, rapid growth put pressure on the surrounding area, requiring stronger management measures. Today environmental pressure still exists, and measures need to be strengthened again.

Introduction

In the 1960s Cancun was deserted, with no permanent residents. Today it is one of the most visited resorts in the world, hosting more than 10 million tourists every year. It is one of the top 10 destinations worldwide. Developing tourism in Cancun took 35 years. In that time, a new city with 143 hotels and 27,518 rooms emerged.[1] Its success, anchored in the original master plan, offers useful lessons in tourism development and serves as a model to emulate.

Tourism Data

Mexico welcomed 86 million international visitors in 2009. International tourism receipts were $12.5 billion. The peak year was 2005, when the country received 103.1 million international visitors (UNWTO 2013).

Arrivals fell yearly at the end of the past decade, as shown in table 10.9. Since then, the world economic recession and increasing drug violence in Mexico have cut into tourism.[2] Total arrivals continued to decline through

Table 10.9 Tourism in Mexico, 2005–09

Indicator	2005	2006	2007	2008	2009
International arrivals (thousands)	103,146	97,701	92,179	91,482	86,189
Expenditure by international tourists (US$, thousands)	12,801	13,329	13,988	14,847	12,309
Trips by nationals in Mexico	—	55,996	61,142	62,020	—
Average daily expenditure (US$)[a]	—	124.6	139.4	145.3	—
Average length of stay (days)	9.93	9.93	9.94	10.0	9.65
Average occupancy (%)[b]	—	51.9	53.4	52.4	—

Source: UNWTO, unless otherwise noted.
Note: — = not available.
a. Includes overnight and same-day visitors.
b. Ministry of Tourism 2009.

2011, but the number of overnight visitors has risen slowly again in the past couple of years. Although in the long run Mexico's tourism seems assured of a privileged place, maintaining that position will require deft management in the short term. Mexico also has a sizable domestic market of approximately 62 million overnight tourist stays in 2008. This is very important, as it complements international travel and may provide a cushion against slowing international markets (many emerging markets have no domestic market). Most foreign travelers are from the United States and Canada (93 percent); Europe accounts for 5 percent. Until quite recently, North America accounted for 73 percent and Europe for 10 percent. This change can be explained by people vacationing for shorter periods of time and closer to home than before the economic recession.

According to the United Nations World Tourism Organization (UNWTO 2013), total expenditure for international tourism in Mexico in 2009 was $12.5 billion, including $1 billion for international transport. Tourism expenditure in 2005 was close to the same level ($12.8 billion), but reached $14.7 billion, before falling back in 2009. The World Travel & Tourism Council (WTTC) estimates that tourism (both directly and indirectly) contributes 14 percent to gross domestic product and will generally retain this share over the next 10 years.[3] Total direct and indirect employment in the sector is 6.8 million jobs and is expected to increase to 7.7 million jobs over the next 10 years.

Local data for Cancun are not readily available, but it is generally estimated that Cancun attracts about one-third of the country's overall volume of visitors. It does well in terms of room rate and occupancy. For example, in 2008 Cancun's average room rate was $133.54, and its occupancy was 62 percent, compared with national averages of $90.03 and 61 percent.[4] However, Cancun's occupancy rate was 79 percent in 2005, and it has slipped every year since then; partial results show that the cumulative occupancy rate reached 71 percent in 2011.[5]

Sector Background and History

Cancun is located on the Caribbean coast of the Yucatán Peninsula in the state of Quintana Roo (map 10.10). In the 1960s Quintana Roo had approximately 40,000 inhabitants, most of them in Chetumal (the southern part of the state) and on the islands of Cozumel and Isla Mujeres (in the north). Cancun had no permanent residents; visitors only came for short stays. Subsequently, divers passed along Cancun's coastal road to take ferries to Isla Mujeres and Cozumel.

Map 10.10 Cancun, Mexico

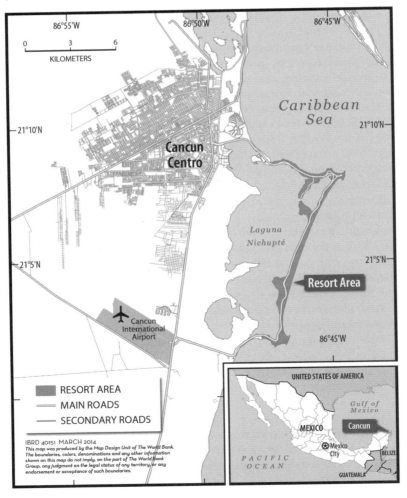

IBRD 40151 MARCH 2014
This map was produced by the Map Design Unit of The World Bank. The boundaries, colors, denominations and any other information shown on this map do not imply, on the part of The World Bank Group, any judgment on the legal status of any territory, or any endorsement or acceptance of such boundaries.

Today Cancun has more than 600,000 residents; the total population along the 130-kilometer Caribbean coastline area is 750,000. The state is divided into eight districts (*municipios*), of which, Benito Juárez (including Cancun) is the largest, with a growing population of 1.1 million. A territory until 1974, Quintana Roo is a young state, populated by immigrants. Its economy revolves around tourism (more than 50 percent of economic activity), with every direct job in a hotel generating 7.5 indirect jobs, according to the tourism office. In 2005, there were 653 hotels in Quintana Roo and 57,830 rooms. Cancun alone has 143 hotels and 27,518 rooms. The other establishments are mostly small and spread along the Caribbean coastline, Cozumel, and Isla Mujeres.

Cancun also represents the northern extremity of what has come to be known as the Mayan Riviera, a stretch of about 130 kilometers of Caribbean coastline that is rapidly becoming a major tourism destination in its own right, focused on the town of Playa del Carmen. Neighboring Isla Mujeres and Cozumel complete one of the most extensive tourism regions in the world. Its juxtaposition to North America and its favorable climate (250 or more days of sun annually) give it a competitive advantage and access to a huge market.[6] Cancun was originally considered a destination hub, housing the area's hotels and key services. Visitors would lodge there and take excursions down the coast to ancient sites and beaches. Over time, the government declared the entire coast to be a series of development areas interspersed with conservation areas. As a result, tourism has grown rapidly along the coast. This carries some risk, as urbanization is deepening (such as in Playa del Carmen), and marine breeding grounds may become threatened.

Cancun covers an area of 12,700 hectares divided into three main zones: the tourist area covering 11 percent, the urban system covering 22 percent, and an area under preservation covering 67 percent (including land and the lagoon). It encompasses a vast array of top-quality service infrastructure for water sports, diving in an unparalleled marine environment, sport fishing, and extreme sports. It has 12 golf courses with extensive views of the Caribbean and Nichupté Lagoon. Cancun is close to such Mayan archeological sites as Tulum, Chichén Itzá, Coba, and Uxmal.

The Case

The origins of Cancun's tourism development can be traced to its original master plan, which included three major elements:

- A *tourism zone* (with no residential area), a kind of tourism corridor (given the characteristics of the land itself) with hotels and shopping centers. The area is divided into three separate hotel zones. In addition, golf courses and marinas serve as activity cores for tourism.

- A *residential zone* for permanent residents, located in the northern part of the delineated area. It has residential and commercial areas, public buildings, schools, hospitals, and markets.
- An *international airport* on the Cancun-Tulum highway, on the mainland south of the city.

The infrastructure program consisted of components for 16 water wells over a 30-kilometer stretch, 100 kilometers of ditches connected to a sewerage treatment plant, and electricity power lines from Tizimín, Yucatán, 150 kilometers away. Engineering for the hotel zone was particularly difficult, given its location and physical conditions.

Cancun's construction caused environmental upheaval. A bridge was constructed at either end of the island, several hectares of mangrove were bulldozed, some land was reclaimed to increase various sections of land, and massive amounts of landfill and topsoil were trucked in. Inevitably, the lagoon suffered damage, sand dunes disappeared, and part of the rain forest surrounding Cancun was damaged. This led to the reduction of animal and fish populations. Although Cancun had environmental regulations in place, it grew so rapidly—the construction of 120 hotels in 20 years—that Quintana Roo had to strengthen its conservation measures. The latter did not, however, contain the expansion of tourism along the Caribbean coast. The number of environmental issues is quite large, complex, and difficult to assess locally,[7] but the government maintains that it pays great attention to environmental conservation. Notwithstanding the challenges, the land was not productive before the tourism projects, and the scant population embraced tourism. Tourism has transformed Quintana Roo and its communities forever. The government had envisaged Cancun as part of Mexico's long-term strategic plan—it has surpassed all expectations. As development proceeds, however, more attention must be paid to fundamental changes in the way environmental conservation is applied to the entire Caribbean coastline.

Investment continues apace. The beaches were recently restored after considerable storm damage. Puerto Cancun, a large marina and hotel complex promoted by FONATUR (National Trust for Tourism Development),[8] is to be built north of the hotel zone. To the southwest, toward the airport, more hotels, golf courses, and a modern hospital are also scheduled for construction. In addition, major resort development is taking place along the 130-kilometer Cancun-Tulum tourism corridor.

The institutions involved in planning and carrying out construction work were critical to Cancún's success. Curiously, the project fell under the responsibility of the local government of Isla Mujeres, a small, offshore island with only modest implementation capacity. Ultimately, the program was transferred to a larger government unit, the district of Benito Juárez. A new federal government agency was created to implement the project. In 1974 FONATUR, a trust fund of the Ministry of Finance, was created to assemble the land, construct the integrated resorts, and manage their development.[9] In rare cases, FONATUR may also finance hotels, but it prefers to restrict itself to promoting investment and to selling or leasing sites to investors and hotel operators. Once a development is well under way, the property can be handed over to a local government, such as a municipality, or FONATUR can remain on-site to manage and maintain the estates created.

Cancun was FONATUR's first integrated planned resort.[10] FONATUR has become one of the largest and most experienced agencies in the world for implementing tourism projects. It provides financing under its federal mandate and is associated with other financing agencies. The Inter-American Development Bank[11] partnered with FONATUR, providing loans in 1971 ($73.1 million) and in 1976 ($49.5 million) for tourism development in Cancun (IDB 2006).

Cancun has a broad range of services. Cancun International Airport is approximately 10 miles southwest of the main tourist areas and has become one of the most modern airports in the Caribbean. The Cancun area offers a multitude of lodging options, with one- to five-star hotels, bed and breakfasts, and rented villas. Sixty-three of Cancun's hotels are all-inclusive, and three-meal options are available at many others. Despite the large number of such hotels, the city offers a broad range of restaurants for all tastes. Cancun is well equipped to handle conferences, with a conference center that can accommodate 8,000 people, located within easy walking distance of nearly 4,700 hotel rooms.[12] The city offers a large range of activities from fine dining to nightclubs and outdoor activities related to the sea and Mexico's culture and history. High season in Cancun is from December to March, but it has become a year-round resort, despite being subject to severe storms from June to November. In late October 2005, it was hit hard by hurricane Wilma, the strongest hurricane ever experienced in the state of Quintana Roo. Wilma struck 76 communities, home to 75 percent of the state's population and most of its hotels, affecting 800,000 people, 30 percent of hotels, and more than 14,000 businesses. Estimates suggest that the hurricane cost Yucatán's tourism industry about $7 million a day (IDB 2006).

Results

Many factors explain Cancun's success, not least of which is the government's foresight in imagining a grand resort, indeed a world-class industry, as part of its long-term strategy for economic development. After analyzing the situation, it wasted no time in taking action. In this regard, FONATUR's creation was an excellent initiative, and it developed into a highly professional and respected organization. Its service, in many ways a one-stop shop, is very efficient.

Cancun has outshone Acapulco, a prized Mexican destination. None of the other integrated planned resorts has come close to reaching Cancun's success. Ixtapa, established at about the same time, has a mere 5,000 rooms today, although it has been quite successful in its own way. Propinquity is a strong argument, especially when the targeted North America market is very large and wealthy. But the product has to be right to appeal to Americans, Canadians, and Mexicans. The Caribbean climate has added enormously to the project's success. Few resorts in the world have sun and sand on the scale enjoyed by the Mayan Riviera. Cancun succeeded with a very broad product line that appeals to middle-income individuals. Moreover, it had substantial help from Spanish hotel groups skilled in offering all-inclusive services that previously held little appeal for Americans. In addition, the project emphasized friendly but high-quality service. Of interest for the future is that Quintana Roo has become a one-industry state, and it must remain open to future trends and respond with agility. Although the typically ideal weather can turn very bad and cause extensive damage, Cancun has become a year-round resort. The environmental lobby, greatly concerned about the carrying capacity of the coastal area and its ability to absorb more tourists, laments the loss of habitat for marine and terrestrial life. Mexico will need to address this issue to protect its precious natural and cultural resources, the loss of which could severely damage the country's capacity to deliver the high-quality tourism products that have been responsible for Mexico's enormous transformation. Cancun underscores Mexico's capacity to develop resorts. It now has five, and more will surely follow.

Notes

1. Total remittances amounted to $21.3 billion in 2010, only 0.1 percent more than in 2009. However, in January 2011, remittances rose 5.8 percent. See World Bank (2012).
2. Eight people were killed in a bar in Cancun on August 31, 2010. The incident, however, occurred in a neighborhood far from the tourism zone.
3. WTTC, Economic Data Search Tool (http://www.wttc.org/research/).
4. Ministry of Tourism (2009). Cancun also scores higher than Mexico City and Punta Cana (in the Dominican Republic, a major competitor).
5. See http://www.cancun.gov.mx.
6. The temperature ranges from 20°C to 30°C (68°F to 86°F) from October to March and from 22°C to 33°C (75°F to 91°F) from April to September.
7. In addition, a combination of federal, state, and local guidelines for environmental protection can lead to a bureaucratic morass.
8. Fondo Nacional de Fomento al Turismo.

9. FONATUR's mandate includes hotels, tourist condominiums, restaurants, and other facilities related to tourism, such as golf courses, marinas, and integrated complexes.

10. It has created five such resorts in Mexico: Cancun, Ixtapa, Los Cabos, Loreto, and the Bahías de Huatulco, and it is working on others in Nayarit and Sinaloa. The five main projects offer more than 245 hotels and 36,800 rooms. On a national scale, these resorts generate more than 50 percent of Mexico's revenue from tourism. They generate approximately $2.78 billion annually in revenues and $300 million in value added taxes. See http://www.fonatur.gob.mx/.

11. IDB loan ME0016 of September 29, 1971, Cancun Infrastructure, and loan number MEOO39 of May 20, 1976, Tourism Cancun II.

12. Cancun Center is situated at the heart of the hotel zone, only 20 minutes from Cancun's International Airport. It has 75,350 square feet of meeting space (13 large rooms that can be broken into 36 breakout rooms), as well as 77,900 square feet of exhibition space, on two levels. See http://cancun.travel/en/groups-and-conventions/convention-centers/.

References

IDB (Inter-American Development Bank). 2006. *Mexico: Economic Reactivation after a Natural Disaster; Support for Small Businesses.* Loan number ME-M1019. Washington, DC: IDB.

Ministry of Tourism. 2009. *Boletín Cuatrimestral de Turismo* 26 (May-August).

UNWTO (United Nations World Tourism Organization). 2013. "Tourism Factbook." UNWTO, Madrid. http://www.e-unwto.org/content/v486k6/?v=search.

World Bank. 2012. "Country at a Glance: Mexico." World Bank, Washington, DC. http://www.worldbank.org/en/country/mexico.

Morocco: Political Challenges and the Bay of Agadir

Key Lessons

- Support from the government and donors along with a feasibility study and an organization to handle project implementation set a solid foundation for the project.
- The commitment to tourism was not fully embraced, and the Agadir project was closed for political reasons, although the construction of infrastructure was well advanced.
- The project was abandoned for 20 years, resulting in a loss of $21 million in investment and much more in potential tourism revenues.

Introduction

Agadir, the fast-growing administrative center of southern Morocco, was the site of this World Bank–supported tourism project. A coastal town with fine beaches, Agadir was destroyed by an earthquake on February 29, 1960, killing 15,000 of the 35,000 residents. In response, the Moroccan government created a specific agency to design and reconstruct a city for 50,000 inhabitants, helping its population to grow rapidly and reach the target population in 1969–70. The Agadir Metropolitan Area's economic activity was based on fishing, agro-industry, ore processing, and tourism. The tourism facilities were built on the city's beachfront. Nonexistent in 1960, tourism boomed, and Agadir had 4,000 hotel beds and 120,000 visitors by 1974. As the rate of demand outpaced the expansion of accommodation capacity, Agadir experienced exceptionally high occupancy rates (75 percent in 1975), but the high volume of demand could not be satisfied. Considerable further growth was expected, due to the strong interest of Moroccan and foreign investors in the area. The future looked bright, and Agadir had regained its position as the leading city in southern Morocco.

However, the situation deteriorated soon after the Bay of Agadir tourism project was approved. Bureaucratic interference hindered the processing of procurement, and the project soon fell behind schedule. A few years later, the government announced the closing of the project and further development ceased.

Tourism Data

According to the United Nations World Tourism Organization (UNWTO 2013), Morocco received 8.7 million international arrivals in 2009. Total international tourist receipts amounted to almost $8 billion. According to the World Travel & Tourism Council (WTTC), in 2009 tourism's contribution to Morocco's gross domestic product was 19.2 percent, and total direct and indirect employment in the sector was equivalent to almost 2 million jobs.[1]

Sector Background and History

Morocco has excellent tourism resources that are within easy reach by car. Its resources include extensive beaches along the Atlantic and Mediterranean coasts; the architectural treasures of the imperial cities of Fez, Rabat, Meknes, and Marrakesh; and the exotic atmosphere of its pre-Saharan oases within sight of the snow-capped Atlas Mountains. The 1973–77 tourism plan called for the construction of three- and four-star hotels to appeal to middle-income Moroccan and international travelers. Under normal circumstances, the infrastructure for such projects would be carried out by the Ministry of Public Works. In this case, a specialized agency was created—Société Nationale d'Aménagement de la Baie d'Agadir (SONABA)—to take the lead in conducting the studies, preparing and launching the bids, supervising implementation of the works, and promoting investment.

Supported by the World Bank, in 1973 the government selected the Agadir area as the recipient of financial support for tourism. The United Nations Development Programme (UNDP) agreed to finance the feasibility studies, with the World Bank as executing agency (World Bank 1976).

The Case

The Bay of Agadir tourism project consisted of (a) infrastructure works and common facilities for a new section of Agadir known as the *unité d'aménagement touristique*, on which 7,000 hotel beds and 2,600 housing units were to be constructed on 260 hectares, (b) regional infrastructure and facilities for the Agadir Greater Metropolitan Area, and (c) related consultancy services. The planning concept for the new tourism zone departed from the usual model of isolated hotel development. It called for the integration of hotels, housing, and commercial activities in a planned area. Although the housing program was designed mainly for upper- and middle-income groups, it was also designed to alleviate the shortage of housing in Agadir. SONABA acquired the land and prepared a land use plan and zoning regulations. Enactment of the regulations was a condition of the loan.

Regional infrastructure and facilities included (a) completing Agadir's ring road to allow heavy traffic from the south and east to reach the harbor without passing through the city center and tourism zones, (b) upgrading a 56-kilometer stretch of road connecting several villages in Imouzzer Valley, and (c) eliminating harbor pollution and the risk of beach contamination by replacing the water pumps used to unload fish in Agadir's port.

The proposed project also included a program of technical assistance and studies intended to help the government to plan the future growth of the area and to develop methods to protect the environment, increasingly threatened by the effects of urbanization and industry. The assistance program would also update and complete the master plan for the area. The plan specified regulations and guidelines for the preservation of traditional architecture in areas surrounding Agadir, thus improving the dwellings of rural families.

The development of Agadir's new tourism zone fell primarily under the responsibility of SONABA, which was to implement all infrastructure and building works through contractors. SONABA was tasked with conducting the detailed planning studies, supervising the final engineering work, advertising requests for tenders, evaluating the bids, entering into contracts, and overseeing the work. Consultancy services were to assist SONABA in preparing the final engineering design and supervising the works in the project zone. SONABA signed contracts for the design, construction, and operation of the water supply, electric power, and telecommunications components with the respective public utility companies. Coordination between SONABA and other government agencies was ensured through an ad hoc interministerial commission at the national level and a local committee chaired by the governor of Agadir.

Once developed, the plots of land for housing, hotels, and shopping facilities were to be sold or leased by SONABA to private investors at market prices. Land revenues were expected to cover all investment costs and provide a satisfactory rate of return for SONABA. Transactions would be subject to regulations, giving SONABA a right of first refusal on plots sold but not developed and imposing construction deadlines and standards to avoid improved land remaining vacant.

To guarantee completion of the project after the infrastructure investment was made, the government strove to ensure that sufficient hotel beds would be built to attain an acceptable rate of return on infrastructure outlays; a minimum of 4,200 beds (or 60 percent of the scheduled total) were to be in operation by 1988. On this basis, the estimated economic rate of return was 13 percent.

Results

When the project was summarily closed, much of the infrastructure had been completed, and a few hotels and houses had been built on the new site. No reason was given for the closure. It became clear, although it was never confirmed, that the explanation was related to the construction of a home for King Hassan II just south of the project area.

The project proved costly for Morocco. The benefits of $21 million in project costs were postponed as infrastructure lay idle for almost 20 years, and the city was unable to respond to the growing demand for tourism in the country.[2]

Notes

1. WTTC, Economic Data Search Tool (http://www.wttc.org/research/).
2. The project was resuscitated in 2000, and development is now under way (see the case study on Morocco that follows).

References

UNWTO (United Nations World Tourism Organization). 2013. "Tourism Factbook." UNWTO, Madrid. http://www.e-unwto.org/content/v486k6/?v=search.

World Bank. 1976. "Morocco: Bay of Agadir Tourism Project." World Bank, Washington, DC. http://documents.worldbank.org/curated/en/1976/01/724607/morocco-bay-agadir-tourism-project.

Morocco: Public Support for Private Action

Key Lessons

- Morocco's discipline and regulatory framework fostered an environment in which private sector actors could invest, while avoiding unfettered and chaotic growth.

- The planned liberalization of Air Maroc, the upgrading of the airport, the signing of open-skies policies, and the opening of new charter routes demonstrated the government's commitment to private sector involvement and spurred investment.

- Donor support built the capacity of the Department of Planning and Investment to initiate sustainable, integrated coastal resort development under public-private partnerships.

- Large-scale private sector development can only succeed if the government is fully committed to the project and remains constant throughout implementation.

Introduction

Tourism industry projects are best run by the private sector. Yet in many countries, particularly after independence, few private operators have experience in the industry. In others, private sector enterprises closely associated with the government rely on privileged contacts to do business. It is now clear that the tourism sector involves a diverse set of activities that are difficult to manage, requiring the skills of various private operators. A sound policy framework and much public investment are needed. The World Bank has worked with many countries to set up tourism, often from a distinctively public sector perspective.

However, a real challenge is to involve the private sector in a project, while avoiding the unfettered growth that often accompanies its involvement, especially in the early years before all regulations and procedures are firmly in place. A disciplined institutional and regulatory framework is key, one that fosters an environment in which the private sector can invest creatively and is a major force. This environment not only is relevant for hotel development but also relates to a broader framework that recognizes tourism as an integrated activity in both urban and rural areas.

Morocco's process balances public and private priorities effectively. Integrated sites take longer to develop than simple hotels and involve high infrastructure costs that translate into high debt levels and capital requirements, greater risks, and complex management. Morocco chose to focus on strengthening the Ministry of Tourism's planning department and to deliver projects that the private sector could bid on. That nexus between economic regulation and private investment promotion is the basis for a modern tourism sector.

Throughout the past three decades, Morocco has embarked on a gradual but solid program of human development and political liberalization. Since the 1970s, gross national income per person increased fivefold from $550 to $2,730. Average life expectancy increased from 55 to 73 years in 2009. Primary school net enrollment increased from 52 percent in 1990/91 to almost 98 percent in 2009/10. Access to safe water expanded rapidly, with quasi-universal access to drinking water in urban areas (83 percent of the population is connected to reliable network service). Furthermore, the Moroccan economy has steadily recovered from the effects of the global crisis. The growth of nonagricultural gross domestic product (GDP) gained 5 percent over the four quarters of 2010, and inflation remained subdued at 0.9 percent. The country has also gained from a progressive diversification of its economy and solid macroeconomic management. As a result, Morocco's overall poverty rate decreased from 15.3 percent in 2000/01 to 9 percent in 2006/07.

Tourism Data

Morocco is experienced in tourism, having catered to sophisticated travelers for many years. Its tourism program consists of three main sectors: mountain tourism and hiking, cultural tourism, and coastal tourism. It has about 1,800 hotels (78,217 rooms) and several world-class chains. In 1999 Morocco received 2.4 million tourists. According to the United Nations World Tourism Organization (UNWTO 2013), by 2009 the number of foreign visitors to Morocco had reached 8.7 million, a 6 percent increase over the previous year, impressive in a year in which tourism declined in most countries. International tourism receipts totaled $8 billion in 2009. According to the World Travel & Tourism Council (WTTC), tourism's contribution to GDP was 19.2 percent in 2009. Tourism also generated 1.8 million direct and indirect jobs in 2009.[1]

Sector Background and History

When the coastal cities tourism project was proposed, the regulatory, management, and financial structures that would be best suited for the integrated development of coastal sites in Morocco were not known. It was clear, however, that the traditional "project unit" model would only be marginally successful and would disappear when the project ended. In its place, it seemed important to build capacity within the Ministry of Tourism in an environment that would emphasize the positive and not seek to solve all of the problems at once. At the time, it was not clear whether the tourism sector had the institutional capacity to bring together all the stakeholders, including the relevant ministries, local and regional authorities, and planning agencies. Agreeing on priorities for promoting sustainable tourism development and attracting private capital for tourism development projects would be complex. Thus the idea was to finance the initial process of defining and evaluating the institutional and organizational mechanisms best suited for the integrated and sustainable development of coastal sites.

The Case

The sustainable coastal tourism development project, a World Bank–supported learning and innovation project, was implemented in 2011 during the slump in international tourism that followed 9/11 (World Bank 2004). Earlier, the May 2003 terrorist attack in Casablanca and the war in Iraq had already increased the risk factor for both public and private investors. In addition, Morocco's local currency rating was downgraded, reflecting the kingdom's large budget deficit. Thus to attract competitive bids from international investors, the government started to privatize Royal Air Maroc[2] and planned to upgrade the airports in Casablanca and Essaouira, which would benefit the Mazagan and Mogador sites. It opened new charter routes and signed contracts with tour operators to promote Morocco aggressively in European markets. These measures demonstrated that the government was serious about promoting private sector involvement, reassuring investors interested in bidding on the project.

The project sought to propose, test, and evaluate the institutional framework and contractual procedures needed to manage the public-private partnerships that are best suited for the integrated and sustainable development of coastal tourism in Morocco. When the project was being prepared in 1999, the tourism sector in Morocco was experiencing accelerated growth and was considered a critical sector for earning foreign exchange and for generating employment by the private sector. In fact, the first pillar of the national strategy was to develop integrated coastal resorts by granting land development concessions to private developers and investors. The project was designed to provide that support. The Department of Planning and Investment (DAI) of the Ministry of Tourism[3] stepped forward as the public "champion" of this effort.

The project included the preparation of master plans that would become the basis for investment projects in three sites, Plage Blanche, Mazagan, and Mogador (map 10.11). In addition, comprehensive prefeasibility studies and standardized requests for proposals (RFPs) based on agreed frameworks were set up as part of project appraisal. The project also had detailed information on

Map 10.11 Morocco

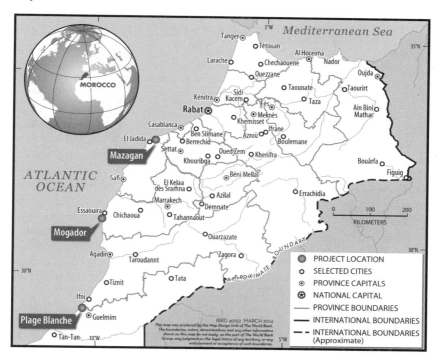

(a) expected public sector participation in each operation, (b) the specific tourism product to be negotiated, based on Morocco's competitive position and government strategy, (c) sensitivity tests, and (d) the proposed contract and incentives to be offered. Technical assistance was also included to advise the DAI on the management and supervision of three new coastal tourism sites and four additional sites, two of which were being prepared with different financing. It included advice on consultant reports and investor proposals. In addition, the project included funding to advise the government on how best to organize itself to manage public-private partnerships in tourism.

The project supported the Ministry of Tourism in building its capacity to program, budget, and implement the tourism strategy with the support of all stakeholders, particularly the Ministry of Finance. To build government commitment and ownership and to mitigate risks, together with the DAI the project team consulted with professionals in the tourism sector and reviewed the latest international experience. The project aimed to foster innovation and learning by the Ministry of Tourism through highly visible and large-scale operations that could not have occurred without the project.

Results

The project achieved its objectives. The DAI learned to initiate sustainable integrated coastal resort development under public-private partnerships. Three development plans were financed under the project, and five RFPs (two more than originally planned) were issued for competitive tendering, drawing the attention of multiple bidders.[4] Four concession agreements (*conventions*) were signed with international consortia. New procedures were established for public-private partnerships in coastal land development (although complicated issues of land acquisition were not resolved). The participation and response rate from the consortia are the best indicators of the project's outcome. For each site, a private site development and management company was established legally, and each developer was required to raise equity financing. The government was charged with managing implementation of these arrangements. The development works have advanced. The promotion and financing of hotel development are under way with private investors, indicating that the public-private partnership approach has been internalized. Before the project, the DAI investment budget was only DH 4 million, with no investment budget for its regional offices. By the end of the project, DAI had an operating budget of DH 12 million and an investment budget of DH 17 million, a fourfold increase.

By project closing, DAI had prepared four large land development concessions on approximately 1,500 hectares, creating 30,000 new beds and 100,000 direct and indirect jobs. The DAI fully prepared and launched the government's action plan, the total investment cost of which amounted to DH 45 billion. Public-private partnerships have not yet been established for two remaining sites, Taghazout and Plage Blanche. Table 10.10 gives the breakdown of projected investments. The public share (not including the cost of land) is below 5 percent of the estimated investment cost.

The project made a major contribution to the environmental aspects of tourism development, as environmental considerations were introduced into

Table 10.10 Investment in Public-Private Partnerships in Morocco in 2004, by Site
DH, millions

Site	Public investment (off-site infrastructure)	Private investment (on-site infrastructure, hotels, and facilities)	Total investment	Share of public investment in total (%)
Lixus	280	5,340	5,620	5
Mazagan	99	5,218	5,317	2
Mogador	150	4,615	4,765	3
Saidia	460	9,000	9,460	5
Total	989	24,173	25,162	4

Source: World Bank 2004.

feasibility studies, RFPs, and final agreements with the private sector. The final agreements included clauses to protect environmentally sensitive areas, natural habitats, and cultural properties within and near the future resorts and to set environmental guidelines for resort management.

Another component was technical assistance to evaluate prefeasibility studies and RFP packages and to conduct bidding and negotiations with resort developers. Two engineering firms provided assistance on infrastructure, environment, and land development. The firms evaluated the studies and plans, discussed them with the DAI team, communicated with the consultants, and incorporated comments in revised plans. A financial management adviser (*banque d'affaires*) worked under a separate contract on financial simulations and a business plan for phased development. It assisted the DAI in marketing, bid evaluation, and negotiation. The DAI commissioned additional topographic studies, reconsidered the feasibility of some of the proposed development plans, defined the public sector contribution for each development program, and used robust criteria to evaluate technical and financial proposals.

During implementation, the DAI evolved in both numbers and acquired skills. At the start of the project, it had 7 managers and 37 staff members. At the end, it had 12 managers and 46 staff members, some recruited from among consultants working on the project. The DAI's capacity, management, and reputation with the private sector improved considerably and internalized more effective management techniques, including improving its organizational structure, establishing effective working relationships with major government agencies and committees, streamlining bureaucratic procedures, and establishing model documents for terms of reference, RFPs, contracts, and simplified administrative communication, all of which improved its efficiency.

The government had earlier failures with projects and did not want to repeat the same mistakes. The project had a major impact on private sector involvement in land development tourism projects by building capacity for project preparation with the private sector, providing inputs into the regulatory framework in cooperation with the private sector, and establishing institutional arrangements to maximize the provision of capital by the private sector and to ensure compliance with the terms of agreements.

The following are the main tools for effective public-private partnerships piloted under the project:

- Contract agreements with detailed technical and urban planning frameworks and guidelines

- Institutional arrangements for resort development and management on completion

- Phased works and use of financial and technical indicators of performance

- Remedies for public and private partners in case of noncompliance with agreements
- Appropriate monitoring and reporting procedures
- Transitional arrangements from construction to operation
- Social and environmental performance criteria for resort development and operation.

The establishment of the public-private partnerships with international and national private developers led to efforts to propose and test "public-public" partnerships between government agencies. The project seems to be sustainable. DAI staff mastered extensive managerial and technical skills, as well as technical skills on land development projects. By the end of the project, the DAI was a visible and respected department and a sound partner for the private sector on future projects.

This type of project involving large-scale private sector development can only succeed if the government is fully committed to the project and remains constant throughout implementation. In this case, the government gave its full commitment to the project, and the continuity of leadership and effort in the lead public agency—the DAI—was a key factor that ensured its success. It is clear that the DAI built credibility through a careful process of learning from and reevaluating its own successes and mistakes.

Notes

1. WTTC, Economic Data Search Tool (http://www.wttc.org/research/).
2. In 2012 the government announced that it would sell 44 percent of shares in Royal Air Maroc to the public. Although this has not yet occurred, the government appears to be slowly moving toward partial privatization.
3. Direction des Aménagements et des Investissements.
4. At the preselection stage, 104 requests were received, and, at the submission stage, 22 proposals were obtained.

References

UNWTO (United Nations World Tourism Organization). 2013. "Tourism Factbook." UNWTO, Madrid. http://www.e-unwto.org/content/v486k6/?v=search.

World Bank. 2004. "Morocco: Sustainable Coastal Tourism Development Project." Implementation Completion Report, World Bank, Washington, DC. http://documents .worldbank.org/curated/en/2004/12/5525092/morocco-sustainable-coastal-tourism -development-project.

Namibia: Using Land Conservancies to Protect Wildlife and Improve Welfare

Key Lessons

- Conservancies offer a stable, transparent platform for negotiating with the private sector and assist communities in working successfully with that sector.
- Conservancy is a useful tool to help local landowners to improve their welfare, protect their land rights, and conserve the environment. It also creates a basis for tourism.
- Understanding the process, obtaining appropriate technical support, and allowing sufficient time for development are essential elements of successful joint ventures.

Introduction

The conservancy program in Namibia, enacted in 1996, uses land tenure and responsibility for wildlife as a mechanism for financial and economic growth (Barnes 2008). It has led to the sustainable use of wildlife resources, stable land tenure by rural Namibians, and improved livelihoods. It has also provided the basis for communities to develop tourism enterprises, either through joint ventures or as community-based operations. More than US$20 million has been invested in communal conservancies by the private sector since 1998.[1]

A conservancy is an area of land in which people acquire the rights and responsibilities for the consumptive and nonconsumptive use and management of wildlife and natural resources on behalf of the community (Ashley and Jones 2001). In particular, a conservancy enables communities to acquire common property rights to manage and use wildlife resources, which was not the case in traditional agro-pastoral and livestock-based livelihoods. It is incentive based and gives people in communal lands the rights to manage and benefit from natural resources (Barnes 2008). The main issue is whether this formula can generate sustainable and viable revenues that outweigh the costs (Spenceley 2010).[2]

Tourism Data

According to the United Nations World Tourism Organization (UNWTO 2013), Namibia received just over 1 million international arrivals in 2009, and total

Table 10.11 Impact of Concessioning Program in Entenda, Palmwag Conservancy, Namibia

Before	After
Existing tented camp, operating 12 years	20-year concession issued
Concession held by private operator	Partnership between conservancy and new investor to run the facilities
Concession awarded to local conservancies in 2007	Capital raised for community ownership of a redeveloped camp
Six staff employed	35 local staff employed
N$40,000 in income for the state	N$300,000 in income for the state
No direct income for communities	N$600,000 for conservancies and ownership; 8% income from land and 10% income for use of infrastructure

Source: Thompson 2008.

international tourist receipts amounted to approximately US$500 million. Four conservancies were registered in 1998; income and benefits have grown from less than N$600,000 to N$41.9 million (US$5.7 million equivalent) in 2008 (Nandi-Ndaitwah 2010). The overall financial rates of return on the projects have ranged from 8 percent (the discount rate) to 19 percent, and financial rates to communities are considerably higher, reflecting the subsidies used. The economic rates of return have ranged from 20 to 130 percent (Spenceley 2010). Most of the revenues in the conservancies come from tourism; in 2008 the concessions generated US$330,000 (Thompson 2008). There are now 31 formal joint-venture lodges, mostly owned by the private sector. Four others are close to signing an agreement, and 11 are in negotiation (Spenceley 2010). Overall, conservancies have created 789 full-time jobs and 250 seasonal positions (Nandi-Ndaitwah 2010). Results from the Entenda, Palmwag Conservancy, are shown in table 10.11.

Sector Background and History

Unlike many top-down processes, participation in the program has been strong and has provided stable land tenure for local communities (Spenceley 2010). It provides a transparent platform for negotiating with the private sector. The program has also led to increases in wildlife populations. Early successes have led to the introduction of the program across the country.

The main difference between Namibian conservancies and others pertains to their main threat: the potential overuse of habitats and resources. Namibians considered the critical factor in wildlife management to be the separation of agriculture and livestock. Therefore, an important challenge for the project was to unify land management to cover agriculture, livestock, and wildlife. This means that, to conserve biodiversity, landowners must be given the right incentives for sustainable land use. Residents then have a vested interest in ensuring the sustainability of wildlife. The combination of economic incentives and proprietorship creates suitable conditions for sustainable use of wildlife. This has been possible in Namibia because population densities are low and the land has few alternative uses (Spenceley 2010).

Results

The conservancy process has extended the coverage of protected areas in Namibia to 19 percent of the country, amounting to more than 130,000 square kilometers—equivalent to a country the size of Greece (Spenceley 2010).[3] In sharp contrast to many other countries, Namibia's wildlife and habitat are increasing substantially. Significant growth has been noted in springbok, oryx, and Hartmann's mountain zebras, as well as in the number of large predators such as lions, spotted hyenas, and cheetahs (NACSO 2009). Namibia has the world's largest population of black rhinoceros; under the program, the country has translocated them out of parks and into communal conservancies. In addition, Namibia is moving wildlife from protected areas to farmland and is contemplating breeding programs there, which will add to community income streams (Nandi-Ndaitwah 2010).

The 29 registered conservancies comprise 230,000 members, or one in eight Namibians (Nandi-Ndaitwah 2010).[4] The Torra Conservancy's partnership with Wilderness Safaris, an operator of wildlife lodges in seven countries, in the Damaraland Camp provides a good example. It took two years to negotiate and set up a resident trust. Its management committee consists of two women and seven men. Meetings between the parties are reported to the broader membership, and the accounts are reviewed four times a year. Seven men and 17 women were employed at Damaraland Camp in 2007. The conservancy's impact on local livelihoods includes small-stock farming, vegetable gardening, and wage labor, along with community jobs (such as receptionist) and subsistence hunting. More than 80 percent of the conservancy's members supported the relocation of black rhinos to their conservancy because of their tourism value and the employment created in managing their welfare (Long 2004; NACSO 2009; Spenceley 2008).

The concessions have been effective from an investment perspective, and donor grants have enhanced community returns. The model offers several key lessons:

- Willingness of communities to work with the private sector proved essential.
- Small improvements in government capacity can unlock numerous opportunities.
- Obtaining appropriate technical advice is vital.
- Governments and communities need to understand how concessions work.
- Joint-venture agreements take time to negotiate (Thompson 2008).

This case study shows that conservancy programs are worth the effort involved, because they can improve human welfare while enhancing biodiversity.

Notes

1. See http://www.met.gov.na/Pages/Protectedareas.aspx.
2. This case study is adapted from Spenceley (2010).
3. See http://www.met.gov.na/Pages/Protectedareas.aspx.
4. See http://www.met.gov.na/Pages/Protectedareas.aspx.

References

Ashley, C., and B. Jones. 2001. "Joint Ventures between Communities and Tourism Investors: Experience in Southern Africa." *International Journal of Tourism Research* 3 (5): 407–23.

Barnes, J. I. 2008. "Community-Based Tourism and Natural Resource Management in Namibia: Local and National Economic Impacts." In *Responsible Tourism: Critical Issues for Conservation and Development*, edited by A. Spenceley, 343–57. London: Earthscan.

Long, S. A. 2004. "Livelihoods in the Conservancy Study Areas." In *Livelihoods and CBNRM in Namibia: The Findings of the WILD Project*. Report of the Wildlife Integration for Livelihood Diversification Project. Windhoek: Namibia Ministry of Environment and Tourism.

NACSO (Namibian Association of Community-Based Natural Resource Management Support Organisations). 2009. "Namibia's Communal Conservancies: A Review of Progress 2008." NACSO, Windhoek.

Nandi-Ndaitwah, Netumbo. 2010. "Statement by Hon. Netumbo Nandi-Ndaitwah, MP Minister Regarding Namibia's Communal Conservancy Tourism Sector Nomination for Top International Award on 24–26 May 2010, Beijing, China." Ministry of Environment and Tourism, Windhoek. http://www.met.gov.na/Pages/Minister'sStatements.aspx.

Spenceley, A. 2008. "Torra Conservancy and Damaraland Camp, Namibia." Presentation to the African Safari Lodges Program, Rosebank, South Africa, May 19–21. www.asl-foundation.org/news.php?id=241&catid= or www.anna.spenceley.co.uk/presentations.htm.

———. 2010. *Tourism Industry: Research and Analysis Phase II: Tourism Product Development, Interventions, and Best Practices in Sub-Saharan Africa. Part 2: Case Studies*. Washington, DC: World Bank.

Thompson, A. 2008. "Concessions in Namibia's Protected Areas." Presentation to the African Safari Lodges Program, Rosebank, South Africa. http://www.asl-foundation.org/news.php?id=241&catid=.

UNWTO (United Nations World Tourism Organization). 2013. "Tourism Factbook." UNWTO, Madrid. http://www.e-unwto.org/content/v486k6/?v=search.

Rwanda: Securing Returns to Community Land and Protecting Gorillas at the Sabyinyo Silverback Lodge

Key Lessons

- A subordinated equity loan is an effective means of minimizing the financial risk of the community in which a tourism project is located.
- The land and physical assets are owned by the community, but the lodge is managed by a well-known tourism operator to meet the needs of the high-end market.
- The community benefits from both the number of bednights and a percentage of after-tax profits, which provides immediate benefits and an incentive to grow the business.
- Funds accruing to the community are managed by a community trust and divided between community projects and household dividends.

Introduction

To mitigate threats to precious land and animals, conservationists and business-people have pioneered conservation enterprises that aim to help communities living near wildlife to promote conservation and protect their economic interests, while generating revenue—making wildlife a valuable asset rather than a costly nuisance. Rwanda's approach, a model project, is a public-private partnership that secures community landownership, protects critical biodiversity, and enhances the welfare of local communities.

Tourism Data

According to the United Nations World Tourism Organization (UNWTO 2013), Rwanda received 694,000 international arrivals in 2009. Total international tourist receipts amounted to $218 million. According to the World Travel & Tourism Council (WTTC), in 2009 tourism's total (direct and indirect) contribution to gross domestic product was 8.9 percent, and total direct and indirect employment in the sector was equivalent to more than 152,000 jobs.[1]

Sector Background and History

Accommodation in the Virunga Mountains of Rwanda, home to endangered gorillas, has always been limited. But the Sabyinyo Silverback Lodge, which opened in 2006, provides both a luxury experience for guests and a model for community involvement in mountain gorilla conservation. The 16-bed lodge is a conservation enterprise on community land adjacent to Volcanoes National Park. At the project's inception, the African Wildlife Foundation brokered a deal for the lodge's development with the Kinigi community, which owns the land. To minimize the community's financial risk, the foundation helped to structure a loan in which interest payments are triggered only by income and interest accrues only when the community realizes commensurate income. This is known as a subordinated equity loan.

The partnerships between the project's various parties are well structured. Musiara Ltd./Governors' Camp, a well-known tourism operator, runs the lodge on behalf of the community, represented by the Sabyinyo Community Lodge Association. The association represents the 12 sectors of the 4 Rwandan districts that border Volcanoes National Park; it has 33 members who represent about 300,000 people. The community owns the land and the lodge's immovable assets, and it is guaranteed new job opportunities. It is also guaranteed $50 per bednight and 7.5 percent of after-tax profits. Funds accruing to the community are managed by a community trust with equal amounts allocated to community projects, microfinance for local enterprises, and household dividend payments.

Results

The Sabyinyo Silverback Lodge has yielded substantial conservation benefits. Its luxury accommodations have attracted more guests to the park, encouraged longer stays, provided communities with a marketable tourism product, and contributed management funds for protected areas. The lodge also compensates local residents for their opportunity costs and is strongly linked to sound con-servation and resource management strategies. It is thus an equitable way of capturing and distributing the rents produced from viewing the region's gorillas, a highly valuable public good.

As part of its support for endangered gorillas, the African Wildlife Foundation also participates in the Kinigi Cultural Center through the International Gorilla Conservation Program. The center is run by the Sabyinyo Community Livelihoods Association and is designed to bring livelihood ben-efits and sustainable development to communities around the Sabyinyo Silverback Lodge. It offers visitors a glimpse of a Rwandan *igikari*, a local king's compound. Trained in hospitality, tourism, and general business management, the employees of the center are all locals. In addition to these activities, the center offers opportunities for local artisans to display their work.[2]

Notes

1. WTTC, Economic Data Search Tool (http://www.wttc.org/research/).
2. See the Africa Wildlife Foundation website (http://www.awf.org/section/wildlife /gorillas).

Reference

UNWTO (United Nations World Tourism Organization). 2013. "Tourism Factbook." UNWTO, Madrid. http://www.e-unwto.org/content/v486k6/?v=search.

Singapore: Promoting Peace and Tranquility on Sentosa Island

Key Lessons

- The developers of Sentosa, a brownfield rehabilitation site, created the proper mix of products and attractions to draw target markets.

- The government established Sentosa Development Corporation, which developed and continues to plan Sentosa's expansion and is a partner in major developments. It has attracted multiple foreign as well as local brands.

- Sentosa has put a premium on providing training and establishing a culinary institute and tourism academy to build local capacity in tourism and to retain staff.

Introduction

In 1970 the government of Singapore decided to transform Sentosa from a military stronghold into a recreational area for Singaporeans and visitors. Its transformation has been slow, with highs and lows as the government sought to create the right mix of assets and attractions. Today the destination attracts approximately 8 million day trippers and vacationers a year. The popular island resort has attained admirable quality of service in its service industries by applying its well-known skills in human resource development.

Tourism Data

According to the United Nations World Tourism Organization (UNWTO 2013), Singapore received almost 9.7 million international arrivals in 2009. Total international tourist receipts amounted to $9.4 billion. In 2008 close to 7 million visitors came to Singapore for leisure, and 2.7 million came for business. According to the World Travel & Tourism Council (WTTC), in 2009 tourism's total (direct and indirect) contribution to gross domestic product was 9.7 percent.[1] Total direct and indirect employment in the sector was equivalent to 203,700 jobs.[2] China (936,747 visitors) and Australia (830,299 visitors) are Singapore's main markets, followed by the United Kingdom (469,756) and the United States (370,704; UNWTO 2013). According to the Sentosa Tourism

Board, the average length of stay is about four days, and the average expenditure per trip is about $1,000 (2008).[3] In Sentosa alone, more than 150,000 people work in tourism-related jobs.[4]

Sector Background and History

Sentosa, which means peace and tranquility in Malay, was formerly called Pulau Blakang Mati and Pulo Panjang. These names did not resonate with foreign visitors, so the authorities appealed to the public for a name, organizing a contest and ultimately choosing Sentosa, a word derived from Sanskrit. Despite its namesake, Sentosa's history was not peaceful. It was used as a garrison by the British army (Fort Siloso, Fort Serapong, and others were built on the island) and became a prisoner of war camp during World War II for British troops captured in the war. In the 1960s after independence, Singapore decided to convert the island into a resort to promote nature and recreational activities. It is close to the center of Singapore, a financial and business hub and a leading distribution center in a strategic location at the crossroads of Asia. Singapore has a major world airline, Singapore Airways, and is also a leader in the meetings, incentives, conferences, and exhibitions (MICE) tourism market. Sentosa offers calm away from the bustle of the city.

Sentosa is a 5-square-kilometer island about a quarter of a mile from the southern coast of the main island. It is the fourth biggest island in Singapore. About 70 percent is covered with rain forest that contains a variety of flora and fauna. It has three beaches stretching for more than 3 kilometers and an impressive array of activities, some of local origin, others imported, including Universal Studios, Sentosa Luge and Skyride, Singapore Cable Car, Sky Tower, Butterfly Kingdom, Sentosa Nature Discovery, and Sentosa Orchid Gardens. The island also has golf courses and casinos. The resort's development has experienced ups and downs, as developers have sought to find the right balance between day trippers and residential tourists and the right mix of attractions. Several activity zones have come and gone, such as Fantasy Island, Volcano Land, Mayan Civilization, and the well-known Musical Fountain, closed after 25 years of operation. The island has excellent transport, with a funicular cable car, high-frequency buses, and trams. Sentosa has numerous hotels and establishments including Shangri-La, Mövenpick, and Hard Rock Cafe as well as other international and local brands.

The Sentosa Development Corporation became active in 1972. It was recently renamed the Sentosa Leisure Group.[5] It is the guiding force behind Sentosa, partnering with many of the attractions and hotels on the island. Its board is composed of private and public directors operating independently but subject to the will of the government. Its revenues come mainly from admission fees, land sales, the rental and hiring of facilities, as well as some interest and other income. In 2010 it had total sales of $189 million and expenses of $252 million before payment of a government subsidy. It had assets of about $2.6 billion, of which 74 percent were cash and 21 percent were fixed assets (Sentosa Development Corporation 2010).

Results

While putting effort into achieving the right mix of products at Sentosa, Singapore has also promoted high-level training in the service industries. Training is the responsibility of Temasek Polytechnic, a public university renowned for its market-oriented and industry-relevant education. It has faculties in trade and professional fields and an operating budget of $153 million. About 20 percent of its revenue comes from student fees and fees for other courses; the balance is funded by the state. It offers two-year associate degree courses in culinary and catering management, leisure and resort management, and hospitality and tourism management, housed in the business school. In 2007 it opened the Temasek Culinary Academy, a $4.6 million institute providing state-of-the-art facilities in the fields of food and beverages. It also operates an overseas student internship program. Temasek Polytechnic receives students from all over Asia. The Tourism Academy at Sentosa is a collaborative effort between the Sentosa Leisure Group and Temasek Polytechnic. Its high-quality training in tourism services attracts students from all over Asia (Temasek Polytechnic 2009).

Notes

1. WTTC, Economic Data Search Tool (http://www.wttc.org/research/).
2. WTTC, Economic Data Search Tool (http://www.wttc.org/research/).
3. See http://www.sentosa.com.sg/en/.
4. For information on the academy, see http://www.tourismacademy.edu.sg.
5. For Sentosa's corporate structure, see http://www.sentosa.com.sg/en/about-us /sentosa-island/corporate-structure/.

References

Sentosa Development Corporation. 2010. *Sentosa 09/10 Annual Report: Think Sentosa.* Singapore: Sentosa Leisure Group. http://www.sentosa.gov.sg/sentosaAR09_10/pdf /Sentosa-AR-2010_Financial-Report.pdf.

Temasek Polytechnic. 2009. *Annual Report 2008*. Singapore: Temasek Polytechnic College. http://www.sentosa.gov.sg/sentosaAR09_10/index.html and http://www.tp.edu.sg/ezines/annual_report/2008_-_9/.

UNWTO (United Nations World Tourism Organization). 2013. "Tourism Factbook." UNWTO, Madrid. http://www.e-unwto.org/content/v486k6/?v=search.

South Africa: Wildlife Tourism and Private Sector Operators

Key Lessons

- The safari lodge model increased local employment, local procurement, capital investment, biodiversity conservation, and corporate social responsibility.
- The public-private partnerships created help to transition from international donor funding for conservation to an entirely domestic economy to support public protected areas.
- The long-term and mutually beneficial joint ventures provide a local stream of income for communities and preserve their land rights.

Introduction

Wilderness Safaris and &Beyond, two tour and lodge operators, have demonstrated that small luxury safari lodges can be scaled up to reach larger numbers of visitors in a broader geographic area in South Africa. They operate mainly in the southern cone of Africa, and their relatively large portfolios of projects can realize significant returns across destinations and generate multiple repeat visits. In addition, they create local employment, local procurement, capital investment, biodiversity conservation, and corporate social responsibility. Underpinning the model is an enabling environment with stable land tenure and infrastructure, medium- to long-term commitment, and, of course, access.[1]

Tourism Data

According to the United Nations World Tourism Organization (UNWTO 2012), South Africa received 9.5 million international arrivals in 2009. Total international tourist receipts were $8.68 billion. According to the World Travel & Tourism Council (WTTC), in 2009 tourism's total (direct and indirect) contribution to gross domestic product (GDP) was 9.6 percent, and total direct and indirect employment in the sector was equivalent to 1.3 million jobs.[2]

The Cases

Wilderness Safaris and &Beyond are two of the most significant and sustainable safari tourism operators-developers in Africa. Each has an impressive track record in the following:

- Conservation of habitats and species
- Sensitive development of infrastructure in ecologically important destinations
- Provision of local economic benefits to communities through employment, procurement, and joint-venture operations.

The two companies have a similar method of generating profits in a synergistic approach that requires both conservation and community development. Each has been in operation at least 20 years. Wilderness Safaris is publicly listed, whereas &Beyond is privately held by two main shareholders. Each operates in seven countries, although not in the same ones. Wilderness Safaris manages more than 2.8 million hectares of land, while &Beyond manages more than 400,000 hectares.[3] Wilderness Safaris's goal is to build sustainable conservation economies, which it achieves through three main mechanisms: tourism, conservation, and building sustainable businesses. The company also shares what has been learned about the model's integration of environmental, economic, and social dimensions (Wilderness Holdings 2010; &Beyond n.d.). Destinations are evaluated on the basis of "four Cs": conservation, commerce, community, and culture.[4]

Wilderness Safaris pioneered the idea of joint ventures with local communities, and it operates in four areas: safari consulting, transfers and tourism, lodge and safari camp operations, and charitable activities (Wilderness Holdings 2010). &Beyond is a camp owner and operator and has a joint venture at Phinda in South Africa. It also operates the &Beyond Foundation, its charitable arm, which channels close to $6 million a year into conservation and community empowerment.[5]

In particular, these companies are notable for their joint-venture operations. Wilderness Safaris's program at Rocktail Beach Camp, South Africa, is used as an example here, as is &Beyond's Phinda operation, which began as a private venture and then was set up as a joint venture.

The land at Rocktail Beach Camp is leased by the iSimangaliso Wetland Park Authority (IWPA) to a joint venture between Wilderness Safaris and the Small Business Development Company. The latter is also a joint venture, between Wilderness Safaris and the KwaMpukane Community Trust. Wilderness Safaris provides technical expertise in business and financial management to the community trust. The arrangements are summarized in figure 10.2.

Figure 10.2 Wilderness Safaris

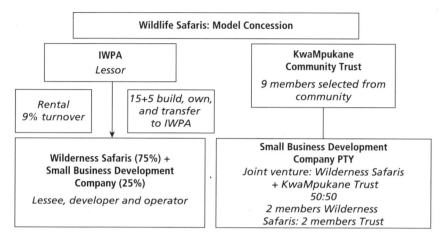

Sources: C. Poultney, personal communication in a meeting to A. Spenceley in 2008; Poultney and Spenceley 2001.
Note: IWPA = iSimangaliso Wetland Park Authority.

Wilderness Safaris employs more than 2,700 employees; 85 percent of staff come from local communities near its lodges (Wilderness Holdings 2010). For this group of staff, there is an average of seven dependents per local employee, and the average salary is R 1,682 ($221).[6] Rocktail itself has 32 local employees out of 35. Hiring local workers helps to maintain staff and their dependents above the poverty line of $1 a day.[7]

For &Beyond, Phinda is an innovation. It became a joint venture with local communities in 2007. &Beyond leases areas of community land and negotiates explicit traversing agreements to operate game drives (figure 10.3).[8] The communities use their rental income for electrification and education projects (&Beyond n.d.). &Beyond employs 3,000 local staff in 46 lodges in six African countries and India, with 90 percent of employees from local communities.[9]

Results

These projects are based on models already used in South African parks. The goal is to transition from international donor funding for conservation to an entirely domestic economy that supports public protected areas: national government or park and conservation authorities lease operating rights to tourism

Figure 10.3 &Beyond Concession, Phinda

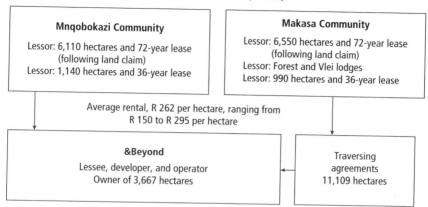

&Beyond Concession (Phinda)

Mnqobokazi Community	Makasa Community
Lessor: 6,110 hectares and 72-year lease (following land claim)	Lessor: 6,550 hectares and 72-year lease (following land claim)
Lessor: 1,140 hectares and 36-year lease	Lessor: Forest and Vlei lodges
	Lessor: 990 hectares and 36-year lease

Average rental, R 262 per hectare, ranging from R 150 to R 295 per hectare

&Beyond	Traversing
Lessee, developer, and operator	agreements
Owner of 3,667 hectares	11,109 hectares

Sources: C. Poultney, personal communication in a meeting with A. Spenceley in 2008; Poultney and Spenceley 2001.

companies. They also provide a stream of income for local communities and preserve their land rights.

One of the strengths of the joint-venture process is the long-term and mutually beneficial relationship built between the community and the private sector. Nevertheless, the transaction costs for the private sector are high, although these could be underwritten by grants or soft loans (Spenceley 2008).

Notes

1. This case study is adapted from Spenceley (2010).
2. WTTC, Economic Data Search Tool (http://www.wttc.org/research/).
3. The area of land in India was not available at the time of writing.
4. See "Our 4Cs Approach" on the Zeitz Foundation website (http://www.zeitzfoundation.org/index.php?page=4cs&subpage=ourapproach).
5. C. Walley, personal communication in an e-mail message to A. Spenceley in 2010. The &Beyond Foundation emphasizes health care, education, income generation, protection of community equity, and assistance to vulnerable children and orphans.
6. C. Roche, personal communication in an e-mail message to A. Spenceley in 2010.
7. C. Poultney, personal communication in a meeting with A. Spenceley in 2008.
8. K. Pretorius and B. Campbell, personal communication in a meeting with A. Spenceley in 2008.
9. C. Walley, personal communication in an e-mail message to A. Spenceley in 2010.

References

&Beyond. n.d. "Give More Take Less: Sustainability Stories from &Beyond; Phinda Private Game Reserve." &Beyond, Johannesburg.

Poultney, C., and A. Spenceley. 2001. "Practical Strategies for Pro-Poor Tourism, Wilderness Safaris South Africa: Rocktail Bay and Ndumu Lodge." Pro-Poor Tourism Working Paper 1, Overseas Development Institute, London.

Spenceley, A. 2008. "Phinda Private Game Reserve, KwaZulu-Natal, South Africa." Presentation to the African Safari Lodges.

———. 2010. *Tourism Industry: Research and Analysis Phase II: Tourism Product Development, Interventions, and Best Practices in Sub-Saharan Africa. Part 2: Case Studies.* Washington, DC: World Bank.

UNWTO (United Nations World Tourism Organization). 2013. "Tourism Factbook." UNWTO, Madrid. http://www.e-unwto.org/content/v486k6/?v=search.

Wilderness Holdings. 2010. *Annual Report 2010.* Rivonia, South Africa: Wilderness Holdings. http://www.wilderness-group.com/news/20.

WTTC (World Travel & Tourism Council). 2013. "Tourism Data Tool." WTTC, London. http://www.wttc.org/research/.

Tanzania: Hiking Tourism on Mount Kilimanjaro

Key Lessons

- The success of Kilimanjaro includes its capacity to generate revenue for the park and the local people.
- The Kilimanjaro National Park's general management plan was developed using public involvement to ensure that the public's interests, cultural traditions, and community surroundings were respected.
- Kilimanjaro staff associations must be strengthened to improve the local regulatory framework, safeguard the rights of members, and increase the pro-poor benefits that hiking on Kilimanjaro brings to the community.
- The government must enhance infrastructure to keep up with rising prices and tourist expectations.

Introduction

This case highlights the distribution of pro-poor financial benefits in an iconic destination, Mount Kilimanjaro in Tanzania (Spenceley 2010). The high level of visitation at the mountain creates the potential for significantly negative environmental impacts, and its protection requires adequate planning, infrastructure, and management. Mount Kilimanjaro supports approximately 400 guides, 10,000 porters, and 500 cooks (Mitchell and Keane 2008). The 35,000 packages sold each year, starting at the base price of $1,205, generate an estimated $50 million in income. Of this, roughly $13 million (28 percent) is pro-poor (Mitchell, Keane, and Laidlaw 2009).[1]

Tourism Data

According to the United Nations World Tourism Organization (UNWTO 2013), Tanzania received 714,000 international arrivals in 2009, and international tourist receipts totaled approximately $1.2 billion. According to the World Travel & Tourism Council (WTTC), in 2009 tourism's total (direct and indirect) contribution to gross domestic product was 13.9 percent, and total direct and indirect employment in the sector was 1.1 million jobs.[2]

Sector Background and History

Mount Kilimanjaro, a world heritage site, is an iconic feature of the Tanzanian landscape, with its trademark snow-capped peak (Spenceley 2010). It is the highest mountain in Africa at 5,895 meters and a habitat for rare, endangered, and endemic plants and animals (UNESCO 2000). The peak can be reached without ropes or technical equipment. A network of tour operators, porters, and guides makes it one of the best-organized treks in Africa. The number of visitors has been increasing rapidly; between 30,000 and 40,000 individuals visit the site annually, 98 percent of whom are foreigners. Tourists tend to stay longer in Kilimanjaro National Park than in other areas to acclimatize themselves for the climb. It is the second highest income earner of Tanzania's national parks, according to the Tanzania National Parks Authority (TANAPA; Mitchell, Keane, and Laidlaw 2009).

In addition to the government of Tanzania, TANAPA, the United Nations Educational, Scientific, and Cultural Organization (UNESCO), the African Wildlife Foundation, and SNV (the Netherlands Development Organization) are active supporters. Local organizations include three nongovernmental organizations: the Kilimanjaro Porters Assistance Project, the Kilimanjaro Environmental Conservation Management Trust Fund, and the Kilimanjaro Guides Association (Spenceley 2010).

The Case

A tourist usually books a package to climb Mount Kilimanjaro as part of a longer trip. For the hike, a TANAPA guide must be hired separately. A typical climb lasts five days, and an all-inclusive package costs $1,205. In addition, tourists spend an additional $171 on discretionary purchases, for a total cost per package of $1,376 (Mitchell, Keane, and Laidlaw 2009). The separate expenditures are shown in figure 10.4.

Parks fees are by far the largest expense, followed by wages and tips and then by tour operator margins. Guides receive an average annual income of $1,830, whereas porters make $842 and chefs make $771. These rates include a gratuity of 25–50 percent of wages, as shown in table 10.12. Many of these jobs are seasonal, although tour operators charging higher prices tend to employ their staff year-round. Compared to farm labor remunerated at $2 a day, these wages are attractive (Mitchell and Keane 2008).

The Kilimanjaro area is endowed with favorable weather conditions and fertile volcanic soil suitable for agriculture. Almost any crop grows, including coffee, bananas and other fruits, vegetables, and cereals; the land also supports dairy cattle.[3] Tourism complements these livelihoods. However,

Figure 10.4 Cost of a Mount Kilimanjaro Tour Package, by Category

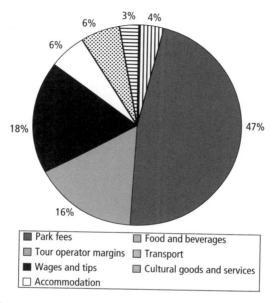

Source: Mitchell and Keane 2008.

Table 10.12 Wages of Mount Kilimanjaro Staff in about 2008

Staff	Daily wage (US$)	Daily tip (US$)	Pay per trip (US$)	Trips per year	Staff annual income (US$)
Guide	10.00	5.38	108	17	1,830
Porter	5.00	3.59	60	14	842
Cook	5.00	2.87	55	14	771

Source: Mitchell, Keane, and Laidlaw 2009.

working conditions for porters and others can be arduous and dangerous. Every year 20 guides and porters die on Mount Kilimanjaro from altitude sickness, hypothermia, and pneumonia (Reid 2008). The Kilimanjaro Guides Association and the Kilimanjaro Porters Assistance Project, which have instituted a form of self-regulation and represent their members in complaints to their employers, need to be strengthened. On the one hand, the Kilimanjaro region remains below the national average in gross national product. On the other hand, the area has the highest school enrollment rate (100 percent) and adult literacy rate (85 percent) in the country (Mitchell and Keane 2008).

Results

Problems have arisen in managing the park and its environment. The Kilimanjaro National Park's general management plan was developed using public involvement to ensure that the public's interests, cultural traditions, and community surroundings are respected (UNESCO 2000; TANAPA 2006). Nonetheless, some key areas have experienced increased environmental degradation (Newmark and Nguye 1991; UNESCO 2000).[4] Trail erosion during wet periods and firewood collection were previously the most widely encountered negative impacts. Firewood collection is no longer allowed on the mountain, and all rubbish must be removed. Environmental problems have also emerged as a result of poor sewerage, in particular, due to the use of pit latrines that infiltrate water systems (UNESCO 2000). Provisions are being made for more permanent infrastructure (TANAPA 2006). The Kilimanjaro National Park Authority and TANAPA are both committed to ecotourism and improved infrastructure, but infrastructure enhancement has not kept up with rapidly rising revenues, including entrance fee increases (TANAPA 2008).[5] Limits have been set for the number of entrances at each gate of the park and on the peak (TANAPA 2006).

The successes of Kilimanjaro include its capacity to generate revenue for the park and for the local people. Thousands of local people benefit from seasonal work, despite the fact that it is hard work performed in difficult conditions primarily by strong young men. Only a few women work on the mountain, with most working in agriculture (TANAPA 2006). The regulatory framework is still weak, and the government does not have the resources to improve conditions quickly. Many of the guides and porters are at the mercy of more powerful forces, so it is critical for the representative bodies to be strengthened to address the abuses against their members. Conditions, however, are improving gradually. Engaging with and empowering these associations may well be the most important action to increase the pro-poor impacts of mountain climbing on Kilimanjaro.

Notes

1. This case study is adapted from Spenceley (2010).
2. WTTC, Economic Data Search Tool (http://www.wttc.org/research/).
3. E. Mtui-Heril, personal communication in an e-mail message to A. Spenceley in 2010.
4. See the Kilimanjaro Environmental Conservation Management Trust Fund website (http://www.kilimanjarotrust.org/). E. Mtui-Heril, personal communication in an e-mail message to A. Spenceley in 2010. These include land degradation, inadequate

water supply, pollution from wastes, habitat fragmentation, loss of biodiversity, deforestation, illegal grazing, and frequent forest fires.

5. E. Mtui-Heril, personal communication in an e-mail message to A. Spenceley in 2010. However, mountain climbing fees apparently are quite inelastic, and higher tariffs have not kept the rising number of tourists in check.

References

Mitchell, J., and J. Keane. 2008. "Tracing the Tourism Dollar in Northern Tanzania." Final report, Overseas Development Institute, London.

Mitchell, J., J. Keane, and J. Laidlaw. 2009. "Making Success Work for the Poor: Package Tourism in Northern Tanzania." Final report, SNV, The Hague.

Newmark, W. D., and P. A. Nguye. 1991. "Recreational Impacts of Tourism along the Marangu Route in Kilimanjaro National Park." In *The Conservation of Mount Kilimanjaro*, edited by W. D. Newmark, 47–51. Gland: International Union for Conservation of Nature.

Reid, M. 2008. "Scandal of the Kilimanjaro Sherpas," *Times*, May 26. http://www.timesonline.co.uk/tol/comment/columnists/melanie_reid/article4003956.ece on.

Spenceley, A. 2010. *Tourism Industry: Research and Analysis Phase II: Tourism Product Development, Interventions, and Best Practices in Sub-Saharan Africa. Part 2: Case Studies.* Washington, DC: World Bank.

TANAPA (Tanzania National Parks). 2006. "Kilimanjaro National Park General Management Plan." TANAPA, Planning Unit, Arusha.

———. 2008. *Tanapa Today: A Quarterly Publication of Tanzania National Parks* (April-June). Arusha: TANAPA.

UNESCO (United Nations Educational, Scientific, and Cultural Organization). 2000. "Convention Concerning the Protection of World Cultural and Natural Heritage: Periodic Reporting of the African Sites Inscribed on the World Heritage List." UNESCO, Paris. http://whc.unesco.org/en/list/403/documents/.

UNWTO (United Nations World Tourism Organization). 2013. "Tourism Factbook." UNWTO, Madrid. http://www.e-unwto.org/content/v486k6/?v=search.

Tunisia: Infrastructure in Six Tourism Zones

Key Lessons

- Initial growth in tourism was led by the government, with adequate public support and technical assistance and funding from donors.

- The government's internal organization responds to the needs of the sector; it includes a ministry, a statutory board for key functions, and a land bank that acts as a semiprivate developer. It believes in integrated development, a path it has followed for more than 30 years.

- As tourism became a major focus, the government prepared young Tunisians for the industry, promoting management and entrepreneurship through a program to ensure that the country produced investors.

- Tunisia needs to diversify its products and deal with the saturation of accommodations if it wants to continue expanding its tourism sector.

- Tourism has the potential to be a driver of growth over the middle to long term if the government can introduce reforms, promote public-private dialogue, restore the balance between supply and demand, and improve the quality of service and training.

Introduction

In the 1960s, Tunisia put major effort into developing tourism as the European charter business grew. It welcomed most of the big European tour operators, who were pleased to have a destination within two to three hours or less of most European capitals. It also created a national carrier, Tunisair, which is still a major player in the Tunisian market. Tunisia shares many of the same assets as Algeria and Morocco: sun and sand, a distinctive culture, fine cuisine and good local wines, outstanding fresh fruits and vegetables, and hospitable people. Morocco has emerged as a tough competitor for Tunisia, whereas Algeria has not emphasized tourism. Tunisia also has a unique blue and white architectural style and surprisingly pristine Roman remains from the ancient culture in Carthage that recall Tunisia's position as the breadbasket of the Roman Empire. Consequently, Tunisia came to be one of the best-recognized destinations in the Mediterranean (map 10.12).

Although the recent freedom movement has disrupted tourism to Tunisia, it is expected to recover as the country stabilizes, given its capacity and tourism infrastructure (World Bank 1972, 1983, 2001).

Map 10.12 Tunisia

IBRD40153 MARCH 2014
This map was produced by the Map Design Unit of The World Bank.
The boundaries, colors, denominations and any other information
shown on this map do not imply, on the part of The World Bank
Group, any judgment on the legal status of any territory, or any
endorsement or acceptance of such boundaries.

Tourism Data

In 1961 Tunisia had 46,110 foreign tourist arrivals; by 1971, the numbers had skyrocketed to 641,000 (World Bank 1972). In 2009 Tunisia hosted more than 7.6 million tourists. Tourist expenditures totaled $2.1 billion in 2005 and had reached $3.5 billion by 2009 (UNWTO 2013). Its tourism offering consists mainly of three- and four-star accommodations, compared with Morocco's higher ratio of five-star hotels and hence higher spending. In 1961 Tunisia had 71 hotels with a total of 4,000 beds; by 2009, it had 856 hotels, with 120,000 rooms and 240,000 beds (World Bank 1972; UNWTO 2013). According to the World Travel & Tourism Council (WTTC), in 2009 tourism contributed about 18 percent (in total) to Tunisia's gross national product, and the sector directly and indirectly employed 530,100 people.[1]

Sector Background and History

Organization and planning were keys to the growth of Tunisian tourism, as was the recognition that sustaining it would require the substantial commitment of resources and effort. Unlike governments in other countries, the authorities did not profess interest in tourism and then fail to provide the support needed to launch it. In the 1960s, the government created a state-owned chain, the Tunisian Tourism Hotel Company, responsible for building four- and five-star hotels that were later privatized as the sector developed. The hotels were built on six sites selected by the government for priority development, including north Tunis, south Tunis, Hammamet and Nabeul, Sousse, Djerba, and Zarsis. Implementation efforts were concentrated in these six zones, and the World Bank was invited to support development of the infrastructure and site planning for these locations. Italconsult, an Italian consulting firm, carried out preparatory studies, funded by the United Nations Development Programme (UNDP) and executed by the World Bank. The World Bank also supported a hotel training project that included academic facilities, practice hotels, and curriculum development.

Tunisia was the first Arab country to invest heavily in upgrading the old cities, both as urban rehabilitation and as tourist markets for the country's fine handicrafts. It focused on upgrading two neighborhoods in the Medina of Tunis. Tunisia also embarked on a cultural heritage project that held great interest for tourism. The International Finance Corporation (IFC) financed many hotels in Tunisia and supported the infrastructure development of financial institutions. The IFC also participated in what was considered a novel project at the time: Sousse Nord, a land development project with a golf course and marina in addition to hotels and real estate.

In addition, the government sponsored young Tunisians as *jeunes promoteurs*. The state provided higher education and technical training for promising students, mostly men, generally in foreign institutions throughout Europe. Many young professionals started their career with such training, but the continued support and promotion of managerial and entrepreneurial success were what made the difference. Suitable candidates were given equity shares in new businesses, allowing them to become shareholders and owners in tourism properties. The funds were paid back out of profits over time. A whole generation of entrepreneurs was formed in this way.

Results

Before the "Arab Spring," Tunisia's tourism sector was already having difficulty. On first appearance, the industry was doing well: hotel capacity was expanding and revenues were increasing. However, the country continued to build luxury hotels when the market appeared to favor three-star accommodations. Tunisia overbuilt in the late 1990s and was obliged to discount its rooms to ensure growing numbers of tourists. To address the pricing issue, the country redefined its product by offering activities away from the sun and sand and by promoting spas and thalassotherapy as well as desert tourism. Other promising areas included incentive travel and sailing. The country also needs to diversify into cultural and adventure tourism and decrease its strong dependence on tour operators. Already in 2004, revenues per client were lower than in competing countries in the Mediterranean, and the sector needed to be relaunched (table 10.13).

The entities and practices that helped Tunisia to expand its tourism sector are outlined in figure 10.5.

Tunisia's institutional model consists of a small, core Ministry of Tourism whose role is to create the vision and policy for the industry's development.

Table 10.13 Tourist Expenditure per Bednight in Selected Mediterranean Countries, 2004
US$

Country	Tourist expenditure per bednight
Tunisia	47
Egypt, Arab Rep.	126
Morocco	158
Greece	192
Turkey	256

Source: Government of Tunisia 2004.

Figure 10.5 Government Tourism Organizations in Tunisia

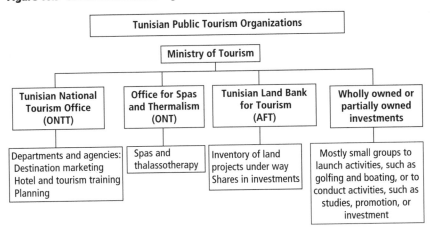

Sources: Based on information from www.TourismTunisia.com and from www.ministeres.tn/html/indexgouv.html.
Note: AFT = Agence Foncière Touristique; ONT = Office National du Thermalism; ONTT = Office National du Tourisme Tunisien. Thermalism is the therapeutic use of hot-water springs.

The National Tourism Office (Office National du Tourisme Tunisien) is responsible for training, classification, destination marketing, and planning. The land bank, Agence Foncière Touristique (AFT), is a state-owned tourism developer that assembles land packages of touristic interest. It holds land until market conditions are right for development. It then launches infrastructure projects and seeks investors for its improved sites. Projects are prepared in close association with the private sector. The AFT interacts with all of the agencies required to launch tourism developments (public works, utilities, and finance).

However, most tourism initiatives have been top-down, which is not surprising given Tunisia's difficult political environment. The state has subsidized the sector heavily with capital investment, interest subsidies, and tax exemptions. The private sector is not well organized, and no sound public-private partnership exists. Little coordination or action is taken directly by the Hotel Federation. It waits for public initiative, is surprisingly silent, and does not influence decisions in the sector. As Tunisia progresses in its infant democracy, more direct action on the part of enterprises and professional associations and a vigorous debate on strategy are expected.

The current move to democracy has caused tourism growth to pause in the short term. However, over the medium to long term, the sector looks set to be a driver of prosperity in Tunisia if it can introduce further reforms, promote public-private dialogue, restore the balance between supply and demand, and improve the quality of service and training. To achieve these aims, the industry will need to learn lessons from its own past: better research is required to make credible assumptions about the expansion of capacity and tourism's target markets.

Note

1. WTTC, Economic Data Search Tool (http://www.wttc.org/research/).

References

Government of Tunisia. 2004. "Tourism Strategy Study: Summary." Unpublished report for the World Bank, Washington, DC.

UNWTO (United Nations World Tourism Organization). 2013. "Tourism Factbook." UNWTO, Madrid. http://www.e-unwto.org/content/v486k6/?v=search.

World Bank. 1972. "Tunisia: Tourism Infrastructure Project." World Bank, Washington, DC. http://documents.worldbank.org/curated/en/1972/05/1558196/tunisia -tourism-infrastructure-project.

———. 1983. "Tunisia: Tourism Infrastructure Project." World Bank, Washington, DC. http://documents.worldbank.org/curated/en/1983/06/725257/tunisia-tourism -infrastructure-project.

———. 2001. "Tunisia: Cultural Heritage Project." World Bank, Washington, DC. http://documents.worldbank.org/curated/en/2001/05/10792808/tunisia-cultural -heritage-project.

Turkey: Government-Led Tourism Development in South Antalya

Key Lessons

- The Antalya model is to acquire land, clear it of any liens, service it with infrastructure, and lease plots to tourism investors and operators for 49 years (renewable). The government has replicated the South Antalya model in several regions.

- The implementation of this complex and multidisciplinary tourism project was managed by the Ministry of Culture and Tourism, which created a project directorate in Ankara and two coordinating committees.

- The government sought external support from the World Bank, the United Nations Development Programme, and the Turkish Tourism Bank, a public sector organization recruited to provide engineering advice for the project and to carry out several components not under the clear responsibility of other agencies.

- The master plan was not finalized and capital was not acquired before the project began causing land acquisition challenges and delays.

- The project produced an economic return barely above the discount rate (10 percent), illustrating the importance of reinforcing links to add value and boost returns.

- As reflected in its Tourism Strategy 2023, Turkey is dealing with rapid growth by slowing growth in coastal resorts, rehabilitating them, and focusing on sustainability. Simultaneously, focus will be placed on the more cultural aspects of tourism, with which Turkey is well endowed, and on new and diverse products.

Introduction

Turkey's South Antalya tourism project is a multisector project carried out by the government, led by the Ministry of Culture and Tourism.[1] A separate government agency was needed for each of the project's components in order to realize the works and commence operations. Despite its complexity, the project was successfully completed. Carrying out additional projects of the same nature using the same model, Turkey's tourism grew to 32 million international visitors in 2009, with tourists spending almost $25 billion (UNWTO 2013). These numbers show great improvement over the 600,000 international visitors Turkey received when the project was being discussed in 1973 (World Bank 1976). The country's tourism strategy has proved beneficial, and in 2009 Turkey was the eleventh largest destination in the world. As it moves forward during a time of recession,[2] extra care will have to be exerted to manage growth in a disciplined way if the sector is to prosper sustainably.

Tourism Data

In 1973, when the project was being prepared, Turkey received just over half a million international visitors (World Bank 1976). At the turn of the century, Turkey received 8 million visitors, and, by 2009, the number had reached 32 million visitors. The Antalya region accounts for about one-third of Turkey's tourism (8.6 million visitors in 2008; UNWTO 2013). According to the World Travel & Tourism Council (WTTC), if direct and indirect impacts are included, tourism contributed about 11.6 percent to Turkey's gross domestic product (GDP) in 2009, forecast to slip to 9.9 percent in 10 years.[3] Turkey's tourism sector employed (directly and indirectly) 1.8 million people in 2009. This number is expected to grow to 2.4 million in 10 years.

Sector Background and History

Turkey stands out among Mediterranean countries for its impressive tourism resources. These include a pleasant climate in the coastal zone with long, dry summers and mild winters; a coastline of several hundred kilometers along the Mediterranean, Aegean, and Black seas, with vast stretches of unspoiled beaches, snow-capped mountain scenery (and skiing in winter), clear waters, and varied vegetation; and a wealth of historical and archeological sites scattered throughout the country, with the remains of some of the oldest civilizations: Byzantine, Greek, Hittite, Ottoman, Roman, and Seljuk.

The South Antalya tourism infrastructure project is set among orange orchards and forests of conifers (within Olympos Beydaglari National Park), which have remained untouched by construction (World Bank 1976, 1986). The area can be reached by air as well as by car and train. Antalya is an old city overlooking a natural harbor. When the commercial port was moved 20 kilometers away, the old port became a marina for fishing boats and yachts. With an ancient Greek amphitheater overlooking the harbor, Antalya is a fine setting for a tourism hub[4] as well as a wealthy market town servicing the region's many agricultural producers. Yet the road southwest of Antalya is relatively new. Its construction required blasting a tunnel through the Tekerlektepe Mountains down to the sea. Before its completion, the coastal area southwest of Antalya had no electricity, water, sanitation, telecommunications, or modern highways.

The Antalya model is to acquire land, clear it of any liens, service it with infrastructure, and lease plots to tourism investors and operators for 49 years (renewable). This model has worked for Turkey, whereas other countries seek more direct and early participation from the private sector. As Turkey's strategy for 2023 suggests, the development of mass tourism on the Aegean and Mediterranean has created a real danger of overdevelopment for a limited prod-uct line (Ministry of Culture and Tourism 2007). The new strategy aims to spread growth more broadly in Turkey, to address shortfalls in infrastructure in current areas through rehabilitation plans, and to focus increasingly on cultural and adventure tourism.

In 1973, as an initial building block, Turkish government officials and a World Bank team selected a 90-kilometer coastal strip southwest of Antalya for an initial tourism infrastructure project, included in a tourism master plan pre-pared for the whole Antalya region (extending from Antalya to Finike). The project is contained entirely within the boundaries of the Olympos-Beydaglari National Park. At the time, five villages (Beldibi, Güney Deniz, Kiziltepe, Tekirova, and Teklerleteke) and three ancient cities (Idyros, Olympos, and Phaselis) existed within the project area. The population of the five villages, initially 10,000, reached more than 53,000 by 2000. A government team, supported by four consultants funded by the United Nations Development Programme (UNDP), prepared a feasibility study for the project, and the World Bank supervised preparation of it.

The Case

The project's objectives were to provide the basis for a new resort with some 5,750 hotel rooms south of Antalya, while preserving the environment, promot-ing economic activities in an area of limited development, and augmenting the country's foreign exchange earnings. The project's appraisal estimated that it would cost $66 million, and the World Bank agreed to finance the foreign exchange component, estimated at $21.9 million. Early delays occurred because the preliminary design had to be scaled up to its final version before tender documents could be prepared. Other impediments included delays in project decisions (for example, pertaining to the acquisition of land). Major civil works were awarded under international competitive bidding for lots greater than $500,000. Ultimately, most if not all of the contracts were awarded to local firms. With regard to equipment contracts, domestic bidders were awarded a preferential margin of 15 percent of the cost, insurance, and freight price of imports. Also under construction, but not part of the project, were an extension to Antalya airport to accommodate large jets and a sanitation project for Antalya that was completed in the 1990s.

The project's complexity was soon recognized, as was the need for special measures to ensure the coordination and implementation of its many components. The lead agency was the Ministry of Culture and Tourism, which created a project directorate in Ankara. In addition, two coordinating committees were established (one in Ankara and the other in Antalya) to assist the project directorate. It was supported by the Turkish Tourism Bank,[5] a public sector organization recruited to serve as an engineering consultant for the project and to carry out several components not under the clear responsibility of other agencies. Table 10.14 gives some idea of the project's complexity.

The implementation of a tourism project is quite complex, requiring multidisciplinary services and the constant balancing of priorities. In the South Antalya undertaking, all plans, tenders, and progress on work were

Table 10.14 Components of the South Antalya Resort Project in Turkey

Executing agency	Activity	Operations and maintenance
Ministry of Culture and Tourism	Master plan and site plans	Ministry of Resettlement
	Land acquisition	Land Registry
	Water supply, sewerage, and solid waste	Province
	Kemer infrastructure	Province and Ministry of Culture and Tourism
	Municipality building	Kemer
	Tourism office	Ministry of Culture and Tourism
	Employee housing	Kemer and Tourism Bank
Tourism Bank	Hotel training school	Tourism Bank and Ministry of Culture and Tourism
	Anchor hotel	Private concession
	Main road artery and network roads	General Directorate of Highways
	Electricity	Kepez Electric, a private power company
General Directorate of Railways, Harbors, and Airports	Kemer yacht marina (150 slips and 150 on-land storage units)	Private concession
State Hydraulic Agency	River works and irrigation	Forestry Ministry
Ministry of Public Works	Health clinics	Ministry of Public Works
Post Telegraph and Telephone	Telecommunications	Post Telegraph and Telephone
General Directorate of Ancient Monuments and Museums	Phaselis works and interpretation center	Department of National Parks
Ministry of Forestry	Forest roads and fire watch towers, camping areas	Department of National Parks
Private sector	65,500 beds	Investors and operators
	Two golf courses	Investors and operators
	Real estate development	Investors and operators

approved not only by the project directorate but also by the appropriate agency (power, water, sanitation, and so forth), such that massive coordination and implementation were necessary, along with the funding and handling of numerous payments. Once works reached the operating stage, tariffs and other cost recovery mechanisms (for example, indirect taxes) were in place and verified. Although standard tariffs may be applied—for example, for power—in similar ventures questions may arise pertaining to step tariffs and cross-subsidization. In the case of tourism, it can be necessary to establish new categories, requiring careful analysis.

Turkey is currently a mature destination. Although little local data are available, three-quarters of visitors are leisure travelers, including Turkish citizens living abroad who are visiting friends and relatives, 10 percent are on business trips, and the rest come to Turkey for other reasons. The peak season extends for eight months. The off-peak season lasts from November to February, although a winter market for skiing exists in some regions, including in Antalya. Turkey's main supplier market is Europe (with 22 million visitors); the two leading generators are Germany (4.4 million) and the Russian Federation (2.8 million). Russia, followed by other Commonwealth of Independent States countries, has been the fastest-growing source market over the last years. Russian arrivals increased 56 percent during the first months of 2011 compared with the same period in 2010, and Turkey is now the top destination for Russians (Mintel Group 2010, 2011). Other Western European countries are also well represented: the United Kingdom (2.1 million), the Netherlands (2.1 million), France (855,000), and Sweden and Denmark (a total of 700,000).[6] The total from the Americas is just short of 1 million visitors. In terms of bednights, some markets have stagnated, including Germany and Benelux. The length of stay has declined, reflecting economic conditions as well as the effects of severe acute respiratory syndrome (SARS) and terrorism.[7]

Since the South Antalya project was launched, Turkey's hotel capacity has grown rapidly (table 10.15).

Table 10.15 Hotel Capacity in Turkey, 1973 and 2008

Indicator	1973	2008
Establishments	367	2,600[a]
Rooms	21,109	266,881
Beds	39,929	563,252
Occupancy (%)	—	51.51[b]
Length of stay (days)	—	2.41

Sources: World Bank 1976, 1986; UNWTO 2013.
Note: — = not available.
a. Estimated.
b. 2007.

In 1973 Turkey had 367 hotels with 21,109 rooms and 39,929 beds. In the project region, an Italian vacation village (Valtur) existed, which later became a Club Méditerranée village, and in Antalya one modern hotel was in operation (Antalya Hotel, owned by Koç Holding). By 2008, Turkey had 266,881 rooms with 563,252 beds.[8] Many establishments were vacation villages, not traditional hotels, offering all-inclusive packages that included food and beverages. By 1990, the 7,500 rooms projected for the South Antalya project were in place. The hotel overlooking the Kemer marina was built with public funds, as an anchor project. This approach is often used to kick-start investment, with the first mover opening the way for others to follow. The hotel was quickly leased to a private operator. Unlike some other projects, investor demand for sites in the project area was high.

In 2008 the United Nations World Tourism Organization (UNWTO) estimated the national average occupancy rate to be 52 percent and the average length of stay to be 2.41 days. The length of stay at the Antalya resort is higher, as most business is generated by tour operators using both scheduled and charter air service; their package trips are either for four or seven days or for two weeks. The average hotel room rate for Turkey was $154.88 in late 2009.[9] While much more data would be needed to estimate expenditures, a crude estimate of hotel room rates at 50–55 percent of total expenditure puts average daily spending by tourists in Turkey at roughly $300–$350 a day, which implies total expenditure of $19.5 billion–$22.8 billion. On this basis, for the South Antalya region, total tourism expenditure would be on the order of $6 billion–$7 billion,[10] including value added tax of 18 percent, or just under one-third of all tourism to Turkey.

Results

In Turkey, the desire to invest was very strong, which helped the project to gather momentum for successful completion, although many obstacles had to be overcome. The project offers several lessons for other countries.

Institutional Model

The model of government as the main developer has caused problems elsewhere. Tourism is complex—as complex as urban development. It entails a broad range of skills that most projects do not have and has economic, social, and environmental impacts that require planning, finance, engineering, sociology, and economics skills, to mention a few. The process of trading one component for another is constant, as resources are limited, whereas the options and problems have no limit. Urban planning and tourism planning are the main sectors that require close consultation with local populations and multisectoral teams that understand the trade-offs. Despite these complexities, Turkey made the large South Antalya project work and has employed the same model in other locations, including Dalaman, Kas, and Kusadasi.

Land

Most of the land for the project belonged to government agencies, and it was expected that access to land would not delay the project. However, 41 hectares belonged to individuals who successfully argued that proper procedures had not been followed in the acquisition process, which delayed implementation. In addition, the master plan was not finalized at the very beginning of the project. Such a plan is a prerequisite to acquiring land, especially if it is being expropriated, as it was for a small part of the project area.

A funding problem also existed such that, when funds eventually materialized, land values had increased, and the negotiated prices were invalidated. The process had to be restarted. A few cases had to be defended in the Supreme Court, a time-consuming process that could have damaged the project's reputation and credibility. The Land Registry Office was slow to handle expropriations. Additionally, since it had been decided that Kemer would become a municipality with a certain level of service, land values again had to be revalued.

This experience shows that nothing is more important than resolving land issues before a project starts: it is always time-consuming to resolve liens on land, and values can escalate rapidly with news of a new project. In a similar vein, having solid knowledge of residents in a project area *before* the project is announced is very useful. Otherwise, residents seem to multiply rapidly before the project can get off the ground. The Bank required the acquisition of land as a condition of the loan, which slowed initial implementation; however, without such a condition, there would have been no project.

Capital Costs

The capital cost of the project at appraisal was $65 million; by completion, the actual cost was $43 million. Minor alterations in the project components changed the costs marginally. Most of the components were awarded to Turkish firms. Given domestic inflation and completion delays, Turkish lira costs were higher and dollar equivalents were lower. At appraisal, in lira terms, the cost was estimated at TL 990 million, whereas at completion it had reached TL 11,022 million. But in dollar terms, more than $20 million were saved, and part of the Bank loan was canceled.

Hotel Projections

The market projections for the project called for an occupancy rate of 75 percent. The rate attained at completion was about 60 percent, still above the national average. Domestic occupancy had been estimated at 20 percent, but it quickly almost doubled (37 percent). However, a critical mass was emerging, and the resort could accommodate large groups. By 1990, 10,350 hotel beds were in place, compared with the appraisal estimate of 11,500 beds (5,750 rooms). The accommodation options also proved quite different from appraisal estimates. At appraisal, 30 percent of beds were allocated to vacation villages and 70 percent to hotels. In reality, the opposite occurred, and vacation villages are still a strong component of the South Antalya mix of accommodations. In addition, whereas the projections allowed for a large share of tourists from Western Europe, the key markets turned out to be Russia and the Middle East as well as Turkey itself. In effect, domestic visitors helped Antalya to withstand the recent international crisis.

Jobs Created

The estimation at appraisal suggested that the project would directly create about 12,500 jobs. By 1990, 7,300 jobs had been created, but these estimates do not include construction jobs or part-time seasonal employment (six to eight months), reducing the number of "equivalent" jobs. The different types of facilities may also have lowered the number of jobs created. A study commissioned by TUI Travel and carried out by the Overseas Development Institute[11] estimated the average wage in a large vacation village (open for eight months of the year) to be €325 a month, compared to the minimum wage of €262. In addition, employees receive accommodation, food, travel, and social security benefits.

Economic Returns

The economic return at appraisal was estimated at 17.2 percent, and the ex post result was 10.5 percent, reflecting the SARS scare, delays in execution of the project, and lower-than-expected tourist expenditures. With devaluation of the lira, Turkey became a "cheap" destination for budget-minded travelers. Occupancies were also lower than forecast. This more than offset the savings in capital costs. The rate of return is conservative, as it does not include the benefits to local residents of having a modern infrastructure system and better public services, such as health clinics and public parks. However, hotel investment was strong, and additional capacity helped to strengthen the returns. In 1985 the government introduced a value added tax, initially set at 11 percent and later increased to 18 percent, resulting in a flow of resources to the government. In terms of financial performance, the Project Completion Report concluded that tariffs and cost recovery mechanisms for public utility services were appropriate and produced positive net present values at a discount rate of 12 percent (World Bank 1986). Land values rose rapidly, and those who sold land generally realized capital gains, although the benefits were not distributed evenly.

Kemer

Before the project, Kemer consisted of a couple of cottages at the crossroads of the main north-south road and the track leading to the beach, where the marina is now located. Today it is a municipality with more than 20,000 residents. This growth was not expected at appraisal, but Kemer's attribution of full municipal functions added an administrative level that helped the project enormously. Moreover, it created a market for real estate that attracted foreign and Turkish investors; this, in turn, inflated land values. Many of the project's components were located there, including the one hotel built by the government, the marina, municipal building, tourist office, and hotel training school as well as the network infrastructure. Although Kemer was built to service tourism, it became a center for tourism.

One issue in Kemer was employee housing. The entire employee complex intended for hotel staff was used for municipal and other administrative employees.[12] While understandable, a typical problem in resorts is the availability of housing for staff; in its absence, hotels must provide housing or transportation for employees. This problem has not yet been resolved, although several options appear feasible: condominiums or cooperatives for staff (a model that works elsewhere in Turkey), traditional sites and services for lower-income families, the conversion and use of older hotel properties, and contractual savings plans for down payments.

Beldibi and Gecekondu

Beldibi is the most northern of the five villages in the resort, closest to Antalya. It has become a preferred location primarily for holiday villas and includes residential housing for Turkish citizens and foreigners. During project implementation, before the infrastructure was finished, a rush to build houses occurred in the project area. In Turkey, a person who constructs the walls of a building and succeeds in roofing it even without the proper permits is immune from sanctions. Building is typically completed at night (the term *gecekondu* in Turkish literally translates as "built by night"). A few *gecekondu* were begun and roofed. However, the plots were bulldozed. Had these few buildings been allowed to stand, a rash of illegal building throughout the project zone would have ensued. As the removal was conducted quickly, there was little public reaction.

Conclusion

The South Antalya project was clearly a success. The government gained early experience from it and, learning from the process, was able to replicate it in several regions. When the difficulties that arose during the initial stage of the enterprise were overcome (some quite time-consuming, such as land acquisition and the launch of tenders), there was great demand from investors for project sites, and a vigorous tourism market developed. The government achieved a broader tax base and collected as much as 18 percent value added tax from tourists. The South Antalya area received high-quality public infrastructure and its first health services. Investors obtained secure access to serviced land, and financing was made available through the Turkish Tourism Bank. The resort created thousands of jobs and now has capacity for about 300,000 tourists and recreational opportunities for approximately 200,000. The orange groves and forest-covered mountains remain unharmed, adding ambience to an amazing landscape.

In a sense, Turkey has become a victim of its own success. Its Mediterranean and Aegean resorts (Alanya, Antalya, Bodrum, Dalaman, Datca, Kusadasi, Marmaris, and Side, to mention a few) have been so successful that they are threatened by too many tourists and too little infrastructure. Unsettled conditions in the Middle East have tempered that enthusiasm for the time being, but it is expected to return as conditions improve. The situation recalls the coastal resorts of Italy and Spain, also threatened by overuse. In its tourism strategy to 2023, however, Turkey has incorporated the need to slow growth in coastal resorts, rehabilitate them, and focus on sustainability (Ministry of Culture and Tourism 2007). Simultaneously, focus will be placed on the cultural aspects of tourism, with which Turkey is well endowed, and on new product lines, including adventure and therapeutic tourism, opening up the sector's great potential even further.

Notes

1. Then called the Ministry of Tourism and Information.
2. According to the World Bank (2010, ii), "Since late-2007, adverse changes in global conditions have taken their toll on Turkey's previously booming economy and business sector. Prior to the global economic crisis, Turkey's economy had been thriving. ... Turkish GDP growth averaged nearly 7 percent per annum between 2002 and 2007. ... Since 2008, though, the external economic environment has deteriorated markedly. ... Turkey's economy is expected to contract by 6 percent, with unemployment estimated to have increased to 14 percent in 2009. A survey carried out by the World Bank in the summer of 2009 shows that most enterprises experienced a sharp contraction in sales, with reported declines between 2008 and 2009 in the region of 40 percent."
3. WTTC, Economic Data Search Tool (http://www.wttc.org/research/).
4. Tourism grew to the east of Antalya around Alanya and Side. Antalya is a hub for both regions.
5. The Turkish Tourism Bank, specialized in hotel finance, has some supplementary functions: financing hotels and other tourism establishments, developing projects, providing technical consultancy, and managing fund transfers from the central government's budget to local administrations.

6. Data from TurkStat.
7. See Mintel Group (2010) on the hotel industry in Turkey in 2009.
8. This includes not only hotels and vacation villages but also bed and breakfasts, hostels, and other forms of lodging.
9. Mintel Group (2010, 2011), using STR Global data.
10. It is hard to reconcile data sources, but these figures approximate the UNWTO data and may therefore be close to reality.
11. See the ODI (2011) report, which examined a large hotel and estimated the total value of the operation at €47 million; €21 million (44 percent) was associated with selling packages in the United Kingdom, flights to the destination, rents to the hotel operator, and out-of-pocket expenses of the tourists. Of the €26 million expenditure in Turkey, only 7 percent represented imports, reflecting Turkey's maturity and the linkages in the country itself.
12. The project had envisaged up to 280 units for employees, a mix of two-bedroom apartments and single-occupancy studios in clusters of six to eight dwellings in two-story buildings (60–100 square meters).

References

Ministry of Culture and Tourism. 2007. *Tourism Strategy of Turkey: 2023*. Ankara: Ministry of Culture and Tourism.

Mintel Group. 2010. "Turkish Hotel Sector." Mintel Group, London, March. http://store .mintel.com/turkish-hotel-sector-turkey-march-2010.

———. 2011. "Travel and Tourism for Turkey." Mintel Group, London, August.

ODI (Overseas Development Institute). 2011. "Measuring and Improving the Socio-Economic Impact of an All-Inclusive Hotel in Turkey." ODI, London.

UNWTO (United Nations World Tourism Organization). 2013. "Tourism Factbook." UNWTO, Madrid. http://www.e-unwto.org/content/v486k6/?v=search.

World Bank. 1976. "Turkey: South Antalya Tourism Infrastructure Project." World Bank, Washington, DC. http://documents.worldbank.org/curated/en/1976/06/724281/turkey -south-antalya-tourism-infrastructure-project.

———. 1986. "Turkey: South Antalya Tourism Infrastructure Project." World Bank, Washington, DC. http://documents.worldbank.org/curated/en/1986/09/740664/turkey -south-antalya-tourism-infrastructure-project.

———. 2010. "Turkey: Investment Climate Assessment: From Crisis to Private Sector–Led Growth." World Bank, Washington, DC. https://openknowledge.worldbank.org /handle/10986/2904.

Index

Boxes, figures, notes, and tables are indicated by *b*, *f*, *n*, and *t*, respectively.

ECO-AUDIT
Environmental Benefits Statement

The World Bank is committed to preserving endangered forests and natural resources. *Tourism in Africa* has been printed on recycled paper with 50 percent post-consumer fiber, in accordance with the recommended standards for paper usage set by the Green Press Initiative, a nonprofit program supporting publishers in using fiber that is not sourced from endangered forests. For more information, visit www.greenpressinitiative.org.

Saved:
- 9 trees
- 4 million British thermal units of total energy
- 827 pounds of net greenhouse gases (CO_2 equivalent)
- 4,488 gallons of waste water
- 300 pounds of solid waste